Goya's Last Works

Goya's Last Works

JONATHAN BROWN

SUSAN GRACE GALASSI

with the assistance of

Joanna Sheers and Iraida Rodríguez-Negrón

THE FRICK COLLECTION, NEW YORK

in association with

YALE UNIVERSITY PRESS, NEW HAVEN & LONDON

Published on the occasion of the exhibition *Goya's Last Works*, organized by Jonathan Brown and Susan Grace Galassi, February 22–May 14, 2006.

Published in 2006 by Yale University Press

Printed and bound in Italy by Conti Tipocolor

Library of Congress Cataloging-in-Publication Data
Galassi, Susan Grace.
  Goya's last works / Susan Grace Galassi and Jonathan Brown.
    p. cm.
  Includes bibliographical references and index.
  ISBN 0-300-11767-1 (cl : alk. paper)
  ISBN 0-912114-27-4 (pbk : alk. paper)
  1. Goya, Francisco, 1746–1828–Last years–Exhibitions. I. Brown, Jonathan, 1939– II. Title.
  N7113.G68A4 2006
  760.092–dc22
                                2005033013

Principal funding for *Goya's Last Works* has been provided by the Robert Lehman Foundation, with major support from Merrill Lynch; Melvin R. Seiden in honor of Jonathan Brown and Susan Grace Galassi; The Widgeon Point Charitable Foundation; The Samuel H. Kress Foundation; and The Getty Grant Program of The J. Paul Getty Trust. The catalogue has been generously underwritten by Lawrence and Julie Salander and made possible, in part, by Furthermore: A program of the J. M. Kaplan Fund. Support for scholarly programming has been provided by the Arthur Ross Foundation. Additional support has been provided by The Helen Clay Frick Foundation and the Fellows of The Frick Collection.

EDITORIAL NOTE
Measurements are given in inches followed in parentheses by centimeters. Height precedes width. Unless otherwise cited, all translations from Spanish to English are by Jonathan Brown and all translations from French to English are by Susan Grace Galassi. Authorship of the catalogue entries is indicated by the following initials: SGG and JB.

Unless otherwise specified, all photographs were supplied by the owners of the works of art, who hold the copyright thereto, and are reproduced with permission. Except when otherwise noted, illustrations are works by Francisco de Goya (1746–1828).

This publication was organized at The Frick Collection by Elaine Koss, Editor in Chief.

For Yale University Press: Gillian Malpass and Emily Lees

FRONT COVER *Portrait of a Lady (María Martínez de Puga?)* (detail), 1824, oil on canvas, 31½ × 23 (80.0 × 58.4), The Frick Collection, New York

BACK COVER *Man on a Swing* (detail), Album H. 58, 1824–28, black crayon on paper, 7½ × 5⅞ (19.0 × 15.1), Courtesy of The Hispanic Society of America, New York

FRONTISPIECE *El Perro volante (The Flying Dog)* (detail), Album G. 5, 1824–28, black crayon on paper, 7½ × 5⅞ (19.0 × 15.0), Museo Nacional del Prado, Madrid

Contents

Foreword   vii
Anne L. Poulet

Preface and Acknowledgments   ix
Jonathan Brown and Susan Grace Galassi

"I Am Still Learning": Goya's Last Works, 1824–1828   1
Jonathan Brown

Goya's Bordeaux: A Chronicle   35
Susan Grace Galassi

CATALOGUE   61

    Goya's Self-Portraits and Portrait of His Son   63

    Portraits on Canvas   77

    Milkmaid of Bordeaux   118

    Miniatures on Ivory   125

    The Bordeaux Lithographs   147

    The Bordeaux Drawings (Albums G and H)   167

        Memories of Spain   174

        Scenes of Daily Life   182

        Social Commentary and Satire   195

        Flights of Imagination   224

Chronology   249
Joanna Sheers

Selected Bibliography   264
Iraida Rodríguez-Negrón

Photograph Credits   274

Index   275

Foreword

Francisco de Goya y Lucientes is one of the most modern artists in The Frick Collection, not necessarily by date—he spent the first fifty of his eighty-two years in the eighteenth century—but through his unvarnished view of the world around him in all its human dimensions at a particularly turbulent time and the simplified, innovative formal language in which he gave it expression. In 1914, at another time of seismic shift, Henry Clay Frick acquired three paintings by the artist: *The Forge* (1815–20) and two portraits, one of the count of Teba (c. 1810) and another of a woman identified as María Martínez de Puga (1824), the latter being the inspiration for this exhibition. These acquisitions completed Frick's holdings of works by Spanish masters, which include examples by El Greco, Murillo, and Velázquez. In later years, the Trustees added two more works by Goya—a pen-and-ink drawing, *The Anglers* (after 1799) and an oil portrait of the duke of Osuna from the 1790s. Despite the number and quality of works by Goya in The Frick Collection, this is the first exhibition we have devoted to the master.

I would like to express my warm thanks to the organizers of this exhibition. Jonathan Brown, Carroll and Milton Petrie Professor at the Institute of Fine Arts, New York University, and one of the world's leading experts in Spanish art, proposed this exhibition and served as its senior scholar. As a valued and longtime member of the Frick Council, he has contributed greatly to the museum's scholarly programs. *Goya's Last Works* is the third in a series of exhibitions on Spanish masters that he has undertaken, the previous two being *Velázquez in New York Collections* (1999) and *El Greco: Themes and Variations* (2001). I also extend my profound gratitude to Susan Grace Galassi, Curator, who brought her extensive scholarly expertise to the organization of the exhibition and to the catalogue, of which she is co-author.

This exhibition could not have taken place without the cooperation of generous lenders. I express my deep gratitude to the following individuals and institutions: Miguel Zugaza Miranda, Director, and Gabriele Finaldi, Chief Curator at the Museo Nacional del Prado; Philippe de Montebello, Director, Everett Fahy, John Pope-Hennessey Chairman of the Department of European Paintings, and George R. Goldner, Drue Heinz Chairman, Department of Drawings and Prints at The Metropolitan Museum of Art; Laurence B. Kanter, Curator, and Dita Amory, Associate Curator, of the Lehman Collection of The Metropolitan Museum of Art; Malcolm Rogers, Director, and Stephanie Stepanek, Curatorial Planning and Project Manager of the Museum of Fine

facing page   *Locos patines (Crazy Skates)* (detail of cat. no. 32; reproduced larger than actual size)

Arts, Boston; Deborah Gribbon, former Director, and Scott Schaefer, Curator of Paintings and Acting Curator of Sculpture at The J. Paul Getty Museum; Evan M. Maurer, former Director, and Patrick Noon, Senior Curator of Paintings of the Minneapolis Institute of Arts; Ana Sánchez-Lassa de los Santos, Curator and Head of Conservation, Museo de Bellas Artes de Bilbao; Ignacio Cano, Director, Museo de Bellas Artes de Sevilla; Earl A. Powell, Director, Alan Shestack, Deputy Director and Chief Curator, and Meg Grasselli, Curator of Old Master Drawings of the National Gallery of Art, and Andrea Woodner and Jennifer E. Jones, Curator, The Woodner Family Collections; Mitchell A. Codding, Director, Marcus Burke, Curator of Paintings, and Patrick Lenaghan, Curator of Prints and Photographs, The Hispanic Society of America; Susan M. Taylor, Director, Princeton University Art Museum; Charles E. Pierce, Jr., Director, The Pierpont Morgan Library; Stephanie Wiles, Curator, Davison Art Center, Wesleyan University; Lora Urbanelli, Interim Director, and Maureen O'Brien, Curator of Painting and Sculpture, Museum of Art, Rhode Island School of Design. I also extend sincere thanks to private collectors who wish to remain anonymous.

The Robert Lehman Foundation provided major support for this exhibition, for which I am deeply grateful; special thanks are due to Michael Thomas of the Lehman Board, who was quick to see the potential of this exhibition. I acknowledge with gratitude as well major support from Merrill Lynch. I extend warm thanks to the Frick's great friend Melvin R. Seiden; and to The Widgeon Point Charitable Foundation; The Samuel H. Kress Foundation; and The Getty Grant Program of The J. Paul Getty Trust. The catalogue has been generously underwritten by Lawrence and Julie Salander and made possible, in part, by Furthermore: A program of the J. M. Kaplan Fund. Support for scholarly programming was provided by the Arthur Ross Foundation. Additional support has been provided by The Helen Clay Frick Foundation and the Fellows of The Frick Collection.

Anne L. Poulet
Director, The Frick Collection

Preface and Acknowledgments

THIS EXHIBITION IS THE THIRD ORGANIZED BY The Frick Collection around masterworks of Spanish artists acquired by Henry Clay Frick. The first and second, devoted to Velázquez (1999) and El Greco (2001), were small in scale and scope, although the works themselves are magnificent. The present exhibition began life four years ago with the idea of following the same pattern. In this instance, the spark was provided by the portrait of María Martínez de Puga, as the sitter has been called. This portrait has been lavishly praised by Goya scholars past and present, although at first glance it is not a spectacular picture. Painted in 1824, it hangs in the East Gallery, where it is somewhat overshadowed by larger, more showy works. Those who do stop to admire the painting are soon impressed by its subtle but bold artistry. *María Martínez de Puga* is a painter's picture, a work stripped of artifice in which not a single brush stroke is wasted in the realization of a daring composition. A kind of artistic miracle is continuously replayed before our eyes.

The year 1824 is a landmark in Goya's life. Then seventy-eight years old, he decided to leave Madrid and emigrate to Bordeaux, home of a sizable colony of Spanish refugees who sought escape from the repressive rule of Ferdinand VII (reigned 1808–33). The move to France was audacious and perhaps risky; Goya was old and in frail health. He had a brush with death in 1819, commemorated in a famous self-portrait (cat. no. 3). And he had been deaf since a near-fatal bout of illness in 1792–93. Two earlier self-portraits in the exhibition document the progress of the artist's physical decline and hint at its psychological impact. Despite these challenges, Goya did not desist from making art; indeed, he fought off the years with undiminished vitality and invention.

A further complicating factor was Goya's personal life. He was accompanied into exile by the fiery Leocadia Zorrilla y Weiss and two of her children, Guillermo and María del Rosario. Rosario, as she is known, was an aspiring artist on whom Goya lavished his affection. Indeed, it is widely believed that she was his illegitimate daughter, although definitive proof of this circumstance is not known to exist. This "second" family was in conflict with his "first," comprising his son, Javier, his daughter-in-law, Gumersinda, and his grandson, Mariano. Both sides aspired to inherit Goya's considerable patrimony and thus were launched on a contest for his favor, with the artist occupying an unstable middle ground.

As we surveyed Goya's life and output during his last four years—he died in the spring of 1828, having just turned eighty-two—we realized that the approach to this exhibition had to differ from that of its predecessors. As far as we know, only one previous exhibition has been devoted to Goya's surprisingly luminous twilight years, although the works have been studied in one way or another by the legion of his admirers. And so the exhibition began to grow and grow until it reached its present size of fifty-one works. Like others who know this final period of Goya's life, we were impressed not only by his sheer fortitude and will to live but also by the regeneration of his art. The aged Goya necessarily worked on a small scale, a consequence of his growing frailty and weakening eyesight. Nevertheless, he achieved a breakthrough in the use of lithography and invented a strikingly innovative technique of miniature painting. He painted just a few pictures, mostly portraits of family and friends who supported him in his final years. (The sequence of the late portraits begins in 1820 with *Don Tiburcio Pérez y Cuervo* [cat. no. 5], which is included here, although it falls outside our chronological boundaries.) A real treasure trove are his album drawings, the largest component of the show. These brilliant compositions range in subject from the mundane to the marvelous and bring us as close as we can expect to come to the workings of the imagination of this great artist.

The sheer strength of Goya's willpower as he faced illness, mortality, and family conflict is impressive, so impressive that we decided to create what we call a "biographical" exhibition, or one that emphasizes the dynamic between personal circumstances and artistic production. For this reason we have decided not to engage in the current debate over the attribution of some of the later works, except for cat. no. 12, the only one that falls within the chronological limits of the exhibition.

Goya himself seems to have explicitly externalized his position in a famous drawing from one of the Bordeaux Albums (too fragile to be lent) entitled *Aun aprendo (I Am Still Learning)* (see fig. 1), which depicts an ancient bearded man, supported by two canes, who hobbles forward in search of new knowledge. In a lighter moment, we spoke of this drawing, and indeed of the entire exhibition, as a "birthday card to the Baby Boomers." The older of us is able to verify that Goya's last works are both telling of advancing age and inspiring about how to confront it.

*   *   *

The six decades of Goya's prolific career bear witness to one of the most turbulent eras in his country's history. Son of a master-gilder father and a mother from an impoverished aristocratic family, Goya was born in 1746 in the village of Fuendetodos (Aragon) and spent his early years in nearby Zaragoza. He received his first training from the Zaragozan painter José Luzán and later worked with Francisco Bayeu, who would become his brother-in-law. After a period in Rome and early commissions for the Church, he moved to Madrid in 1774 and began to paint cartoons depicting Spanish themes for the Royal Tapestry Factory of Santa Barbara. He was elected in 1780 to the Real Academia de Bellas Artes de San Fernando in Madrid, appointed Painter to the King in 1786 by Charles III, and elevated to Court Painter in 1789 by Charles IV. Goya attained renown for his brilliant portraits of the Bourbon kings and their families, aristocrats, merchants, and *ilustrados* (men and women of the Enlightenment). A near-fatal illness in 1792–93 left him totally deaf and marked a turning point in his art. Alongside his commissioned pieces, he began to create a more personal, inventive, and often bitterly satirical body of work, in which he gave free rein to his imagination in etchings, notably Los Caprichos of 1799, as well as in small paintings and sketchbook drawings.

The late 1790s ushered in a period of extreme political and social instability, as ideas emanating from the Enlightenment and the French Revolution clashed with the absolutism of the Spanish monarchy and the rigid authority of the Church. Napoleon's invasion of Spain in 1808 and the forced abdications of Charles IV and his son Ferdinand VII initiated five years of French occupation and continual patriot resistance, with bloody reprisals on both sides. Goya maintained his position at court (without collecting a salary) under the reign of the progressive "intruder king," Joseph Bonaparte (1810–13), while producing his series of etchings the Disasters of War—an unmitigated indictment in images of brutal intensity of the atrocities he witnessed and imagined—and other works of a dark and private nature.

With the restoration in 1814 of the repressive Ferdinand VII and the reinstatement of the Inquisition, patriots, supporters of Joseph Bonaparte, sympathizers with the French, and *ilustrados* were ruthlessly persecuted, and many took refuge in France. Although a Liberal, Goya remained in Spain and carried out occasional commissions for Ferdinand VII, while pushing further his exploration of the irrational in his enigmatic series of etchings, Los Disparates (1816–23), and in phantasmagoric images of witchcraft, old age, and death in the Black Paintings of 1820–23.

Goya left Spain in 1824 for Bordeaux, a prosperous city 750 kilometers from Madrid, with a population of 90,000. There he and Leocadia Weiss and her children joined a large community of Spanish émigrés from both the Peninsula and South America, among them his friends Leandro Fernández de Moratín, the playwright and poet, and Manuel Silvela, a former government official who opened a school for Spaniards. Goya spent two months in Paris in the summer of 1824, where he saw works by Delacroix, and made the acquaintance of several Bordelais artists in his new home. He returned to Madrid twice during his years in exile and died in Bordeaux on April 16, 1828.

Goya's triumph over adversity and the dramatic nature of the political events that shaped his final years have been examined in biographies, film, and psychological studies and have even inspired an opera, while the late work has been the subject of extensive art historical study. Yet the small-scale, intimate works created in Bordeaux, now scattered throughout North American and European public and private collections, are little known to the American public. This exhibition and its accompanying catalogue aim to promote a greater understanding of the culminating achievement of a great artist who was "still learning" as he faced death and the conflictive world in which he lived his last years.

Acknowledgments

It gives us great pleasure to thank the many persons who contributed to the realization of *Goya's Last Works*. First of all, we acknowledge Anne L. Poulet, Director of The Frick Collection, for her continuous support and enthusiasm for this project over several years. We are very grateful to Helen Clay Chace, former President of the Board of Trustees, and all the members of the Board and of the Frick Council for their generous support. Colin B. Bailey, Chief Curator, has been characteristically forthcoming with his advice, interest, and help at every turn. We express our thanks as well to Robert Goldsmith, Deputy Director, and to Jessica London, Vice Director for External Affairs, as well as her predecessor, Martin Duus, and to Amy Busam, Manager of Corporate and Foundation Relations, for their essential contributions. We also thank former Director Samuel Sachs II, for his encouragement at the outset and help in securing certain key loans.

In Bordeaux, we are grateful for the generous help in research and hospitality from the following museum directors, curators, librarians, and archivists: Agnès Vatican, Conservateur, Archives Municipales de Bordeaux; Françoise Garcia, Conservateur et chef du patrimoine, Agnès Biron, Conservateur des dessins, and Marie Cathala, Librarian of the Musée des Beaux-Arts, Bordeaux; Bernadette de Boysson, Directeur, and Valerie de Raignac, Règisseur des oeuvres, Musée des arts décoratifs, Bordeaux; Geneviève Dupuis-Sabron, Conservateur, Musée d'Aquitaine, Bordeaux; Hélène de Bellaigue, Conservateur of the Fonds patrimoniaux of the Bibliothèque municipale de Bordeaux, as well as Agnès Verret, Assistante qualifiée, and Suzanne Faugère; and Sebastian Quesada, Directeur, Instituto Cervantes, Bordeaux. We owe special thanks to Pierre-lin Renié, Curator at the Musée Goupil in Bordeaux, for his guidance on the city and introductions to colleagues, and to DeCourcy McIntosh, who also shared his familiarity with Bordeaux. In Madrid, we owe warm thanks to Gabriele Finaldi, Chief Curator at the Prado, for his generous support. We express as well our gratitude to Marcus Burke and The Hispanic Society of America for their essential collaboration. At The Metropolitan Museum of Art, Dorothy Mahon, Conservator in the Paintings Conservation Department, provided us with valuable information on Goya's painting technique.

In New York, we owe a great debt of gratitude to the entire staff of the Frick Art Reference Library for their expertise and support, especially Patricia Barnett, Andrew W. Mellon Librarian, Inge Reist, Chief of Collections, Development and Research, and Lydia Dufour, Chief of Public Services, a Hispanist herself and most generous collaborator.

This catalogue rests on the foundations of the pioneering scholarship of several distinguished Goya experts. We are particularly indebted to the fundamental work of Juliet Wilson-Bareau and are grateful for her help in refining our loan list and directing us to works in a private collection. The scholarship of Janis Tomlinson is reflected throughout these pages, and we turned often to the work of Nigel Glendinning, Priscilla Muller, and Carmen Garrido. Jacques Fauqué and Ramón Villanueva Etcheverría's authoritative study of Goya in Bordeaux was an essential reference.

A number of staff members of The Frick Collection contributed substantially to the carrying out of this exhibition and catalogue with characteristic professionalism and collegiality. It was a pleasure to work with Diane Farynyk,

Registrar and Exhibition Manager, her assistant, Allison Galea, and former assistant, Christine Minas, who handled the organization of the show. We are equally indebted to Joseph Godla, Conservator, William Trachet, Senior Conservation Technician, and Adrian Anderson, Senior Galleries Technician, for their fine work on the installation, and to Barbara Roberts, former Conservator. It gives us pleasure to acknowledge the beautiful installation design of Stephen Saitas. Heidi Rosenau, Manager of Media Relations, Rebecca Brook, Manager of Publications, and Amy Herman, Head of Education, have also contributed substantially to this undertaking. Edgar Munhall, Curator Emeritus, provided guidance and warm encouragement. Curatorial summer intern Margot Weller and Library intern Amanda Young were also very helpful.

We are much indebted to Elaine Koss, Editor in Chief, for her expert shaping of the text and buoyant good will which carried us through. We also thank Michael Bodycomb, Photographer, and Kristine Potter, Digital Imaging Coordinator. At Yale University Press in London, we were privileged to work with Gillian Malpass and thank her for her faith in the project and exquisite design of the book.

From the outset, Joanna Sheers, Curatorial Assistant, handled the lion's share of the administrative end of the exhibition and catalogue with the utmost care and efficiency. She also contributed significantly to the research and editing and wrote the Chronology that appears at the end of the catalogue. Iraida Rodríguez-Negrón, a doctoral candidate at the Institute of Fine Arts, New York University, joined us as a part-time research assistant in the fall of 2005; the remarkably thorough files she assembled are a testament to her ingenuity and the foundation for the entries. She is responsible for the Bibliography. To both our young partners we express our deepest thanks and admiration; the exhibition and catalogue could not have been accomplished without their collaboration. We also thank each other for a most enjoyable and rewarding partnership; and last but by no means least, we gratefully acknowledge our spouses, Sandra Brown and Jonathan Galassi, for their sustaining interest and encouragement throughout the phases of this fascinating project.

Jonathan Brown

Susan Grace Galassi

facing page Self-Portrait after Illness of 1792–93 (detail of cat. 2; reproduced larger than actual size)

Aun aprendo

54

JONATHAN BROWN   *"I Am Still Learning":*
Goya's Last Works, 1824–1828

Emerging from dark shadows, a bent and ancient man inches his way forward, supported by a cane in each gnarled hand (fig. 1). His hair is scraggly and unkempt, an impressive white beard falls almost to the waist. He is clad in a shapeless gown that covers his feet. Although he is weak and feeble, diminished by time, his eyes blaze with life and intensity, as he focuses his gaze outward. In the upper right corner, a terse inscription explains the scene—*Aun aprendo (I Am Still Learning)*. Although the body may be failing, the mind is alert and curious.

This drawing in black crayon is part of an album created by Francisco de Goya in the final years of his life, 1824–28. Although Goya's facial features do not closely resemble those of the old man, the drawing has long been interpreted as a metaphorical self-portrait. In June 1824 Goya, then seventy-eight years old, began a self-imposed exile in France, settling in Bordeaux. Despite waning physical powers and severe bouts of illness, Goya worked without surcease, often in innovative ways. From time to time, he painted the portraits of friends and supporters, achieving a marvelous breadth of execution. These portraits, with their subtle, muted tonalities and vigorous brushwork, breathe the air of modernity. And he drew incessantly. Since 1796 Goya had made albums of drawings in which he created a private universe inhabited by subjects real and imagined. During his time in Bordeaux, he executed some 123 drawings in black crayon. The pages of the Bordeaux albums, known as Album G and Album H, testify to unceasing powers of observation and imagination.

Another facet of his activity was lithography, a newly invented graphic medium with which he had experimented in Madrid. Late in 1825, he created four lithographs of bullfighting scenes known as the Bulls of Bordeaux. Using the medium with extraordinary freedom, Goya anticipated an unbridled approach to lithography that would not become current until the closing decades of the century.

Finally, he invented an entirely new technique, a type of miniature painting in which the subject was determined not by previous intention but by patterns haphazardly created on the surface of small slivers of ivory. Goya was as good as his word: he continued to learn and discover ways to invigorate his art and, through his art, his old age.

*   *   *

Fig. 1   *Aun aprendo (I Am Still Learning)*, Album G. 54, 1824–28, black crayon on paper, $7^1/_2 \times 5^3/_4$ (19.1 × 14.5) (reproduced larger than actual size), Museo Nacional del Prado, Madrid

Turmoil in Spain

Goya's decision to leave Madrid and move to France, made in the spring of 1824, must be seen in the context of the violent, convoluted course of Spanish politics in the wake of the French Revolution.[1] Spanish society from around 1800 to 1828, the year of Goya's death, was marked by an unending, brutal struggle between conservative and progressive forces and by invasions of foreign armies. The reign of Charles IV (1789–1808) had made a promising start in continuing the enlightened policies of the previous Bourbon king, Charles III. However, the French Revolution struck fear into the minds of the monarch and his advisers, who saw the republican contagion spreading to Spain. Charles twice placed the government in the hands of the upstart Manuel Godoy (an important patron of Goya's), who was first minister from November 1792 to May 1798 and returned to power in 1799. This highly unpopular figure played a game of international politics and played it badly. His main opponent was Napoleon Bonaparte, who took advantage of a Franco-Spanish alliance and in 1808 sent the French army to Spain. The occupation coincided with a popular uprising against Charles IV and Godoy, forcing the king to abdicate in favor of his son, Prince Ferdinand, who had masterminded the revolt. Napoleon, taking advantage of the confusion, made them all prisoners and brought them to France. He then installed his brother Joseph on the throne of Spain.

The French annexation of Spain immediately sparked a war of resistance and liberation against King Joseph. True, some Spaniards decided to join his government, which promised to effect much-needed changes in the economic and social order. They became know known as *afrancesados* or *josefinos*. Between 1808 and 1813, the so-called Peninsular War raged on, pitting the Spanish irregulars, known as guerrillas (later joined by the English), against the might of the French army. At the same time, a group of loyalists, called the Regency Council, assembled in Cádiz and convoked a meeting of the Cortes, a body representative of the people of Spain. The Cortes declared its sovereignty, establishing a constitutional monarchy, and proposed a thorough revision of Spanish law and institutions, which was embodied in the constitution of 1812.

Defeated by the Spanish guerrillas and the English army, commanded by the duke of Wellington, the French retreated in 1813, and in the following year Ferdinand (fig. 2) returned to Madrid to become king, amid high hopes for the future. These were soon dashed, as he quickly abrogated the constitution and

Fig. 2 *Ferdinand VII*, 1814–15, oil on canvas, 81⅞ × 56⅛ (208 × 142.5), Museo Nacional del Prado, Madrid

restored absolute monarchy and all its regressive policies and institutions. Collaborators and Liberals were persecuted; many fled to France, others were summarily imprisoned.

For all the brutality of the reprisals, pockets of resistance to the monarch remained active, and in 1820 one group staged a successful revolt. This was led by an army officer, Rafael del Riego (1785–1823), who rallied his soldiers and proclaimed allegiance to the constitution. In 1823 the constitutional government took the king prisoner and brought him to Cádiz. However, the Spanish "spring" quickly turned to winter. A year earlier, the Holy Alliance, comprising the conservative powers of Europe, had decided to intervene and reverse the course of events. The French organized an expeditionary force, known as the 100,000 Sons of Saint Louis, which entered Spain in the spring of 1823 and, encountering little resistance, occupied Madrid on May 24. On August 30–31, the French defeated the constitutional army at Trocadero. Ferdinand was freed and Riego was taken prisoner; he was executed in Madrid on November 7, and six days later the king was again in the capital and in control. The expected reign of terror was soon unleashed.

Goya's activities during the so-called Liberal Triennium are not well known. On February 27, 1819, he had purchased a small house and garden on the western outskirts of Madrid, the famous Quinta del Sordo. Later that year, he fell deathly ill but made an almost miraculous recovery, commemorated in a fascinating composition, the *Self-Portrait with Dr. Arrieta* (cat. no. 3). On April 4, 1820, he attended a meeting of the Royal Academy for the last time. Over the next two years, there is no trace of the painter.

Although direct evidence of Goya's support of the constitutional government is tenuous, it is nearly certain that his sentiments veered in that direction. Indeed, one of the interpretations of the mural decorations of the Quinta del Sordo, the Black Paintings, is based on that very premise, and Los Caprichos are thoroughly imbued with the spirit of the Enlightenment.[2] More revealing are Goya's actions, which confirm that, whatever the strength of his support for the Liberals, it would be perceived as solid. Little imagination was needed to foresee the consequences that would be inflicted on supporters of the constitution. Thus, on September 17, 1823, less than three weeks after Trocadero, Goya transferred the deed of the Quinta to his grandson, Mariano, then seventeen years old. His motive could only have been to protect this asset from expropriation. (In 1832 Mariano would make the property over to his father, Javier

Goya, from whom he ultimately reinherited it in 1854.) It was not a moment too soon; with the return of the king to Madrid on November 13, 1823, the absolutist mobs launched violent reprisals against suspected Liberals. By a decree of January 8, 1824, the police force was organized and joined the hunt, the ferocity of which finally persuaded the European allies to insist that the purge be ended. On May 1, 1824, amnesty for the Liberals was decreed, and only then did Goya come out of hiding.

Goya's place of refuge was the home of a distinguished Aragonese priest, José Duaso y Latre (1775–1849; cat. no. 6), who had quarters in the Hospital del Buen Suceso in the Puerta del Sol. Although highly placed in civil and ecclesiastical circles, he took the risk of harboring Goya and other Liberals during the violent early months of 1824. Goya may have moved in with Duaso in January, when the police and military commissions were organized. By February 19 he appears to have been considering leaving Madrid. On that date, he assigned a power of attorney to collect his royal salary.[3] One of the witnesses was Dionisio Antonio de Puga, whose wife, María Martínez, has tentatively been identified as the sitter in the Frick portrait (cat. no. 7). This subtle portrait is the masterpiece of Goya's last years, a bold invention of flattened space and a limited palette of somber hues.

In the event, Goya stayed with Duaso until the amnesty, and once it was declared he wasted no time. On May 2 he petitioned the king for a leave of six months to take the mineral waters at the spa of Plombières-les-Bains (Vosges), which was granted on May 30.[4] This was merely a pretext to leave Spain. By June 27 he was in Bordeaux, some 750 kilometers from Madrid (the coach trip from Madrid to Bordeaux took six or seven days), where he would join a large community of political refugees from Spain, some of whom, the *josefinos*, had been living in the city on the Garonne River since the fall of Joseph Bonaparte. Goya probably had nothing to fear from the king, who treated him with generosity in the final years of his life. But how could he be confident of the sovereign's disposition beforehand? The evidence was all to the contrary.

It has also been speculated that Goya was motivated by a desire to protect his companion, Leocadia Zorrilla y Weiss (fig. 3), and her two younger children, Guillermo and Rosario.[5] Leocadia later claimed to have been an outspoken Liberal, and if so she could have been in grave danger. She had also been accused of adultery by her husband, a charge that might have made her a target of the ultraconservative supporters of the king. For some reason, this infor-

Fig. 3   Artist unknown, *Leocadia Weiss*, oil on canvas, 13⅛ × 10⅜ (33.5 × 26.5), Fundación Lázaro Galdiano, Madrid

mal family appears to have split up briefly in early 1824, when Goya, about to leave for France, entrusted Rosario to a friend, the architect Don Tiburcio Pérez y Cuervo (cat. no. 5). Cuervo's portrait, painted in 1820, is the first in the series of intimate portraits of the last years. With their broad execution and subdued tonal harmonies, they mark a new phase of the artist's development. In any event, Leocadia and her children were soon reunited and by September 20, 1824, were with Goya in Bordeaux.

Goya in Bordeaux

Goya's arrival in Bordeaux was reported by the renowned playwright Leandro Fernández de Moratín (1760–1828), who had been a close friend in earlier times (cat. no. 10).[6] A supporter of Joseph Bonaparte's, Moratín had been expelled from Madrid and lived mostly in Barcelona before moving to Bordeaux in 1821. There he joined forces with another exile, Manuel Silvela y García de Aragón (1781–1832), an official of Bonaparte's government, who had started a school for the children of émigrés (cat. no. 11). Moratín maintained a regular correspondence with a friend in Madrid, Abate Juan Antonio Melón, and his often pungent letters are the principal contemporary source of information about Goya's years in Bordeaux up to September 1827, when the playwright moved to Paris. His letter to Melón dated June 27, 1824, provides the leitmotif of Goya's last years—precarious health, undaunted spirit.

> In effect, Goya arrived, deaf, old, clumsy and weak, and without knowing a word of French and without bringing a servant (which no one needs more than he), and so content and so desirous of seeing the world. He was here three days; on two of them he ate with us as if he were a young student.[7]

As Moratín states, Goya was only making a brief stop in Bordeaux en route to Paris. "I've exhorted him to return around September and not to linger in Paris and be surprised by the winter that would finish him off. . . . We'll see if such a journey leaves him alive."

Goya's haste to reach Paris is a mystery, although some educated guesses can be made. To the eyes of the Paris police, who spied on the Spanish exile community, Goya was a harmless old man. A police report, dated July 15, revealed a placid routine of daily life.

The foreigner arrived in Paris on June 30 and he has descended on 5 rue Marivaux. The surveillance of which he has been the object has not been able to discover that he has habitual relations with any of his compatriots. He receives no one at his place and the difficulty he has in speaking and understanding French often keeps him at home, from where he does not leave except to visit monuments and take a walk in public places. Although he is seventy years old [actually seventy-eight], he appears older than his age and is extremely deaf.[8]

Either the surveillance was careless or it stopped too soon. Paris was swarming with Spanish émigrés, some of whom were in contact with Goya, including a few noblewomen who had known the painter or sat for their portraits in what must have seemed another life—the countess of Chinchón (Museo Nacional del Prado, Madrid) and her younger sister, the duchess of San Fernando (to whom he would write on November 30, 1824) and the marquise of Pontejos (fig. 4). Goya's entry into their circle was arranged by Moratín's introduction to Vicente González Arnao, a wealthy lawyer who had served in Joseph Bonaparte's government and had fled to Bordeaux after the defeat of the French. In 1824 he moved to Paris, where he handled the affairs of the Spanish exile community and established relationships with important French and Spanish bankers.

More important for Goya's plans were Joaquín María de Ferrer and his wife, Manuela de Álvarez Coiñas y Thomas. Ferrer had joined the constitutional government and, as a leading voice in calling for the removal of Ferdinand VII, had been sentenced to death. He made his escape via Gibraltar and Falmouth and then went to Paris in late December 1823. Having earlier conducted business in the French capital, Ferrer was able to establish himself in the world of banking. He was also an aficionado of prints and a devoted bibliophile, who supported a small publishing venture. These interests were an obvious attraction for Goya and perhaps explain why he painted portraits of the Ferrers (cat. nos. 8 and 9) and made for them a painting of a bullfighting scene (cat. no. 22).

José María Cardano (1782–after 1827), a friend from Madrid, was another of Goya's contacts in Paris. In 1819 Cardano had founded the Real Establecimiento Litográfico in Madrid, where Goya made his first, rather unsatisfactory lithographs.[9] In July 1822 Cardano traveled to Paris to learn the latest techniques and refinements of the medium. We may suppose that Cardano took Goya around the ateliers so that he could see what was going on.

Fig. 4 *The Marquesa de Pontejos*, c. 1786, oil on canvas, 82³/₄ × 50 (210.3 × 127), Andrew W. Mellon Collection, National Gallery of Art, Washington D.C.

It has always seemed strange that, as far as is known, Goya had no contacts with the leading artists of Paris. One of the giants on the art scene was Eugène Delacroix, who was an admirer of Los Caprichos. In his diary entry of April 7, 1824, just a few months before Goya's arrival in Paris, Delacroix noted his intention to make lithographs in the "manner of Goya." Furthermore, Goya stayed in Paris just long enough to visit the Salon of 1824, inaugurated on August 25, which included Delacroix's *Massacre at Chios*, Gérard's *Daphnis and Chloe*, Ingres's *Vow of Louis XIII*, and Prud'hon's *Christ on the Cross*. Another star of the show was Constable's *White Horse*, now a prized possession of The Frick Collection. Given his insatiable curiosity, he probably took the opportunity to see what his French colleagues were doing, but it was very late in the day for him to be more than a spectator. From what we know of his artistic ideas, Goya would have admired Delacroix and loathed Ingres.

A final contact was Jerónimo Goicoechea, a young cousin of Javier Goya's wife, Gumersinda Goicoechea. Jerónimo was already in residence at the Hôtel Favart, where Goya was sent to stay. Also stationed in Paris was Javier's father-in-law, Martín Miguel de Goicoechea, a wealthy merchant, who was accompanied by his daughter Manuela and her husband, José Francisco Muguiro, all exiles from the troubles in Spain. Goya may have intended to meet them from the start, but Martín, Manuela, and José Francisco had left for London on June 19, just missing Goya's arrival.[10] By mid-August they had returned to Paris and on September 1, with the artist in tow, boarded a stagecoach and departed for Bordeaux. According to a letter written by Goya to the duchess of San Fernando on November 30, the arrival of the Goicoechea family had been timely, as he had completely run out of money.[11] This welter of random information does little to satisfy our curiosity about what should have been a momentous encounter—Goya, Paris, 1824. Yet he did have at least one possible purpose in mind: the painter, who always kept a close eye on his purse, was trying to establish a network of support and a market for future artistic projects. Subsequent events tend to confirm this conjecture.

Almost as soon as he had returned to Bordeaux, Goya was reunited with Leocadia Weiss and her two younger children. They had crossed the frontier on September 14 and by the twentieth were living with Goya in an apartment on 24 Cours de Tourny in the center of the city. Their arrival was noted by Moratín in a letter to Melón, dated September 20.

Goya is here again, with madame and the little ones, in good furnished quarters and in a good location. I believe they will pass the winter very comfortably in it. He wants to do my portrait, and from that I infer how pretty I am when such skilled paintbrushes aspire to multiply my copies.[12]

Ten days later, Moratín was a bit less sanguine. "Goya is here with his doña Leocadia; I do not perceive the greatest harmony between them."[13]

La Leocadia

Leocadia Zorrilla y Weiss (1788–1856) was a powerful force in Goya's final years, and their relationship has been the locus of much speculation.[14] This centers primarily on the paternity of her second and third children, Guillermo, born on January 31, 1811, and Rosario, born on October 3, 1814. Seven months after the birth of Guillermo, Leocadia's husband, Isidoro Weiss (they were married in 1807), accused her of infidelity, a charge he renewed the following year. This leaves a margin to suppose that Guillermo's father was not Leocadia's husband.

As for Goya's relationship to Rosario, this is a much-disputed question. Goya's wife, Josefa Bayeu, had died on June 20, 1812, which placed him at liberty to begin a new relationship. Goya's affection for Rosario, as expressed in letters written in Bordeaux, is unmistakable, although in one of these he explicitly distances himself from a paternal relationship with the little girl. Another factor that weighs against Goya's paternity of Rosario is his failure to make some sort of financial provision for her in a will or deed of gift. During his Bordeaux years, Goya assiduously saved his royal pension to create a fund for his grandson, Mariano, but left Rosario without a penny. Goya's paternal emotions, as evidenced by his relationship with his son and grandson, were very powerful, and the failure to provide a legacy for Rosario suggests that she was not a blood relative. However, he certainly took what might be called a grandfatherly interest in her artistic training. The idea of Goya involved in an intimate May-December relationship—he was after all no less than forty-two years older than Leocadia—has a certain fascination. However, these suspicions have never been confirmed.

Still, there is no doubt that the Weiss marriage was not a success. In the accusations of adultery, Isidoro did not pull his punches and accused his wife of having a "haughty, threatening spirit." Weiss, for his part, had invested Leocadia's

Fig. 5 *La Leocadia*, 1820–23, oil transferred
to canvas, 57⅞ × 52 (147 × 132), Museo
Nacional del Prado, Madrid

considerable dowry in the family jewelry shop, which in 1817 was facing bank-
ruptcy. The marriage was disintegrating and Goya was in the picture; he probably knew her through her family ties to Javier Goya's mother-in-law. It is now
supposed that their alliance began in 1820, when Goya moved to his country
house, the Quinta del Sordo. One of the paintings on the walls has tradition-
ally been identified as "La Leocadia" (fig. 5); the image is of an attractive woman
striking the pose of a melancholic, which was all too prophetic.

Once settled, Goya soon turned his attention to Rosario, now ten years old
and a fledgling artist. Goya had been teaching her the rudiments of drawing in
Madrid and decided that her talents were best suited to miniature painting.[15]
With this in mind, on October 28 he wrote to his new acquaintance in Paris,
Joaquín María de Ferrer, asking if he could send Rosario to live in his house
while she studied the art, treating her "as if she were my daughter."[16] (Despite
Goya's disclaimer, it is this phrase that has sparked the speculation that Rosario

Fig. 6 (*above left*) *Javier Goya,"* 1805, oil on copper, diameter: $3^{1}/_{8}$ (8.0) (reproduced larger than actual size), Museo de Zaragoza

Fig. 7 (*above right*) *Gumersinda Goicoechea,* 1805, oil on copper, diameter: $3^{1}/_{8}$ (8.0) (reproduced larger than actual size), Museo de Zaragoza

was his child.) Goya praised her to the skies and sent a small sample of her work which, he said, "had astounded all the professors [of painting] in Madrid as I hope will be the same there." Goya was asking a very big favor, which was not granted; Rosario remained in Bordeaux and studied with local artists.

Just a month later, Goya tried to interest another of his Parisian contacts in becoming a patron. On November 30 he drafted a letter to the duchess of San Fernando, accompanied by a drawing of what he called "three commissioners (agents or go-betweens)."[17] This represented three dwarfs who had recently appeared in the fair of Bordeaux; Goya carefully specified the height of each. The work must have been a drawing in the vein of the street scenes that appear in Albums G and H, the Bordeaux Albums, but the "commissioners" do not appear to have been well received. As far as we know, Goya never heard from the duchess again.

Only one more autograph letter survives from 1824, addressed to his son, Javier, in Madrid and dated December 24.[18] Javier was the unworthy star of Goya's affective universe (fig. 6).[19] Born on December 4, 1784, he was the last and only surviving child of the six who were born to Goya and Josefa Bayeu. Goya appears to have regarded him as the vehicle that would carry the family to new heights of respectability and wealth, hopes that ultimately came crashing to earth. On July 8, 1805, Javier married Gumersinda Goicoechea (1788–1852) (fig. 7), the daughter of Martín Miguel de Goicoechea and Juana Galarza, both members of prosperous families of merchants and bankers.

Overnight the newlyweds became wealthy by dint of the considerable sums bestowed on them by their relatives. Javier already enjoyed an annual royal pension of 12,000 reales, the result of the sale of the plates and remaining impressions of the Caprichos to the crown, and an additional 3,000 per annum, a bequest from the duchess of Alba. On top of this, Goya offered another annual sum of 13,000 reales should the couple move from his house, which they promptly did. Some years later, following the death of Josefa Bayeu (1812), Javier was given half the common property of his parents. From the bride's side came a dowry of 249,186 reales. These young people were rich and they were covetous.

Javier, who is described on the marriage certificate as a painter, did not have to work for a living and never did.[20] He seems to have kept his finances on track by occasionally selling works bequeathed to him by his father. Goya loved his idle son, but as revealed in a merciless portrait drawing of 1824 (cat. no. 4), he had no illusions about his character. His surviving letters to Javier from Bordeaux, admittedly few in number, talk only about Javier's failure to stay in touch and financial matters. Goya's finances were handled by Goicoechea (his death in 1825 was a severe blow to Goya, who visited him almost daily) and Jacques Galos, a French merchant and banker whose portrait was painted by Goya in 1826 (see fig. 33), another of the monochromatic masterpieces of the late years.[21]

Most of Goya's correspondence for 1825 is lost, but crucial pieces of information are recorded in other sources. Most important was the extension of his leave of absence. On January 13, 1825, Ferdinand VII granted the artist another six-month period, ostensibly to take the waters at Bagnères-en-Bigorre (Hautes-Pyrénées) in the hope that he would recover his health.[22] However, Goya was no invalid. As we learn from an informative letter written to Ferrer late in the year (December 20), he had spent the winter months of 1824–25 working on an entirely new project.

> It is true that last winter I painted on ivory and I have a collection of nearly forty exercises, but they are original miniatures which I have never seen the like of before because the whole is made up of points and things which look more like Velázquez' brushwork than that of Mengs.[23]

Goya possessed an unflagging curiosity about the possibilities of pictorial art and an eagerness to try new things. Proof of this assertion are the Bordeaux

Fig. 8   *A Seated Majo and Maja*, 1824–25,
carbon black and watercolor on ivory,
$3^1/_2 \times 3^3/_8$ (9 × 8.5), The National Museum of
Fine Arts, Stockholm

miniatures, which were executed in an experimental technique described by Antonio de Brugada, a young painter from Madrid who was Goya's mainstay in the final four years of his life. Brugada's observations were recorded by an early biographer of Goya, the French writer Laurent Matheron.[24]

Goya had long professed his belief in the power of imagination as the driving force of artistic creation. In the miniatures, this conviction assumes dramatic shape.[25] Often likened to the Black Paintings, these little chips of ivory are pure essences of Goya's late style. As for the subjects, not surprisingly they often reprise some of the "capricious" themes that had appeared in earlier works. *A Seated Majo and Maja* (fig. 8) represents the popular characters who first appear in the tapestry cartoons of the 1780s and are leading players in Los Caprichos (1799). The manic intensity of the Black Paintings, to which the term *capricho* has also been applied, is echoed in the *Monk and Old Woman* (cat. no. 14) and in the strange, leering figures in the *Heads of a Child and an Old Woman* (cat. no. 18). Goya's "images made by chance," as the Surrealists would have called them, turn out to be shaped by personal demons and obsessions.

Much of the information about Goya's life and well-being during 1825 comes from Moratín's letters to his friend Melón. Sometimes these are only scraps, but there are also choice morsels. The letter dated April 14 is particularly informative, revealing a restless Goya who was thinking about returning to Madrid, an idea that made no sense to Moratín.

Goya, with his seventy-nine Easters and his chronic complaints, doesn't know what he expects or wants. I'm exhorting him to stay quiet until his license [leave of absence] is finished. He likes the city, the countryside, the climate, the food, the independence, the tranquillity that he enjoys. Since he's here, he's had none of the illnesses that discomfited him there. And nevertheless, if they allowed him, he would put himself on the road, mounted on a chestnut-colored mule, with his cloth cap, his walnut stirrups, his wineskin and his saddlebags.[26]

Moratín's description of Goya's daily routine is confirmed by Brugada, who observed that Goya lived a modest, simple life. Most of his time was spent with Leocadia and the children and a few friends. Like many an exile, he sought the company of his compatriots. The Liberals and *josefinos* in Bordeaux gathered at the shop of Braulio Poc, like Goya, a native of Zaragoza, who would be a pallbearer at the artist's funeral. Over cups of chocolate, the expatriates would gossip about the latest political news and relive earlier, happier times. Goya communicated in sign language and spoke little, although he never lost the use of his voice. Brugada provides some information that helps us imagine how Goya participated in the *tertulias*.

> He still had his expansive moments of good humor and then, with that discordant voice of the deaf, he enjoyed telling the adventures of the good old days. There were clear moments of malice and joy, when the man of earlier times suddenly appeared whole. He rarely spoke of painting and almost never answered when you pushed him onto this territory.[27]

According to Brugada, Goya did break his silence on his art on at least one occasion. Although the words appear within quotation marks, they may not be verbatim. Yet the statement, which mocks academic painters and their tutelage of drawing, coincides with Goya's most important observations on the art of painting, his critique of the teaching program of the Real Academia de Bellas Artes de San Fernando, delivered on October 14, 1792.[28] Goya regarded the academic emphasis on line, contour, and precise modeling as against nature. The words are certainly colorful enough to have been spoken by him.

> My eye never perceives features or details. I don't count the hairs of the beard of the man who passes [my way], and the buttonholes of his suit do not stop my eye. My paintbrush should not see better than I do.[29]

Goya's artistic energies may have been little diminished, but his rugged constitution, which had allowed him to survive previous close encounters with death, was now starting to fail him. A medical report by two Bordeaux physicians, a Spanish translation of which is dated May 29, paints a disturbing picture.[30] Goya was suffering from an accumulation of ailments in the region of his groin. The doctors observed a paralysis of the bladder, a hardening of the bowels, and a large tumor on the perineum. They concluded "that the infirmity is incurable and the patient presently finds it impossible to do any exercise."

Writing to another friend in Madrid two and half weeks later, on June 16, Moratín observed that Goya had been at death's door but had managed to recover. Flushed with the exhilaration of having cheated death again, he was described by the playwright on June 28 with these words: "He is very full of himself and paints like nobody's business without ever wanting to correct anything he paints."[31]

Sick though he was, Goya did manage to formulate a petition to the king for the renewal of his leave of absence. The annual stipend, 50,000 reales, was the major source of income and provided more than enough to live on. The surplus was being invested in government bonds through the agency of Jacques Galos and was being patiently accumulated for the benefit of Goya's grandson, Mariano. Goya's petition, this time for a year's extension, was accompanied by the certificate from his French doctors. Ferdinand hastened to approve the action. The request was presented on June 21 and granted on July 4; due notice was taken of the "decaying condition" of Goya's health.[32]

We next hear from Moratín on October 30, 1825, informing Melón that the Goya ménage had moved from the Cours de Tourny to the suburb of Saint-Seurin, occupying the house at 10 Chemin de la Croix-Blanche.

> Goya has taken a very comfortable little house with a northern and southern light and a little bit of a garden; it is a new, self-standing house which suits him very well. . . . Doña Leocadia, with her customary fearlessness, swears at times and enjoys herself at others. La Mariquita [Rosario's nickname] now speaks French like a woodlark, sews and skips and amuses herself with a few little toads of her own age.[33]

After a year in Bordeaux, Goya, the volatile Leocadia, and the two children seemed to be putting down roots.

Lithographs and Drawings

Amid this domestic tranquillity, Goya decided to return to the art of lithography, which he had practiced in Madrid before leaving for France. Writing once more to Ferrer on December 6, Goya asked his Parisian acquaintance about a lithograph he had earlier sent via an intermediary.[34] The print in question is one of the series known as the Bulls of Bordeaux, four large lithographs depicting

Fig. 9   Gustave de Galard (1779–1841),
Gaulon's Workshop, 1823, lithograph,
Bibliothèque municipale de Bordeaux,
Fonds Delpit

scenes of bullfighting. Goya added his address and a very curious postscript: "And if we die, then let us be buried." Was this an appeal for sympathy or an outburst of fatalism? Ferrer seems to have been unmoved; his negative reaction can be inferred from Goya's answer (December 20, 1825) to his now-lost letter. Goya had to swallow the bitter pill and asked if Ferrer would be willing to find a print dealer who could sell them cheaply as works of an anonymous artist.[35]

Lithography was a recent invention (1796–99), and Goya had first experimented with the medium in 1819, working with José María Cardano. The results are somewhat uneven. (As can be inferred from Goya's letter to Ferrer of December 6, Goya and Cardano were staying in touch.) He was tempted to try again by the superior quality of French lithographers and by one in particular, Cyprien Gaulon (1777–1858), whose atelier (fig. 9) was quite near the residence of his financial agent, Jacques Galos. Gaulon's superb craftsmanship made it possible for Goya to return to the art of lithography with renewed interest and improved results. As a token of gratitude and demonstration of his mastery of the technique, Goya made a beautiful lithographic portrait of his printer friend (cat. no. 27).

In choosing bullfights to attract the Parisian public, Goya was taking a risk; the French were experiencing one of their periodic aversions to the spectacle. Presumably Ferrer had offered some encouragement; why else would Goya have painted that small bullfight for him in the summer of 1824? However, Goya's previous set of bullfight prints does not appear to have enjoyed great success. In 1816 he had published the Tauromaquia, but this did not offer much competition to an earlier series by Antonio Carnicero (1790). These are regarded as banal in comparison to Goya's dramatic compositions, but Carnicero's were more widely circulated; pirated editions were published in France, Italy, and England.[36]

The Bulls of Bordeaux in fact opens with a reprise of Plate 24 of La Tauromaquia, *El famoso Americano, Mariano Ceballos*, depicting the daring feat of the South American matador who made his debut in the ring at Pamplona in 1775. Riding a wild bull, he closes in for the kill with a short sword. Even more extraordinary than this maneuver is the execution of the lithograph with its novel use of crayon and scraper. Goya carefully depicts the foreground scene, paying close attention to the bulls but drawing the *torero* in a more sketchy manner. The crowd, which has spilled over the barrier onto the arena, is a tangle of lines, suggesting human forms without defining them. *Aficionados* seated in the stands are composed entirely of circular shapes, representing their heads, and enlivened by vigorous, irregular patches of white where the crayon has been scraped away to reveal the stone. Ferrer probably did not know what to make of these experimental works; nor did anyone else. (For the set, see cat. nos. 23–26.) The entire edition of one hundred was quickly sent to a warehouse owned by Jacques Galos.[37]

Fig. 10   *Claudio Ambrosio Surat/Llamado el Esquelete vibiente/ en Bordeux año 1826 (Claude Ambroise Seurat, Known as the Living Skeleton, in Bordeaux the Year 1826)*, Album H. 45, 1826, black crayon on paper, 7$\frac{1}{2}$ × 5$\frac{3}{4}$ (19.2 × 14.7), The State Hermitage Museum, St. Petersburg

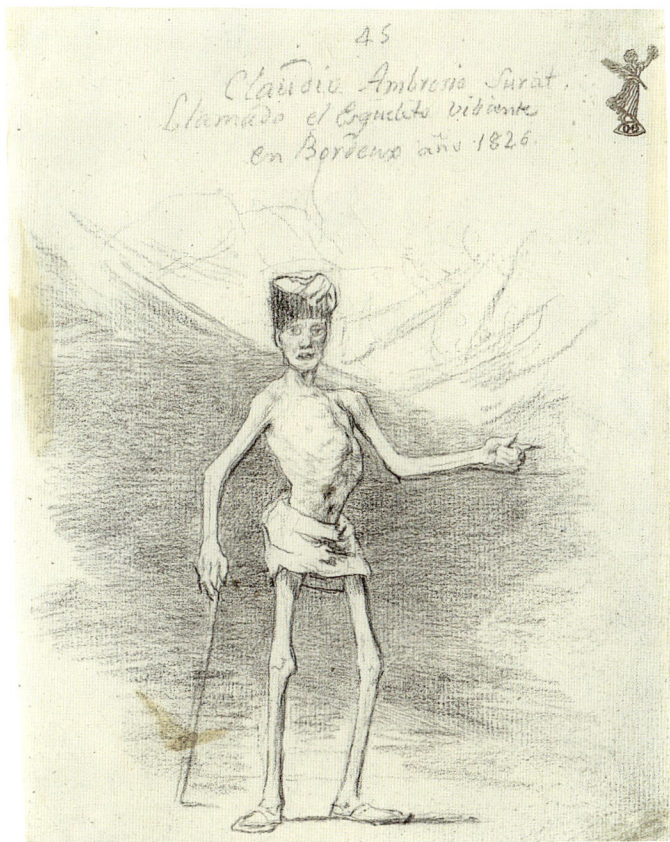

Goya's use of graphic media was not confined to lithography. From a quantitative point of view, his drawings represent the majority of his Bordeaux output. Upon reflection, this is logical. The art of drawing is at once economical and supple, permitting a master artist to transmute ideas into images with facility. Goya was a prolific draftsman throughout his career, and the Bordeaux Albums, G and H as they are known, open wide the doors of his private world.

The drawings done in Bordeaux are a fascinating anthology of fact, memory, and fantasy. One real-life character who makes an appearance is Claude Ambroise Seurat, the human skeleton, who was seen by Goya at the fair of 1826 (fig. 10). He had arrived in October and placed himself on public display for a fee of ten sous. In a contemporary newspaper article, it is reported that the "human skeleton," age twenty-eight, was five feet, three and a quarter inches tall and weighed a mere forty-six pounds.[38]

Goya moves from the factual to the fanciful in *Gran coloso durmido (Great Sleeping Colossus)* (fig. 11). This arresting image represents the head of a giant swarming with tiny human figures who scale the heights, some with

Fig. 11   *Gran coloso durmido (Great Sleeping Colossus)*, Album G. 3, 1824–28, black crayon on paper, 7$\frac{1}{2}$ × 6 (19.2 × 15.4), The State Hermitage Museum, St. Petersburg

the aid of a ladder. Upon attaining the summit, one of them raises a celebratory flag. A venture into the subconscious is *Mal sueño* (G. a., Museo Nacional del Prado, Madrid), a quintessential bad dream in which a flock of magpies flies away with the terrified human face in their beaks as the dreamer emits a scream. In the ample space between dream and reality Goya exposes human frailties. *Who Will Win? (Quien vencerá?)* he asks of two men consumed with rage and hatred (fig. 12). They fire at each other at point-blank range and achieve only their mutual self-destruction. As he approached his eightieth birthday, Goya, despite his infirmities, was still going strong.

Goya at Eighty

Goya completed eighty years on March 30, 1826, and decided to petition the king to retire at full salary. This request required him to be present in Madrid, and thus in May he began the long, taxing journey back to the Spanish court. Moratín alerted Melón of Goya's impending departure in a letter of May 7. He had his doubts that he was strong enough to survive the trip.

Fig. 12 *Quien vencerá? (Who Will Win?)*, Album G. 58, 1824–28, black crayon on paper, 7½ × 5¼ (19.2 × 13.5), The State Hermitage Museum, St. Petersburg

The news there is to communicate to you from here is of very little importance. One thing is Goya's trip, which will be within two or three days, and arranged as he always arranges his travels; he is going alone and unhappy with the French. If he has the good fortune that nothing harms him on the road, you can welcome him when he arrives; if he doesn't arrive, don't find it strange because the tiniest little ailment can leave him stiff in the corner of an inn.[39]

The trip went smoothly; the petition was presented on May 30 and was authorized by the king on June 17.[40] As the appropriate royal official stated, the artist was eighty years old and had served with distinction in the royal household for fifty-three.[41] His works had been widely praised, and as a further consideration, his advanced age implied that he would enjoy the favor for very little time. He was free to return to France to enjoy, as the royal official had correctly surmised, a brief period of official retirement. (In fact, Goya had not received a royal commission since 1802.)

Little more is known about this brief stay in Madrid. Obviously he lodged with his son and his family, and obviously he was not tempted to remain with them, reinforcing Javier's fears about the disposition of his father's estate. The only other record is the idealized portrait by the court painter Vicente López (1772–1850), in which a robust Goya sits bolt upright, brush and palette firmly held in his hands, barely marked by signs of advanced old age (fig. 13). By July Goya was again in Bordeaux and, as Moratín reported, was eating, napping, drawing, and living in peace with his second family. Late in that year, they moved again to another house in the same district, 13 rue Saint-Seurin.

After the surge of creativity experienced in late 1824, which carried through to the end of the following year, Goya's output declined. The one signed portrait of 1826 depicts his friend and financial agent, Jacques Galos (see fig. 34). It is inscribed *Dn. Santiago/Galos pintado por Goya de edad de 80 años de 1826*, and thus was painted between March 30 and the end of the year.[42] As is the case with most of the late portraits, Goya proudly cites his age, offering proof of his unflagging artistic energy and skill.

More accurately, it should be said that Goya's known production declined, because according to Brugada's colorful testimony, never a day went by that Goya did not paint.

> Goya painted; he produced until his final day. Less careful than ever, he painted carelessly on any piece of wood, cardboard or paper. Each day brought its work. He often covered in the morning what he had painted the night before. It may be remembered that in Madrid he did not always make use of brushes; in Bordeaux he did not use them at all. He replaced them with a knife, a piece of cloth anything at all. In this way he did some bullfights, to rejuvenate his heart [spirit], some of his Caprichos and a large number of small still lifes.[43]

The whereabouts of most of these works is not known; it is not impossible that they were thrown away because, according to Matheron, "the majority of these last paintings of the artist were feeble and slack; the touch was weak, the drawing lost its precision and firmness. But for him to do otherwise would have surely surpassed the limits of the marvelous."[44]

Proof of Goya's continued mastery of portraiture, and indeed of painting, is *Juan de Muguiro* (see fig. 35), precisely dated May 1827 by Goya himself, and giving his age as eighty-one. Like other sitters of the Bordeaux years, Muguiro was a friend and distant relative of the artist's. His brother was the husband of Manuela Goicoechea, the sister of Javier Goya's wife. A banker, Juan de Muguiro also exercised power of attorney in Bordeaux for Javier Goya. The

Fig. 13   Vicente López Portaña (1772–1850), *The Painter Francisco de Goya*, 1827, oil on canvas, 36⅝ × 29½ (93 × 75), Museo Nacional del Prado, Madrid

20

oper a su Amigo Goya

portrait of Muguiro is one of the masterpieces of the final years. Using a limited range of colors, essentially tones of dark green and greenish blue, except for the face, hands, and shirt, Goya produced a chiseled image of his friend. The brush strokes, which are tremulous in places, are heavily loaded with paint, enlivening the surface of the subdued image. Muguiro appears as if attending to business; he holds a just-opened letter and gazes expectantly at the viewer. To his left is a writing table, on top of which, and rendered with the fewest possible number of brush strokes, are an inkwell and quill pen and more papers. Goya added a signature that is almost ostentatious; perhaps he was brimming with pride that, at his advanced age, he was still the best painter in the world.

Goya's friendship with Muguiro seems to have led to a wholly unexpected development. On July 2, 1827, Muguiro obtained a pass to go to Madrid; his traveling companion must have been Goya. Although this second trip to Madrid has sometimes been doubted, it certainly happened. We even know the date when the painter returned to France, September 20.[45] What remains mysterious is the motive for this daring displacement. Why would the ancient Goya endure the hardships of travel, made doubly uncomfortable and dangerous by his tumor? That he saw his son and grandson is not only obvious but documented by a portrait of Mariano, dedicated with an inscription on the verso: *Goya a su nieto/a los 81 años de su edad* (Goya, to his grandson at 81 years of age).[46] The handsome young man in this sketchy portrait (fig. 14) would dissipate his inheritance in dubious financial schemes and be forced to sell the many works of Goya's bequeathed to him by his father.

Only one document of this 1827 trip has come to light, a unique letter from Goya to Leocadia.[47] It is dated "Madrid, 13 of August" and hence could only have been written in 1827, the previous year's journey having ended in July. As in any informal or intimate letter, most of the references are oblique or written in response to topics mentioned by the sender. The name of Lord Wellington appears but, as will be seen, in connection with an inquiry from Leocadia. Reference is made to the "matter of Silvela and Moratín," referring to their intention to move to Paris. More than anything, however, is the affection expressed by Goya toward his companion, affection that goes beyond mere formulas.

I have just read your most beautiful letter right through and it has made me so happy that even if I tell you it has made me completely better I am not exaggerating at all. A million thanks.

Fig. 14 *Mariano Goya*, 1827, oil on canvas
20$\frac{1}{2}$ × 16$\frac{1}{4}$ (52 × 41.2), private collection,
Switzerland

And the valediction reads: "A thousand kisses and a thousand things from your most affectionate Goya."

The Last Months

At this point, we enter into the tangled web of Goya's family and finances. Goya had two families, one comprising Javier, Gumersinda, and Mariano, the other, Leocadia, Guillermo, and Rosario. For understandable reasons, Javier was deeply worried that Goya would provide for Leocadia at his expense. The mere fact that his father was returning to Bordeaux was cause enough to be concerned, if indeed the visit to Madrid was not motivated by the intention to provide money or property to support Leocadia and her children. Javier must have pressed his claims to be sole heir in the most emphatic terms and persuaded Goya to leave his will untouched. As a further measure, he decided to send his wife and son to Bordeaux to safeguard their interests.

Upon returning to Bordeaux in late September, Goya discovered that he would have to move again, his landlord having decided to rebuild the house. He returned to the center of town, to a third-floor apartment at 39 Fossés de l'Intendance. A neighboring occupant was José Pío de Molina, a prominent member of the exile community. Matheron, relying on Brugada, provides a few poignant details of Goya's final months.

> He resumed his peaceful, bourgeois habits. But his energy was going away, his walks became less frequent, his paintbrushes less active, his spirits darker. Soon he could not go out except with the help of M. de Brugada. He leaned on his arm and in isolated places he tried to walk alone. But the efforts were useless. He didn't have the legs for it. He then became angry. "What humiliation. At eighty years," he cried out, "they have to walk me like a baby. I have to learn to walk!"[48]

As the old man and his young friend inched their way along the streets of the city, Brugada used sign language to communicate, and here again he aroused Goya's ire. "Can't you make your signs more discreetly? Does it give you pleasure to allow the whole world to see that the old Goya can neither walk nor hear?"

Another anecdote takes us into Goya's apartment, where a piano had been rented for Rosario. Brugada would play once in a while, and Goya hit on an idea that would enable him to hear the music, or so he thought. He went to the piano, placed his hands on the piano strings, and told his friend, "Play a chord, play a chord!" hoping that the sound would be transmitted through his fingertips. But all he could apprehend was that someone had touched the keyboard. "'Nothing, nothing,' he said sadly, and went to sit down."[49]

During the first months of 1828, which would be the last of his life, Goya found renewed enthusiasm from the pending visit of the family of Javier Goya. The trip to Madrid in the summer of 1827 had indeed heightened Javier's anxiety about the provisions of his father's will. Goya had drafted a will in 1811, a year before the death of his wife, and, as far as anyone knew, it had never been amended. But Goya was in distant Bordeaux, living with Leocadia, who naturally would try to secure at least some of Goya's property. Three letters from Goya to Javier exist, written in January and March, which are informative and imply that the son was as much attached to his father's pursestrings as he was to his heartstrings.

In the letter of January 17, Goya expressed his joy that Gumersinda and Mariano were on their way to Bordeaux. For the moment, Javier was remaining in Madrid to protect his interests, but Goya was already making arrangements for their stay, which he hoped would last a couple of years. Javier could come whenever he wished; everything would be ready after he returned from a planned trip to Paris.[50]

Two months later, on March 12, Goya wrote again, in answer to Javier's letter of the third.[51] It appears that Javier was now planning to take his family to Paris, to Goya's great consternation. "This is a better city and more appropriate for Mariano's needs." And speaking of Mariano, he reminded his son that he had been patiently accumulating the capital that would yield a pension for Mariano of 12,000 reales per year. This money was being saved from his royal salary (50,000 reales or 12,500 francs d'or per year) and being deposited regularly with Galos, who had just informed him that he needed only 3,000 francs more to reach the goal. Goya seems to have harbored no illusions about the motives of Javier's affection.

In the letter to his son of March 26, Goya was still awaiting the arrival of the "travelers" and expressed great joy that Javier had canceled his plans to go to Paris and would be coming to Bordeaux, he hoped in the summer.[52] The pension for Mariano was now only 979 francs short, which would be covered when Javier remitted two more payments from the crown. Goya reported that he had been ill but was now feeling better, thanks to a remedy of powdered valerian given him by his neighbor Pío de Molina. Two days later, on March 28, Gumersinda and Mariano at last arrived, just in time for Goya's eighty-second birthday (March 30). In an undated note written at this very time, Goya sent a brief message to Javier.

> I can't tell you how much happiness I have. I'm slightly indisposed and in bed. God willing that you come to join them for my pleasure to be complete.[53]

We learn of Goya's final days in a letter from Leocadia to Moratín of April 28.[54] Following lunch on April 1, Goya felt ill and went to bed. At 5 a.m. of the

following morning, he awoke, having suffered a stroke; he was unable to speak, and his right side was paralyzed. Although he recovered his speech, he could not move and remained in this condition for two weeks, able to recognize people but in a state of confusion and bewilderment. He expressed a desire to make a will in favor of Leocadia and her children but was told by his duplicitous daughter-in-law that one had already been written. At 2 a.m. on April 16, he passed away in the presence of Brugada and Pío de Molina (fig. 15). He was interred in the cemetery of the church of Notre Dame on April 17, in the family tomb of Martín Miguel de Goicoechea.

A coda to this chapter remains to be told: the fate of Leocadia Weiss and her family. Upon receiving news of his father's illness, Javier Goya began the process to secure his inheritance before leaving for France.[55] After assembling the necessary documentation, namely a copy of his own birth certificate and of his father's will, dated June 3, 1811, he departed for Bordeaux. He arrived at the frontier on April 21, where he encountered Pío de Molina, en route to Madrid to see if Goya had made provision for Leocadia in his will. Javier did not see fit to spare him the trip.

Two days later, he was in Bordeaux and immediately engaged a lawyer to establish his sole claim to his father's estate. Javier would inherit everything, including the significant sum amassed by Goya during his years at Bordeaux. Nothing was left to Leocadia, and Javier was pitiless. Her letter to Moratín of April 28 is sad and touching.

> He [Javier] has come to see me three times, and after having collected the silver, the clock and the pistols, he told me what accounts his father had had and said, "As you are in a foreign country, if you wish to return to your own, here is a bill of 1,000 francs and you can keep the furniture and clothes."[56]

The rent had been paid to the end of the month, and she was looking for a place to live.

On May 13 Leocadia wrote another letter to Moratín, who must have been her last hope.[57] She was requesting his assistance in tracking down a certain Mr. Hoogen, a German who formerly had been secretary to the duke of Wellington and obviously an intimate friend of the family of Isidoro Weiss. In fact, it has recently been suggested that he was Leocadia's paramour and the father of Guillermo.[58] This is undoubtedly the same person whom Leocadia had been attempting to trace in 1827 via Abate Melón. Evidently he could not be found and, with Moratín's death on June 21, the quest seems to have been dropped.

Late in 1829 Leocadia sold her last remaining valuable possession, the painting by Goya which she called the "Milkmaid" and is now known as the *Milkmaid of Bordeaux* (cat. no. 12). On December 9 she addressed a letter to Juan de Muguiro, who had offered to buy the painting on previous occasions.[59] The time had come and the picture was sold. (It remained in Muguiro's family until donated to the Prado in 1945.) Although its authenticity has recently been questioned, it is likely that this picture is among the many that Goya, no longer in full command of his powers, rapidly executed in the final stage of his life.

In his last works, Goya fought the fight against old age, armed with paintbrush, crayons, and a fecund imagination. Summoning remarkable energy and fortitude, he kept on creating and trying new things; he continued to learn. As he wrote to Ferrer in 1825, "I lack everything and the only thing I have in excess is willpower." His passion for experimentation and his refusal to play out his days with a repertory of old habits and stale routines sustained him, keeping his mind engaged even as his physical powers declined. The story is inspiring except for Leocadia's fate; she played no small part in keeping Goya vital and comfortable during his last years, and yet he failed to provide for her. He kept faith with his art, only to break it with the woman who dearly loved him. As she wrote to Moratín with a sense of foreboding shortly after Goya's death, "In spite of his disposition, our sorrow will be eternal, whatever luck befalls us."[60]

A Tale of Two Families

In the last four years of his life, Goya was caught in the middle of a struggle between Javier and Leocadia over the disposition of his money and property, including a large collection of the master's paintings, prints, and drawings, which remained in Madrid. Goya and his wife, Josefa Bayeu, had drafted a will in favor of Javier in 1811, which became the focal point of the battle. Leocadia was understandably anxious about her financial future, and it may well be that she coerced Goya to return to Madrid in 1827 to amend his will and to include her as a beneficiary. This codicil was never realized, probably because Javier and

Fig. 16 Rosario Weiss (1814–43), *Self-Portrait at Drawing Board*, pencil on paper, 8¼ × 10⅛ (21.0 × 25.6), Colección Rodríguez-Moñino-Brey, Real Academia Española, Madrid

Fig. 17   Rosario Weiss (1814–43), *Virgin of Contemplation*, 1840, oil on canvas, The Museum of the Royal Academy of Fine Arts of San Fernando, Madrid

Gumersinda exerted heavy pressure on his father to leave the will intact. In the event, Leocadia and her children were not mentioned and they were destitute. In 1831 she appealed for assistance to the French Ministry of Finance but was refused.

Leocadia, Guillermo, and Rosario returned to Spain in July 1833, and Rosario began a career as an artist, attempting to realize the promise seen in her by Goya (fig. 16).[61] Her path to success took many turns, not least because of the obstacles routinely placed in the way of a female artist. At first she worked as a copyist in the Prado, an activity that seems to have led her into the murky world of making fakes of old masters for an unscrupulous art dealer. She also achieved a modicum of fame as a portraitist in pencil and was a skilled lithographer. In 1840 her luck began to improve; in June she was admitted as a member of the Real Academia de Bellas Artes de San Fernando and presented the *Virgin of Contemplation* as her reception piece (fig. 17). Her next step up was important indeed. On January 18, 1842, Rosario was appointed drawing teacher to the queen of Spain, Isabella II, and her sister Infanta Luisa Fernanda at an annual salary of 8,000 reales. Unfortunately, just six months later, she was felled by a

serious illness and was obliged to ask for a leave of absence. The medical report of her condition was dire. She was suffering from convulsions, heart palpitations, and incontinence. Rosario could not return to the palace until December, and seven months later she was dead at the age of twenty-nine (July 3, 1843). Leocadia survived her daughter by thirteen years and died in obscurity in Madrid on August 7, 1856.

Goya's legitimate family fared much better, at least for a while. Javier was supported by his pensions from the crown and the duchess of Alba. He and his wife had also received a considerable amount of cash and property on the occasion of their marriage. And, of course, Javier inherited a sizable collection of his father's works, which he could and did sell to raise cash from time to time. The first recorded sale was put into motion as quickly as May 23–24, 1828 (Goya had been dead just over a month), when he offered a number of pictures to Infante Sebastián Gabriel, an avid collector and amateur painter.[62] The history of Javier's activities as an art dealer and possibly as a forger of his father's works is now too tangled to tell. However, on his death in 1854, he still owned a stock of pictures, prints, copperplates, and most of the drawings. These were to be liquidated by Goya's grandson, the ne'er-do-well Mariano (see fig. 14).

Growing up in the midst of plenty, Mariano saw no need to acquire a profession and turned his attention to speculating in real estate and mining properties, the latter of which failed and thoroughly depleted his financial resources.[63] A vain man, he aspired to join the ranks of the nobility and in 1846 purchased the title of marquis of Espinar, a transaction that was never officially recognized, although Mariano continued to use the distinction. As his financial situation deteriorated, he fell back on his last remaining asset, the collection of his grandfather's art. In one way or another, everything seems to have been sold. Many of the drawings, which had been kept intact by Javier, were acquired surreptitiously by Federico de Madrazo (1815–1894), the renowned society portraitist and director of the Museo del Prado from 1860 to 1868.[64] His life in ruins, Mariano moved to the austere mountain village of La Cabrera, north of Madrid, and went into seclusion. Although he dressed like a peasant, he continued to insist on the use of his bogus title. The last male of the Goya line died on January 8, 1874. Two daughters from Mariano's second marriage seem to have left no descendants.

facing page *La Leocadia* (detail of fig. 5)

NOTES

1 The following is a much-abbreviated account of the complex period from 1789 to 1828. For a fuller history of events from 1808 to 1833, see Carr 1982, pp. 79–154.

2 Muller 1984. The case that Goya is not the author of the Black Paintings remains unproven. See Glendinning 2004.

3 Virtually all Goya's writings as well as a variety of contemporary texts relating to him are collected in Canellas López 1981. For the text cited above, see p. 385, no. 266.

4 Ibid., pp. 385–86, no. 267.

5 Cruz Valdovinos 1987.

6 The fundamental sources for Goya in France are Núñez de Arenas 1950; Andioc 1973; and Fauqué and Villanueva Etcheverría 1982. The last is trilingual; citations are to the English version of the text. Also important is Ribemont and Garcia 1998 (Spanish version 1999).

7 Canellas López 1981, p. 497, no. CXLVII.

8 Ibid., p. 498, no. CL.

9 See Vega 1990 for the Real Establecimiento Litográfico.

10 Baticle 1998, p. 83.

11 Canellas López 1981, pp. 387–88, no. 270.

12 Ibid., p. 498, no. CLII.

13 Ibid., no. CLIII.

14 For Leocadia Weiss, see Fauqué and Villanueva Etcheverría 1982, pp. 568–74, and Cruz Valdovinos 1987.

15 For Rosario's artistic career, see Álvarez Lopera 2001 and 2003. Her tutelage by Goya is examined by López-Rey 1956 and in Ribemont and Garcia 1998, pp. 197–99.

16 Canellas López 1981, p. 386, no. 268.

17 Ibid., pp. 387–88, no. 270.

18 Ibid., p. 388, no. 271.

19 For biographical data on Javier, see Sánchez Cantón 1946; Saltillo 1952; and Matilla Tascón 1978.

20 Javier's career as a painter and imitator of his father is now being discussed, especially by those who challenge the attribution of some of Goya's later paintings. As yet, no work has been securely attributed to him. See Wilson-Bareau 1996(a) and Junquera 2003(a), the latter of which should be read with the correctives of Glendinning 2004.

21 Gassier and Wilson 1971, no. 1662. Hereafter cited as GW.

22 Canellas López 1981, p. 499, no. CLVI.

23 Ibid., pp. 389–90, no. 273; translation Wilson-Bareau and Mena Marqués 1994, p. 324.

24 For Brugada, see Arías Anglés 1989 and Junquera 2003(a). His observations are recorded by Matheron (1858), ed. cited 1996.

25 For the technique of the miniatures, see Sayre 1966.

26 Canellas López 1981, p. 501, no. CLX.

27 Matheron 1996, p. 256.

28 For the text in English, see Tomlinson 1994, pp. 306–7.

29 Matheron 1996, p. 168.

30 Canellas López 1981, pp. 501–2, no. CLXI.

31 Ibid., p. 503, no. CLXIV.

32 Ibid., pp. 502–4, nos. CLXIII and CLXIV.

33 Ibid., p. 505, no. CLXVIII.

34 Ibid., p. 389, no. 272.

35 Ibid., nos. 273–74.

36 See Sayre 1974, p. 197, for Carnicero's prints.

37 Matheron 1996, p. 262.

38 Fauqué and Villanueva Etcheverría 1982, p. 605.

39 Canellas López 1981, p. 505, no. CLXIX.

40 Ibid., pp. 390–91, no. 275.

41 Ibid., pp. 505–7, no. CLXX.

42 GW no. 1662.

43 Matheron 1996, p. 256. The extant still lifes are now dated to 1808–12. See Vischer 1997.

44 Ibid., p. 258.

45 Núñez de Arenas 1950, p. 258.

46 GW no. 1664.

47 Young 1972.

48 Matheron 1996, p. 270.

49 Ibid.

50 Canellas López 1981, pp. 392–93, no. 277.

51 Ibid., pp. 393–94, no. 279.

52 Ibid., p. 394, no. 280.

53 Ibid., p. 395, no. 281.

54 Ibid., pp. 512–13, no. CLXXXIII.

55 For Javier's movements after the death of his father, see Fauqué and Villanueva Etcheverría 1982, pp. 675–82.

56 Canellas López 1981, pp. 512–13, no. CLXXXI.

57 Ibid., pp. 514–15, no. CLXXXIII.

58 Cruz Valdovinos 1987, p. 149.

59 Canellas López 1981, p. 515, no. CLXXXIV.

60 Ibid., p. 514, no. CLXXXIII. "A pesar de su jenio, sera eterno nuestro dolor, qué-panos la suerte que nos quepa." Presumably Leocadia refers to Goya's failure to provide for her and Rosario.

61 For Rosario's life and career in Madrid, see note 15.

62 For Javier's biography, see note 20. For his art sales, see Wilson-Bareau 1996(a) and 2001, p. 24.

63 For Mariano's checkered career, see Lafuente Ferrari 1947, pp. 295–300, and Saltillo 1952, pp. 43–56.

64 Wilson-Bareau 2001, p. 24

SUSAN GRACE GALASSI   *Goya's Bordeaux: A Chronicle*

Goya's years in Bordeaux fall under the reign of Charles X, the reactionary brother of Louis XVI and Louis XVIII and the last of the Bourbon monarchs of France. The Bordelais welcomed the stability of the monarchy after a long period of economic downturn following the Revolution and the Napoleonic Wars, but though the Restoration saw a resumption of commercial activity in Bordeaux, the regional capital of Aquitaine would never again rise to the level of its *âge d'or* of 1730 to 1790, when its port was the second largest in the world after London. At the time of Goya's departure from Spain in 1824, Madrid had a population of 120,000; at its peak just before the Revolution, Bordeaux had reached the same level, but by the 1820s it had fallen to 90,000.[1] A commercial center rather than a capital, Bordeaux during Charles X's reign (1824–30) was nevertheless a cosmopolitan city with a vibrant cultural life and a rich past that dated back to Roman times, all of which formed part of Goya's experience. In taking up residence in Bordeaux, the painter followed in the footsteps of legions of émigrés who throughout the city's 2000-year history had sought work in its vineyards and wine trade, education in its centers of learning, profits in its colonial trade and stock exchange, as well as religious and political refuge, and had contributed substantially to the city's power and prestige.

Early History

The first settlement on the curve of the tidal Garonne River, where it meets the Devèze about sixty miles upriver from the Atlantic coast and on the shortest land link between the Atlantic and the Mediterranean Sea, was established by the Bituriges Vivisci, Celtic tin traders. The Romans colonized the town, known as Burdigala, in the first century AD and introduced vineyards, and a prosperous commercial, cosmopolitan city developed, hospitable to Iberians, Jews, Greeks, and Bretons. The fourth-century poet and rhetorician Ausonius describes Burdigala, his birthplace, as a square walled city and one of the greatest centers of learning in Gaul.[2] Two of the major commercial arteries of present-day Bordeaux—the rue Sainte Cathérine, which runs from the center of the city to its southern end, and the rue de Porte Dijeaux, perpendicular to it—were laid out in Roman times.

Bordeaux reached a second flowering during the period of English domination in the Middle Ages. Eleanor of Aquitaine divorced her French husband,

facing page   Louis Garneray, *Vue du port du Bordeaux prise du quai de la Bastide* (detail of fig. 28)

35

the future Louis VII, and in 1154 married Henry Plantagenet, Duke of Normandy, Count of Anjou, the future Henry II. Her dowry included all of Guyenne (the English corruption of Aquitaine) and most of southwestern France. When Henry succeeded to the throne of England two months after their marriage, the couple's vast domain rivaled the holdings of the king of France. Over the next three centuries, Bordeaux prospered and expanded, largely owing to the northerners' taste for its red wine (called claret because of its clear, light color). The citizens of Bordeaux enjoyed a certain degree of independence, with a mayor and a Jurade or municipal council, but it was not until the battle of Castillon in 1453 (the end of the Hundred Years' War) that Bordeaux and Aquitaine finally reverted to France.

Le vif pourtraict de la Cité de Bourdeaux (fig. 18)

The centurylong struggle for the prosperous wine city is evident in this sixteenth-century bird's-eye view. The densely built-up city enclosed in its fourteenth-century *carcan* (iron girdle or wall) and massive gates, protected by major fortifications, stands on the west bank of the Garonne with its back to the river.[3] The Fort du Hâ, on the left side of the image, and the first Château Trompette, on the right, guarding the river and access to the sea, were built at the end of the Hundred Years' War to prevent further invasions. By the end of the eighteenth century, most of the wall had been torn down, though the forts remained standing until just a few years before Goya's arrival—major impediments to urban development.

On his entry into Bordeaux, Goya would have seen the large and imposing église Saint Michel (in the lower left quadrant close to the river), begun in 1350 and built over two centuries, and its fifteenth-century hexagonal bell tower, the highest in southwestern France. Familiarly known as *La Flêche* (The Arrow), it can still be seen from any point in the city. From his last home in Bordeaux on the Fossés (now Cours) de l'Intendance, Goya could see the towers of the nearby cathedral dedicated to Saint André, built between the eleventh and twelfth centuries and modified in the thirteenth and fifteenth. Here the cathedral appears at the back of the city against the wall. Today, however, it marks the center of town. Beyond the walls in the upper right corner of the image stands a Roman coliseum, known as the Palais Galien, named for a Princess Galienne, who traveled from Ethiopia to Burdigala to marry a son of the Emperor

Le vif pourtraict de la Cité de Bourdeaux.

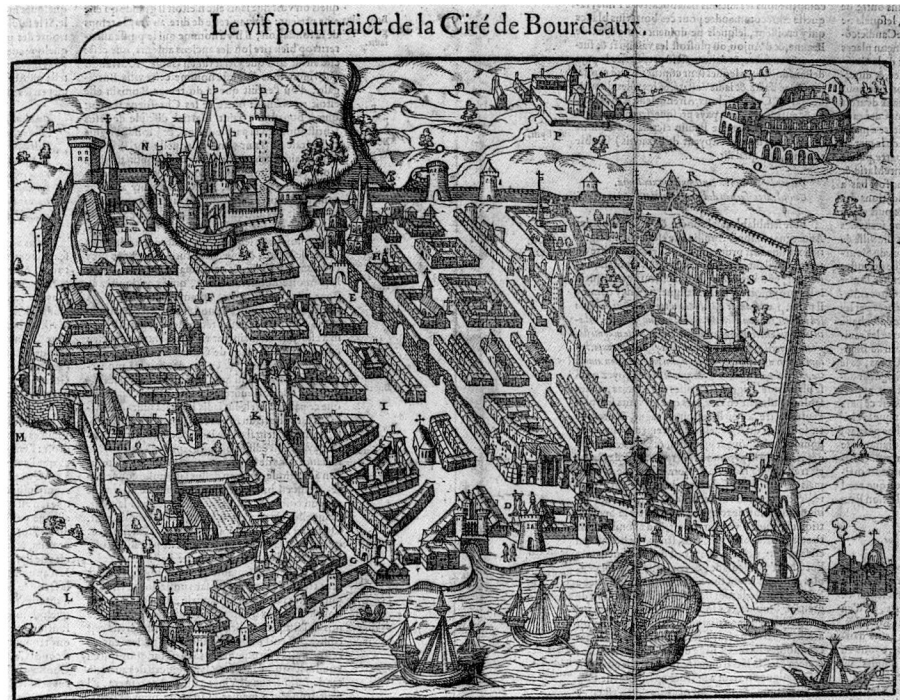

Fig. 18 Artist unknown, *Le vif pourtraict de la Cité de Bourdeaux [sic] (Bird's eye view of Bordeaux)*, 1550, engraving, Archives municipales de Bordeaux

Vespasian in the third century. It once sat 15,000 spectators and remained largely intact until the French Revolution when much of it was destroyed.[4] Goya would have known the picturesque remnants of the amphitheater in the vicinity of the suburb of Saint Seurin, northwest of the city proper, where he lived for two years with his companion, Leocadia Weiss, and her children, Rosario and Guillermo.

Bordeaux flourished as a humanist center in the sixteenth century. The Collège de Guyenne was established in 1533, and one of the region's most notable figures, the philosopher and essayist Michel de Montaigne (1533–1592), studied there. (He served as mayor of the city from 1581 to 1585.) Visiting professors from the north brought with them the ideas of the Reformation, resulting in rising numbers of Huguenots. From 1562 to 1598, many regions of France witnessed violent conflicts between this Protestant group and the Roman Catholic Church. The Wars of Religion began in 1563 with the massacre of thirty Huguenots at Vassy and were ended in 1598 by Henry IV (a converted Catholic) with the Edict of Nantes, which guaranteed religious and political rights to the Protestants.[5] The peace was not long lasting. Bordeaux became a center for the Counter-Reformation in the seventeenth century, a period of severe persecution of Protestants.

The Seventeenth and Eighteenth Centuries

Further fortifications were added under the reign of Louis XIV (1643–1715) following the uprisings in 1648 to 1652 of discontented princes and nobles in Paris and the provinces, known as the Fronde, against the policies of Cardinal Mazarin, who served as chief minister under the young king from 1643 to 1661.[6] Bordeaux, which had enjoyed a certain amount of administrative independence, opposed the central authority of the monarchy and was one of the strongholds of the Fronde. Under Louis XIV, the ruins of a Gallo-Roman temple known as the Piliers de Tutelle (seen on the right-hand side of fig. 18) were razed to make way for the enlargement of the Château Trompette, designed by Louis's famous military architect Sébastien Le Prestre de Vauban. Fort Louis was built near the waterfront at the opposite corner of Bordeaux so the rebellious city could be kept under surveillance from three points.

The ground was laid in seventeenth-century France for the economic boom that would launch Bordeaux's era of *haut commerce* and make it one of the leading ports in Europe. During the second quarter of the seventeenth century France added to her holdings in North America (including Nova Scotia and Quebec and parts of the present-day United States) a large number of West Indian islands, among them Haiti, Martinique, and Guadeloupe. Outposts in India and in the Indian Ocean were acquired as well as trading posts in Senegal on the West African coast in the 1670s. Louis XIV's minister of finance, Jean-Baptiste Colbert, encouraged the Bordelais to develop a merchant fleet to participate in the transatlantic trade.[7] With its advantageous geographic position, far-flung outposts, and a chamber of commerce established in 1705 to safeguard the interests of the merchants, Bordeaux at the turn of eighteenth century was poised to reap the rewards of a dawning era of intense commercial activity.

As the historian Camille Julian has noted: "Bordeaux now had two fields of exploitation in which it could create its fortune: the vineyards of its countryside and the plantations of the islands. It would soon have a third which would be no less productive. . . ."[8] Though to a lesser extent than Nantes, the leading *port négrier* in France, the slave trade contributed substantially to the enormous wealth of Bordeaux.[9] Ship owners left Bordeaux for the coast of Africa with manufactured objects and local produce, which they exchanged at inflated prices with slave dealers in Africa.[10] They transported slaves to America (often Guyana), selling them at a great profit, and were remunerated with the exotic island commodities of sugar, coffee, cocoa, cotton, and indigo that were in high demand in Europe.[11] Bordeaux's economy grew by leaps and bounds. While the French defeat at the end of the Seven Years' War (1756–63) resulted in the cession of all of New France and many West Indian colonies to Britain, France was able to retain some of its major outposts—Guadeloupe and Martinique, for example, which were vital sources of sugar—and Bordeaux's colonial trade continued and even flourished. In one year, 1774, 562 ships returned to France from the West Indies; almost half of them came into Bordeaux.[12] Even the disruption to the city's wine trade during the American Revolution did not have immediate repercussions.

During this time Bordeaux enjoyed the position of the primary port of France and third largest city after Paris and Lyon and an annual growth rate close to 4 percent above the country's gross national product.[13] Workers flooded into the city from the nearby southwest, the further provinces of Limousin and Brittany, while British, Irish, German, and Jewish merchants took up residence in the seaport, giving the city an enduring cosmopolitan character.[14] The population, made up in large part of immigrants working in the port and stock exchange, had doubled since the beginning of the century. On the eve of the French Revolution, Bordeaux reached the peak of its commercial trade with the colonies. Paradoxically, as Eric Saugera has noted, during the years when such issues as liberty and the rights of all men were under intense discussion and the end of slavery was being called for, the slave trade reached its apogee in Bordeaux.[15]

Under the dynamic leadership of a succession of enlightened Intendants—provincial governors granted extensive power by the king[16]—the Bordelais ploughed back much of the profits of the colonial trade into the embellishment of their city. Over the course of the eighteenth century, the Intendants and their architects transformed a decaying medieval walled city with large areas of swamp into a modern metropolis of broad avenues, open squares, and quays lined with blond limestone houses. While preserving the charm of its ancient quarters, they also built some of the finest classical and neoclassical architecture

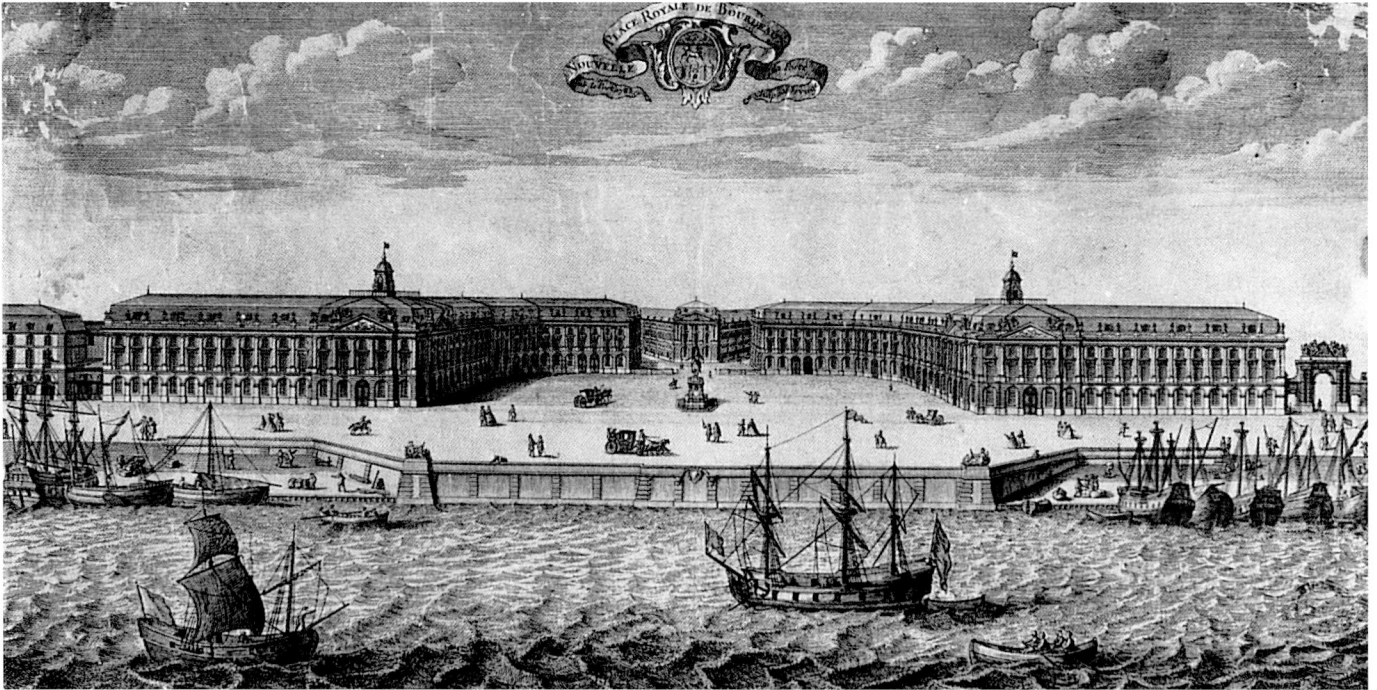

Fig. 19 Artist unknown, *Nouvelle Place Royale de Bordeaux*, 1743–89(?), engraving, Archives municipales de Bordeaux

in the kingdom.[17] The widely traveled English gentleman farmer Arthur Young offers the following description of Bordeaux in 1787 in his *Travels in France*:

> Much as I had read and heard of the commerce, wealth, and magnificence of the city, they greatly surpassed my expectation. Paris did not answer at all, for it is not to be compared to London; but we must not name Liverpool in competition with Bourdeaux [sic]. . . . The *place royale*, with the statue of Lewis XV in the middle, is a fine opening, and the buildings which form it [are] regular and handsome. . . . But the quarter of the *chapeau rouge* is truly magnificent, consisting of noble houses, built, like the rest of the city, of white hewn stone. It joins the *château trompette*, which occupies nearly a half mile of the shore. This fort is bought of the king, by a company of speculators, who are now pulling it down with an intention of building a fine square and many new streets, to the amount of 1800 houses. I have seen the design of the square and the streets, and it would, if executed, be one of the most splendid additions to a city that is to be seen in Europe. . . . The theater, built about ten or twelve years ago, is by far the most magnificent in France.[18]

Nouvelle Place Royale de Bordeaux (fig. 19)

The first major urbanization project in eighteenth-century Bordeaux—and the first to breach the walls—was the Place Royale, initiated in 1729 by Claude Boucher, Intendant of Guyenne from 1720 to 1743. The Place Royale is situat-

ed on the curve of the river, southeast of the Château Trompette. The buildings, designed in the prevailing French classical style by Jacques Jules Gabriel, *premier architecte du roi* under Louis XV, were richly ornamented with sculpture. On either side of the central building, flanked by two streets that connect the city with the waterfront, are two wings with pavilions bordering the quays: the Hôtel des Fermes (house of the tax assessor) to the left of the image, and the Bourse (stock exchange) at right. In 1743 a bronze equestrian statue by Jean-Baptiste Lemoyne representing Louis XV in Roman garb, his arm extended in a gesture of peace, was installed in the center of the Place.[19] From 1749 through the mid-nineteenth century, the two major annual fairs of May and October were held in the Place Royale (renamed after the Revolution the Place de la Bourse), which Goya attended with Leocadia and her children.[20]

Nicolas Ozanne, *Le Port de Bordeaux vu du quai des Farines* (fig. 20)

Gabriel's Place Royale and the cluster of apartment houses he designed that extend eastward down the quai from the Hôtel des Fermes (known as the Ilôt Gabriel) set a high standard for architecture and urbanization projects for the rest of the century. These and later grand residences appear in the foreground of Ozanne's engraving of 1776 of the Port de la Lune (named for the curve in the river) looking from the Quai Richelieu toward Les Chartrons and the distant suburb of Bacalan. In the middle distance, we see the wrought iron gates that then enclosed the Place Royale.[21] On the right, a large sailing ship is anchored in the middle of the river, as the water was too shallow at the edge for it to pull up to the quay. Casks and barrels containing wine and other products are assembled on the shore and moved by men and oxen to barges, which conveyed the cargo to and from the ships.[22]

The combination of grand architecture lining the broad sweeping quay (part of a five-mile stretch of the riverfront) and the intense activity of the port, filled with ships from all over the world, made scenes such as this the quintessential image of Bordeaux, drawn, painted, and etched by artists over several centuries. The port was the nodal center of the city and the engine of its economy; from here, Bordeaux reached out to far-flung places on the globe. Goya would have walked along the quay and been familiar with images of the scenic port in prints by local artists and may have known Pierre Lacour's monumental canvas of 1804–6,[23] though the port appears in none of his drawings of Bordeaux street life.[24]

Tourny's Bordeaux

More than any of the other provincial governors, it was Louis Urbain Aubert, Marquis de Tourny, Intendant of Guyenne from 1743 to 1757, who left his imprint on the city. He vowed on his arrival to make Bordeaux the most beautiful city in the kingdom in four or five years.[25] With Ange-Jacques Gabriel, who had succeeded his father as first architect to the king, Tourny completed the Place Royale (inaugurated in 1755) and engaged a number of architects to continue the line of houses from the Ilôt Gabriel to the Porte de la Grave and carried out more comprehensive changes that modified the face of the city.

During his tenure, Tourny opened up congested spaces and linked the city with the suburbs, imposing a rational plan and architectural consistency on large sections of the center. He demolished squalid old quarters, pierced new streets into the heart of the city, and gave a harmonious rhythm to the new squares, avenues, and the quays thanks to the uniformity of the facades of the many new houses built under his administration. The old walls largely disappeared at this time, and most of the heavy, fortified gates were replaced with graceful triumphal arches, such as the Porte Dijeaux designed by André Portier, one of Tourny's chief architects.[26]

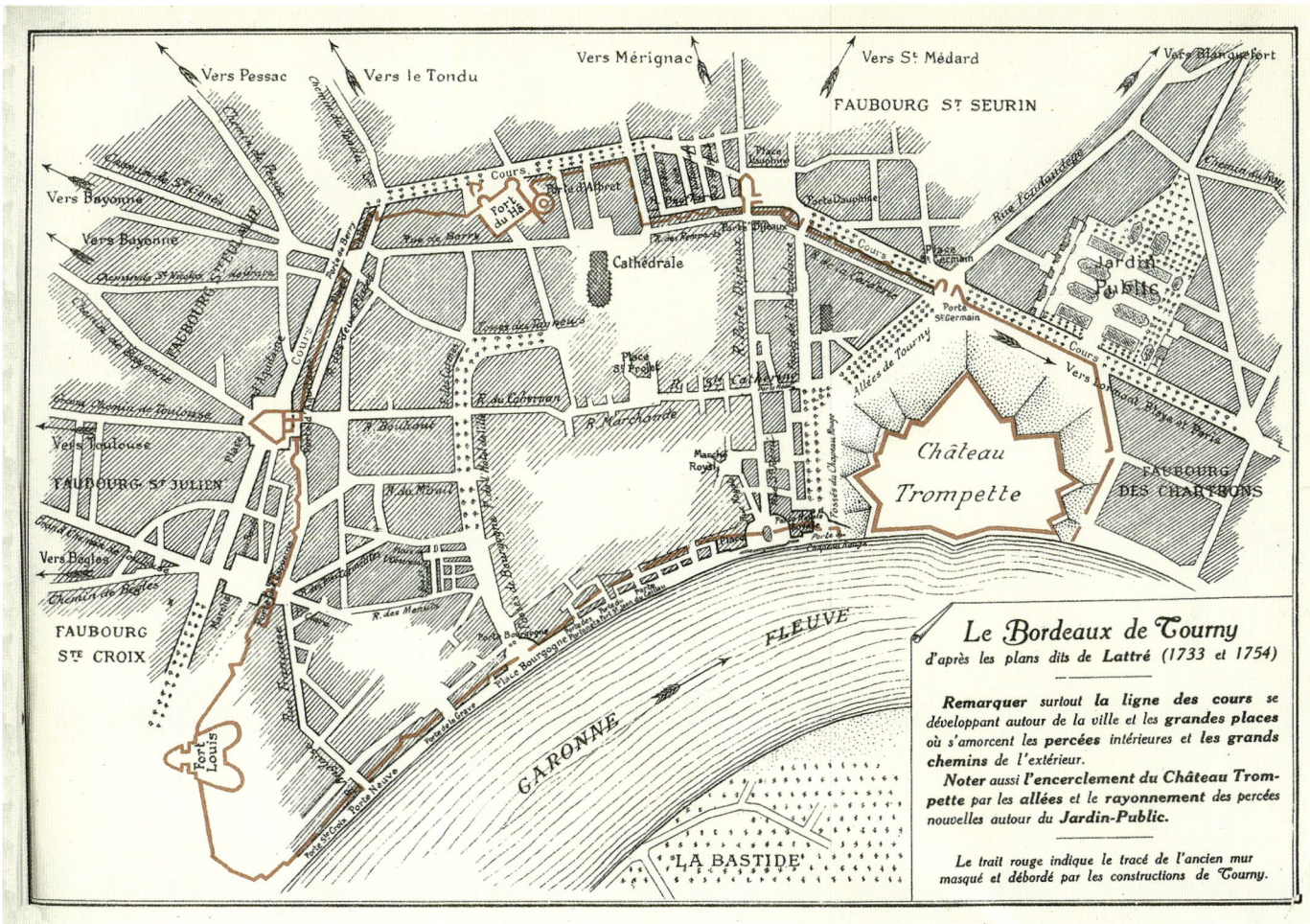

Fig. 21 Artist unknown, *Le Bordeaux de Tourny, d'après les plans dits de Lattré*, published in Michel Lhéritier's *L'Intendant Tourny*, vol. II, Paris: Librairie Félix Alcan, 1920

Le Bordeaux de Tourny d'après les plans dits de Lattré (fig. 21)

This map was commissioned by Tourny for Louis XV's geographers to show the changes that he and his predecessor had carried out.[27] Tourny created promenades (marked by the red line) around the perimeter of the city and broad avenues that cut through it, connecting the center with the waterfront (skirting the huge impediment of the Château Trompette) and the suburb of Les Chartrons, where Protestant and Jewish merchants had built their mansions on the riverbank, beyond the city walls.[28] There, Tourny established a public garden, designed by Ange-Jacques Gabriel in a formal French style. (Under Napoleon III it was enlarged and transformed in an English style, as it remains today.)

Central to the Intendant's transformations are the famous Allées de Tourny, built between 1746 and 1757, a long rectangular space originally planted with rows of lindens and elms, which became the enduring social center of the city. Tourny laid out the Allées between the embankment of the Château Trompette,

Fig. 22   Jean-Jacques Alban de Lesgallery (1808–?), *Les Allées de Tourny et le Grand Théâtre*, after 1831, gouache on paper, 9⅝ × 17½ (24.5 × 44.6), Archives municipales de Bordeaux

which dominated much of the center of the city and the waterfront, and the buildings and land of the convents of the Jacobins and the Récollets. On the convent side, Tourny built a row of harmonious two-story houses designed by Portier; the side along the embankment remained largely undeveloped until the huge outmoded fort was finally demolished in 1818.

Jean-Jacques Alban de Lesgallery, *Les Allées de Tourny et le Grand Théâtre* (fig. 22) and *Les Allées de Tourny et la maison Meyer* (fig. 23)

The Allées de Tourny were at the heart of Goya's life in Bordeaux. By the 1820s, they were a place to stroll, linger in cafés along the perimeter, attend a performance at the theater, visit the purveyors of luxury goods, hire a fiacre, embark on a journey—to Paris or Madrid—in a high-speed diligence, and above all, to see and be seen, much as they remain today. In figs. 22 and 23 we see the Allées from two directions in the 1830s, much as Goya knew them. (In 1831 the last of

Fig. 23 Jean-Jacques Alban de Lesgallery (1808–?), *Les Allées de Tourny et la Maison Meyer*, after 1831, gouache on paper, 7¼ × 11¾ (18.5 × 30), Archives municipales de Bordeaux

the trees planted by Tourny were cut down, affording a more open appearance.) Portier's houses can be seen in fig. 22 on the side of the former convents. By then, new stories had been added to the original structures. At the southeastern end, in the Place de la Comédie, stands the magnificent Grand Théâtre. It was near the theater that Goya first set foot in Bordeaux after an arduous seven-day journey from Madrid.[29] He may have traveled in a diligence similar to the one seen in fig. 23 showing the Allées from the Place de la Comédie looking northwest.

Constant, *2me vue des Allées de Tourny* (fig. 24)

The Cours de Tourny (the street to the far right of this image, now called Cours Georges Clémenceau) formed one arm of the so-called golden triangle, then as now the most elegant section of town and the heart of the eighteenth-century district. (The Allées formed another arm.) A number of streets radiated from

Fig. 24 Constant, *2me Vue des Allées de Tourny prise de la place Tourny*, after 1831, lithograph, Archives municipales de Bordeaux

the Place Tourny, among them the rue de la Petite Taupe (now rue Huguerie), where Goya met his friends at Braulio Poc's *chocolatería*, the "lion's den," which was the social center of the Spanish expatriate community.[30] The bronze statue of the marquis de Tourny by Joseph-Charles Marin (1759–1834) in the center of the Place Tourny, facing the Allées, was unveiled in July 1825.[31] Goya's first home in Bordeaux—the "good furnished quarters in a good location" referred to by Moratín in a letter—was located at 24 Cours de Tourny, from which he could have witnessed the ceremony.[32] It was here in the center of the city that he lived with Leocadia and her children from September 1824 to the autumn of 1825 and he painted his experimental miniatures on ivory. After spending the following two years in the working-class faubourg of Saint-Seurin, within walking distance from the center, living first in what Moratín described as one of the new self-standing houses "with a northern and southern light and a bit of garden,"[33] they returned to the Tourny district at the end of 1827, moving into a spacious apartment at 39 Fossés de l'Intendance—a broad avenue with grand houses in a neoclassical style built in the early nineteenth century.

* * *

Dupré de Saint Maur's Bordeaux

The city continued to expand throughout the 1760s and 1770s. It became a formidable cultural center: the Académie des Arts was created by a group of local artists and Enlightenment philosophers in 1768; exhibitions of art and architectural projects were held annually from 1771 to 1787; the Musée de Bordeaux was founded in 1783.[34] Bordeaux reached a peak of opulence and sophistication under the administration of Nicolas Dupré de Saint Maur, Intendant from 1776 to 1785. The most important architectural addition to the quartier Tourny at this time was the Grand Théâtre, built between 1773 and 1779. This architectural masterpiece in the new neoclassical style would be a model for future theaters in France. Though completed under Dupré de Saint-Maur's tenure, the theater had been instigated by the famously sybaritic Louis-Armand Duplessis, Maréchal de Richelieu, governor of Guyenne from 1758 to 1788, who commissioned the Parisian architect Victor Louis to design it. Goya spent his first nights in Bordeaux in Richelieu's former residence, the magnificent Hôtel du Gouvernement on the rue de Porte Dijeaux, where Manuel Silvela and his family and Moratín lived from 1823 to 1827. It was there that Silvela ran his school for the children of bankers, merchants, aristocrats, and former military officers from Spain and Latin America who had sought refuge in Bordeaux.[35]

Joseph Basire, *Le Grand Théâtre* (fig. 25)

With its imposing colonnaded porch, the Grand Théâtre evokes Bernini's Rome as well as ancient Burdigala.[36] It was built on the site of a Gallo-Roman temple, the remains of which (the Piliers de Tutelle) were ruthlessly torn down by Louis XIV to make way for the enlargement of the Château Trompette. The porch or peristyle is made up of twelve columns in a composite style, surmounted by an entablature and carved stone sculptures representing the nine muses and the goddesses Juno, Minerva, and Venus. The building initially stood flush with the ground of the surrounding square, as seen in this watercolor from the Revolutionary period, and would have been so during the Restoration. In midcentury, however, the ground was lowered and the steps surrounding the building were added.

It seems unlikely that Goya, who had been long deaf, would have attended the theater; for Moratín, however, it was a second home, which he referred to affectionately as "mi oficina."[37] "I have a season ticket for the theater," he wrote

Fig. 25   Joseph Basire, *Le Grand Théâtre*, 1796, watercolor on paper, $8^1/_4 \times 11^3/_4$ (21 × 30), Musée d'Aquitaine, Bordeaux

to Melón, "and you will find me there every night without fail, from seven to eleven."[38] The repertoire consisted mainly of traditional tragedies, comedies, and opera; there were also occasional vaudeville performances, though these were usually held in the smaller theaters throughout the city.[39] Liszt performed there in Goya's time.

New public buildings were erected in the Tourny district under Dupré de Saint Maur's administration throughout the boom years of the 1770s and 1780s. The cluster of grand *hôtels particuliers* along the rue du Chapeau Rouge and the rue Esprit des Lois designed in a neoclassical style by Victor Louis (built between 1774 and 1778)—and praised by Arthur Young in 1787—however, are the most telling testimony of the opulent taste and way of life of the enormously wealthy merchants from all quarters of Europe that made up the cosmopolitan society of the city during the last years of the ancien régime.

Revolution to Restoration

Despite its outward appearance of prosperity, Bordeaux's dominance of the colonial trade was slowly eroding throughout the 1770s and 1780s,[40] and the upheaval of the French Revolution and the reign of Napoleon brought its golden age to a close. The fall of the Bastille in Paris on July 14, 1789, was greeted with enthusiasm in Bordeaux, and a representational government was peacefully established.[41] The new local administration, consisting of conservative wealthy merchants and lawyers, embraced the progressive principles of the Revolution, but by 1792 the solidarity and optimism of the early years of the new nation had begun to dissipate. The Bordeaux clergy were among the first to express opposition to the Revolutionary government; 73 percent refused to take the oath of allegiance to the state, which was required by the civil constitution of 1790.[42] On July 15, 1792, three of the so-called refractory priests were seized, and two of them were summarily executed and their heads were paraded through the city on lances—a macabre and disturbing sight witnessed by Moratín, who was passing through the city at that time.[43]

Extreme food shortages in 1792 prompted riots by the poor, whose basic needs were not being met by the new government. Angry mobs also attacked symbols of the ancien régime: the statue of Louis XV by Lemoyne in the center of the Place Royale was torn down, along with the grillwork surrounding the square.[44] The Roman amphitheater, the Palais Galien, was also a temporary target of collective rage, and all but the section that remains today was torn down.

A turning point in the history of the department of the Gironde, of which Bordeaux was the prefecture, occurred in 1793. One of the two leading national political parties, the moderate and idealistic Girondins (so called because most of the leaders were from the Gironde) were committed to safeguarding newly won individual liberties. They clashed with the radical faction of the Jacobin party, the Montagnards, who were willing to sacrifice certain individual rights for the perceived greater good of preserving the integrity of the new nation.[45] In a coup at the national convention in Paris on June 2, 1793, the twenty-two Girondin deputies were seized and imprisoned and later accused of treason; twenty-one were guillotined.[46] The Bordelais condemned the tyrannical measures of the Jacobins under Robespierre's leadership and withdrew their recognition of the convention's authority. Designated an outlaw city, Bordeaux (along with other rebellious provincial cities) was a target of Robespierre's retribution. A military commission was installed in the city, and between October 1793 and Robespierre's death on July 31, 1794, 301 suspected insurgents or enemies of the Republic went to the guillotine, which was set up on the Place Dauphine, and many more were incarcerated in deplorable conditions.[47] Following the bloody interlude of the Terror, the city returned to order, but, as the historian Michel Figeac has noted, not without a deep blow to its economy and social fabric, as well as its architectural patrimony; during the Revolution the city "seemed to have lost its antique splendor."[48]

With the Decree of February 13, 1790, which suppressed religious communities and confiscated their land holdings, the large area in the center of the triangle occupied by convents in Tourny's time had become available for development. The selling off of property and tearing down of buildings began in 1792. The same year, work began on the Place des Grands Hommes, the city's major surviving Revolutionary landmark; its construction was interrupted by the Terror of 1793–94 and completed at the turn of the century. The architect Chalifour oversaw the creation of the Place des Grands Hommes in a star-shaped configuration, with streets named for the philosophers and writers, whose ideas were influential in the Revolution, radiating from the center.[49]

Gradually the old convent area was largely transformed into a quartier of clubs and theaters and is today a commercial center.[50] Goya's last home in Bordeaux on the grand Fossés de l'Intendance was just steps away from the Théâtre Français (designed by Jean-Baptiste Dufart and completed in 1800), the Place des Grands Hommes, and the beautiful baroque Dominican convent church of Notre Dame. His funeral on April 17, 1828, was held there and was attended by the entire Spanish community. (He was buried in the church's cemetery, La Chartreuse.)

Following the slave revolt of 1791 in Haiti, France lost its richest and most important colony in the Antilles, while ongoing war with England from 1793 through the end of the empire in 1814—with a brief respite during the Peace of Amiens in 1802–3—cut off trade with its few remaining West Indian colonies. Napoleon's Continental Blockade of 1806, an attempt to destroy England's trade with Europe by preventing any British ship from docking in French ports, had the ultimate effect of injuring France's economy by creating a shortage of colonial goods brought to the Continent via England. Britain responded in 1807 by forcing neutral countries' trade vessels to go through its ports, thus restricting French trade to a critical degree. The blockades were lifted in 1812, but the severe damage to France's trade relations had already been done, particularly in port cities like Bordeaux, for which maritime trade was the backbone of the economy.

On a visit to Bordeaux in April 1808, Napoleon witnessed for himself the dismal state of affairs in the port and the disastrous effects on the Bourse; his attempts to revive the city's economy, however, were not successful. According to a report of 1809 on the financial situation of imperial France by the German economist Philippe-André Nemnich, Bordeaux's population had fallen to 60,000 to 70,000 inhabitants: "instead of progress one fears greater regression . . . hundreds of houses stand empty, and one laughs at the old plans for expansion. Ships are parsimoniously distributed across the water; the view is no longer cut to infinity by a forest of masts."[51]

Napoleon's visit, in fact, occurred only a few weeks before the uprisings in Madrid against General Joachim Murat's occupying troops on the second of May, which were responded to by the brutal reprisals of French soldiers on the third of May 1808. (Goya's eponymous pair of paintings of 1814 commemorates these events.) By June 1808, Napoleon's brother Joseph was installed on the Spanish throne, which he occupied until 1813. Many of the Spaniards who sympathized with the Liberal-leaning regime of the "intruder king" or held a post in his administration—*afrancesados* or *josefinos*—emigrated to Bordeaux in 1813, and some received financial aid from the French state.[52]

It was not until hostilities with England ceased at the end of the empire in 1814 and the Bourbons were restored to power, that Bordelais merchants resumed the export of wine to Britain and northern ports. The Treaty of Paris of May 30, 1814, gave France back many of its old colonies, and the colonial trade, the other mainstay of Bordeaux's economy, started up again as well, though the slave trade, which had contributed to the soaring profits of the *âge d'or*, had been abolished with the Congress of Vienna in 1815.[53] The city slowly revived but it was never to return to its former glory; Bordeaux slipped to third rank as a French port, after Marseilles and Le Havre.[54]

Building resumed in Bordeaux under the Restoration (the reigns of Louis XVIII, 1814–24, and Charles X, 1824–30), and some of the urbanization plans of the Intendants of the ancien régime were finally carried out, among them the demolition of the royal forts dating from the period of the Fronde. At long last the plans for a "fine square and many new streets" that Arthur Young had seen on his 1787 visit took shape in the form of the enormous fifteen-hectare Place des Quinconces laid out on the empty site of the former Château Trompette.[55]

Légé, lithograph, after a drawing by Jules Philippe, *Bains des Quinconces* (fig. 26)

The riverfront of the Quinconces is at the center of the five-mile stretch of quays that run along the Garonne. This esplanade, only a few years old on Goya's arrival, was a short distance from the artist's first home on the Cours de Tourny. Goya's close friend and relation through marriage, Martín Miguel de Goicoechea, the father of Javier's wife, Gumersinda, lived on the Quinconces,

Fig. 26 Légé, after a drawing by Jules Philippe, *Bains des Quinconces (Bordeaux)*, after 1825, lithograph, 12¹/₂ × 19¹/₄ (31.7 × 49), Bibliothèque municipale de Bordeaux, Fonds Delpit

and Goya visited him frequently.[56] (Martín's death in June 1825 was a notable loss for Goya.) One wonders if the aged and infirm artist, who left Spain on the pretence of taking the waters at Plombières, may have frequented the luxurious new medicinal baths that opened in the Quinconces in 1826, designed by Michel Laclotte.[57] He may have seen the work in progress on the two rostral columns glorifying Commerce and Navigation that stand at the water's edge, prominent landmarks in the city, which were completed in 1829. The Fossés de l'Intendance—the most elegant axis of the city—where Goya spent the last six months of his life from the autumn of 1827 to April 1828, was urbanized during the Restoration. Many of the grand residences with interior courtyards combined apartments above street level commercial spaces; Goya's building had a bookstore or lending library on the ground floor.[58] From the windows facing the street, Goya could see the towers of the nearby cathedral of Saint André (though the street directly in front of the house, which today leads straight to the cathedral, was not cut through until the mid-nineteenth century). There Goya installed a piano for Rosario and continued to paint every day, often hastily and carelessly, as his young friend the marine painter Antonio de Brugada noted, "on any piece of wood cardboard or paper. . . ."[59] On Brugada's arm, Goya navigated the three flights of the steep, curved stone stairs with extreme difficulty and continued his habitual walks. It was along the Fossés de l'Intendance and the Allées de Tourny (fig. 27) that the wealthy expatriate Spanish community was centered.[60] Goya's friend José Pío de Molina, former mayor of Madrid, lived in the same building. The banker and entrepreneur Jacques Galos, Goya's financial adviser, and Juan de Muguiro y Iribarren (a

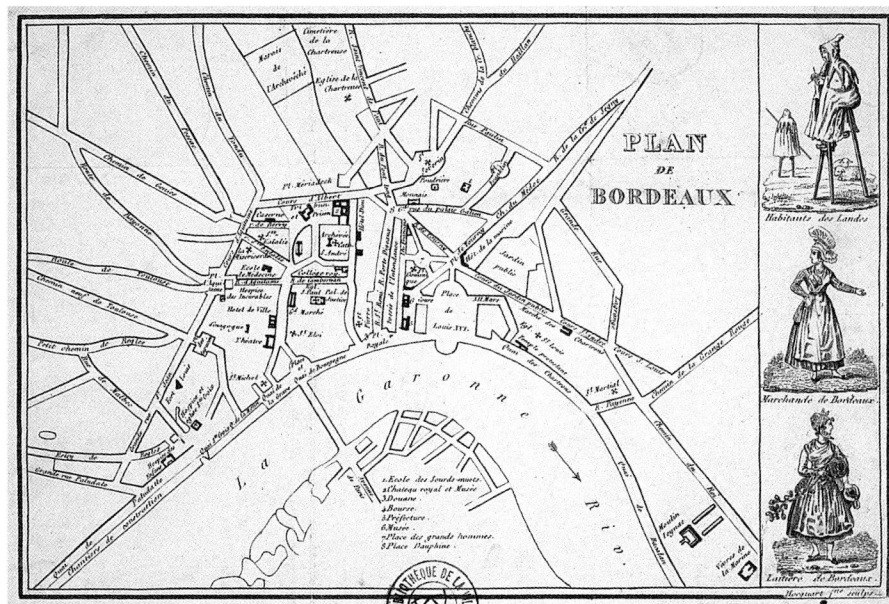

Fig. 27 Artist unknown, *Plan de Bordeaux*, from Richard's *Guide classique du voyageur en France*, Paris: L. Maison, successeur de M. Audin, 1842. Bibliothèque municipale de Bordeaux, Fonds Delpit

cousin of the Goicoechea family) were lodged nearby. The printer Cyprien Gaulon's atelier on the rue Saint Rémi, where Goya had carried out his lithographs, was a few steps away. They, as well Moratín and Silvela (who in 1827 moved on to Paris), sat for portraits by Goya in Bordeaux (see cat. nos. 10, 11).

Louis Garneray, *Vue du port de Bordeaux prise du quai de la Bastide* (fig. 28)

The most significant and spectacular of the urbanization projects carried out during the Restoration was the building of the Pont de Pierre, which spans the Garonne and made possible the development of the city on both sides of the river. Tourny and his successors had all recognized the need for such a bridge, and over time various solutions had been proposed and rejected.[61] Plans were given a new impetus in the early nineteenth century for political reasons: Napoleon needed to be able to marshal troops quickly to Spain during the Peninsular War and ordered work on a bridge to begin in 1810. He summoned the most brilliant engineer of the time, Claude Deschamps, to design it. The moorings for his first plan for a wooden bridge on metal arches were swept away in a storm, and Deschamps eventually opted for a combination of masonry and brick—materials used by the Romans as seen in the remnants of the Palais Galien—and completed the project under Louis XVIII.

The fully completed bridge, approximately 1,595 feet in length, and of Roman inspiration in design, opened to the public on May 22, 1822. The viewpoint in Louis Garneray's famous painting from La Bastide with the tollhouses

Fig. 28   Louis Garneray (1783–1857), *Vue du port de Bordeaux prise du quai de la Bastide*, after 1822, oil on canvas, 13⅛ × 17¾ (33.5 × 45), © Chambre de commerce et d'industrie de Paris.

in the foreground (fees were charged for the bridge's first ninety-nine years) presents a panoramic view of the façade of the quays that had replaced the old city ramparts during the city's *âge d'or*. Rising above the houses at left is the medieval Église Saint Michel, and its *Flèche*. With the bridge in place, only one part of the river remained open to maritime traffic as larger vessels, such as the three-masted ships seen here at the right, could not pass under it; smaller boats, however, continue to navigate the full length.[62]

The red brick bridge is embellished with white stone medallions bearing the oak leaves and insignia of Louis XVIII, glorifying the king who saw through its completion and presided over the city's revived prosperity. As noted by Bordeaux historians Coustet and Saboya, "To the pride of possessing a superb monument worthy of the great achievements of the ancients or of the *âge d'or*, was added the pleasure of the contemplation of ships anchored in the middle of the river, the manifest sign of the long awaited return of commercial activity."[63]

*   *   *

Two years after the bridge's completion, Goya and his second family joined the expatriate community in Bordeaux as part of a wave of Liberals fleeing the brutal repression and vengeance of Ferdinand VII on his return to the throne in 1823 following the revolt of 1820 and the so-called Liberal triennium. The new arrivals joined the *afrancesados* who had arrived in 1813, some of whom, like Silvela, chose to remain in exile after the establishment of a constitutional government in Spain in 1820, when they were invited back. As in earlier eras of Bordeaux's history, particularly its golden age, when immigrants made their fortunes in the flourishing transatlantic trade, the Spanish community of the period between 1813 and Ferdinand's death in 1833 contributed substantially to the city's economic growth and cultural life, some of them investing large sums in the newly revived port commerce and urban development.[64]

The modern nineteenth-century city, with its bucolic suburbs, magnificent eighteenth-century core, and medieval and Roman monuments, formed the backdrop of Goya's everyday life in Bordeaux. There the aged court painter who had served three Spanish monarchs and one French "intruder" king found tranquillity and produced a brilliant body of experimental work in a variety of media; almost none of it, however, remains in Bordeaux.[65] What survives of Goya's "Burdeos" is a series of intimate portraits of friends and family who formed part of his last *tertulia* and vivid drawings of the city's singular inhabitants—many of them misfits and outcasts who aroused the curiosity and sympathy of the artist, an outsider himself in more ways than one. The Bordeaux albums of drawings include depictions of fairground freaks, cripples, beggars, the mentally ill, a pitiful criminal about to be executed, as well as more lighthearted images of reckless roller skaters and women being carried on the backs of men in shoulder chairs, all of whom formed a bizarre sideshow to Bordeaux's well-ordered city and bourgeois society.

For a broader vista of Bordeaux in Goya's time and intriguing details of everyday life (such as the price of chocolate and a theater subscription) from the perspective of a fellow expatriate, we must turn to the poet-flâneur Moratín, who sang its praises in his copious letters to his friends in Spain. "Amongst the principal pleasures offered by the city," he noted in a letter of November 30, 1823, "must be included the theater (an essential necessity for me); availability of all the newspapers; a well-stocked library; meetings of educated and refined people; grand balls; beautiful walks some formed by art and others made by nature herself; a wealth of different foods; shepherds and their flocks; peasant dances; rustic flutes and songs."[66] Moratín, who settled in Bordeaux in 1821, comments in another letter on the flood of Spaniards into the city: "We are inundated with Spaniards. . . . As for marquises, I assure you we are up to our necks in them here; I have only to step into the street and I can't look in any direction without my eye falling on a marquis or a little marquise."[67] He had little patience with those fellow countrymen who failed to see the city's merits. In a letter of July 17, 1825, Moratín writes: "Aylloncito came and spent two days here, but left on the third, fed up with the river, the bridge, the theater, Chartron's [sic], the Chapeau Rouge, the public gardens, the new avenue, by these heavenly wooded groves, the shops, the Stock Exchange, the ships in the port, in sum, by everything, because none of it could be exchanged for a tub of straw in his native Manzanares, a little eating den in the Madrid *Rastro* or even a dungheap by the Gates of Gil Imón."[68] Goya, as described by Moratín, fell in between: "pleased with the city, the countryside, the climate, the food" but if allowed "would put himself on the road [to Madrid] mounted on a chestnut-colored mule . . ."[69] Goya, in fact, did return to Madrid twice during his four-year stay, but both times he chose to come back to his second family and to live out his remaining days on the banks of the Garonne.

Two years after Goya's death in 1828, the July Revolution of 1830 brought about the abdication of the ultraconservative Charles X, who had been unwilling to cede any of his power to the people, and a constitutional monarchy was established in France under Louis Philippe, which endured until 1848. The death of Ferdinand VII in Madrid in 1833 marked the end of absolutism in the peninsula as well, and most of the Spanish expatriates in Bordeaux returned home, among them Leocadia Weiss and her now-grown children. The turbulent era in Spain's history set off by the French Revolution of 1789, which had propelled Goya and many of his countrymen into exile, had come to a close. Finally, following the first great retrospective of Goya's art in Madrid in 1900, the painter's remains were also repatriated (though his skull was missing) and buried in the Pantheon in the cemetery of San Isidro in Madrid. In 1929 they were transferred once again to his final resting place below the cupola of the hermitage of San Antonio de la Florida in Madrid, decorated with his celebrated murals carried out at the height of his fame in the waning years of the eighteenth century.

NOTES

The research for this essay was carried out during a monthlong stay in Bordeaux in the summer of 2004 made possible by a Getty Curatorial Travel Grant, for which I am most grateful. I also thank Pierre-lin Renié, Curator at the Musée Goupil in Bordeaux, and Pamela and Jay Hill for their comments; Joanna Sheers, Curatorial Assistant at The Frick Collection, for her contribution to the research; and my Bordeaux companion, Jonathan Galassi.

1   Fauqué and Villanueva Etcheverría 1982, p. 538.

2   *Encyclopaedia Britannica,* Eleventh Edition, 1910, IV, p. 245.

3   The image is oriented with west at the top.

4   MacDonald 1976, pp. 42–43.

5   The Edict simultaneously protected Catholic interests by discouraging the establishment of Protestant churches in certain areas.

6   The French word *fronde* means sling, or slingshot, and refers to the pelting of windows with stones that characterized the uprisings.

7   Rèche 1996, p. 389. See also López 1988, p. 5.

8   Cited in Hiéret 1986, pp. 23–24.

9   See Saugera 1995, the major study on this subject. My thanks to Pierre-lin Renié for this reference. Saugera notes on p. 17 that 40 percent of the expeditions left from Nantes. He remarks on p. 21 that the colonial commerce in Bordeaux could not have existed without the massive transplanting of blacks to another continent, and that great fortunes were founded on their labor. Le Harvre and La Rochelle are also designated as *ports négriers.*

10   Hiéret 1986, p. 24.

11   Ibid.; see also Saugera 1995, pp. 25–26, on the triangle trade.

12   Worldfacts n.d.

13   Rèche 1996, p. 389; Forrest 1975, p. 7.

14   López 1988, pp. 4–5. See also Moniot 1986, pp. 19–20.

15   Saugera 1995, p. 111. The slave trade continued illegally into Goya's time in Bordeaux.

16   Intendants were first employed in France under the reign of Louis XIII (1610–43) but were established in this capacity and given greater authority by Louis XIV (1643–1715).

17   Bernadau 1844, p. 12, describes Bordeaux at the outset of the eighteenth century as a city "surrounded by ancient and high walls, at the foot of which lay large ditches, which bordered the sinuous streets of wasteland or cultivated land, and large areas of swamp. The city, isolated from the neighboring suburbs . . . resembled a war zone. . . ."

18   Young 1900, p. 67.

19   Taillard 1997, pp. 76–79.

20   The annual fairs were moved to the Quinconces in 1853; see Dupuis-Sabron 1993–94, pp. 130–31, nos. 138–40.

21   The grillwork was designed by Joseph Fuet in 1755, under Tourny's administration, and demolished during the Revolution.

22   Dupuis-Sabron 1993–94, p. 78.

23   Lacour presented the painting, *Vue d'une partie du port et des quais de Bordeaux dits des Chartrons et de Bacalan,* to Empress Josephine when she passed through Bordeaux in 1808. It is believed to have remained in the Lacour family until 1872, when it was purchased by the City of Bordeaux, presumably for the Musée

des Beaux-Arts, where it remains today. With thanks to Valérie de Raignac of the Musées des Arts Décoratifs of Bordeaux for providing this information.

24 Lafond 1907, pp. 130–31, presents an image of the restless Leocadia "dragging her obedient slave from one end of Bordeaux to the other, attending fairs and circuses with little Rosario," though states no source.

25 Letter of August 1746 from Tourny to the *contrôleur général*, cited in Lheritier 1920, II, p. 217.

26 A few medieval gates, such as those known as "La grosse cloche" and the Porte de Cailhau, remain.

27 Hiéret 1986, p. 23.

28 MacDonald 1976, p. 25.

29 Fauqué and Villanueva Etcheverría 1982, p. 541.

30 Ibid., p. 624. On Braulio Poc, see also Nuñez de Arenas 1950, p. 249. Poc was an Aragonese Liberal and defender of Zaragoza and served as a pall bearer for Goya.

31 The statue was replaced in 1900 with the currently standing version by Gaston Leroux-Veunevot.

32 Fauqué and Villanueva Etcheverría 1982, p. 545.

33 Canellas López 1981, p. 505, no. CLXVIII.

34 Rèche 1996, p. 391. The museum was closed by the end of the century but was soon replaced by the Musée des Beaux-Arts de Bordeaux, founded in 1801 by Pierre Lacour.

35 Fauqué 1988(a), p. 19.

36 Taillard 1997, p. 152.

37 Andioc 1998, p. 31.

38 Letter of October 15, 1821, cited in Fauqué and Villanueva Etcheverría 1982, p. 544.

39 Bordeaux 1988, p. 24.

40 For percentages, see Poussou 1989, p. 15.

41 For background on the Revolution in Bordeaux, see Forrest 1975 and Figeac 2002.

42 Figeac 2002, p. 255.

43 Diary entry dated July 15, 1792, Ruiz Morcuende 1962, p. xvi.

44 A reduced version of the statue is in the Musée des Arts Décoratifs in Bordeaux. The allegorical reliefs on the pedestal by Claude Francin glorifying Louis's military exploits with symbols of the four continents at the base are preserved today in the Museé d'Aquitaine.

45 Figeac 2002, p. 265.

46 A monument to the Girondins deputies was erected in the Places des Quinconces in Bordeaux between 1898 and 1904.

47 Figeac 2002, p. 272.

48 Ibid., p. 249.

49 Desgraves 1954, p. 137.

50 Ibid.

51 Cited in Desgraves 1954, p. 134.

52 López 1988, p. 10, speculates on the basis of lists of names of those receiving aid that there may have been "more than a thousand Spaniards living in Bordeaux between July 25, 1813, and February 26, 1814."

53 Britain exerted pressure on Spain, Portugal, France, and the Netherlands to abolish the Atlantic slave trade, which had been banned earlier in Britain and the United States.

54 Desgraves 1954, p. 152.

55 See Coustet and Saboya n.d., pp. 27–43, on the development of the park.

56 Fauqué and Villanueva Etcheverría 1982, pp. 630–31.

57 Dupuis-Sabron 1993–94, p. 150.

58 Fauqué 1988(a), p. 24. From 1981 to 1991 the Casa de Goya was installed in what was presumed to be the artist's apartment; an exhibition commemorating his life in Bordeaux was on view during

this period (see Fauqué and Villanueva Etcheverría 1982). Today, however, much of the building is occupied by the Instituto Cervantes. A plaque hangs above the main entrance in honor of Goya.

59 Matheron 1966, p. 256.

60 Fauqué 1988(a), p. 20.

61 Coustet and Saboya n.d., pp. 62–63.

62 Ibid., p. 101.

63 Coustet and Saboya n.d., p. 67.

64 Fauqué 1988(a), p. 19, notes that members of this wealthy expatriate community involved themselves in port commerce and invested fortunes in Bordeaux through Jacques Galos, representative of Mexico and Goya's friend and financial adviser.

65 Of Goya's work from his years in Bordeaux, the Musée des Beaux-Arts in Bordeaux, however, owns the unique impression of the fifth state of the Bulls of Bordeaux.

66 Andioc 1973, p. 573, no. 293, translation in Fauqué and Villanueva Etcheverría 1982, p. 544.

67 Letter to Melón, February 5, 1824; Andioc 1973, p. 580, no. 298.

68 Ibid., p. 633, no. 341, translation in Fauqué and Villanueva Etcheverría 1982, p. 544.

69 Canellas López 1981, p. 501, no. CLX.

CATALOGUE

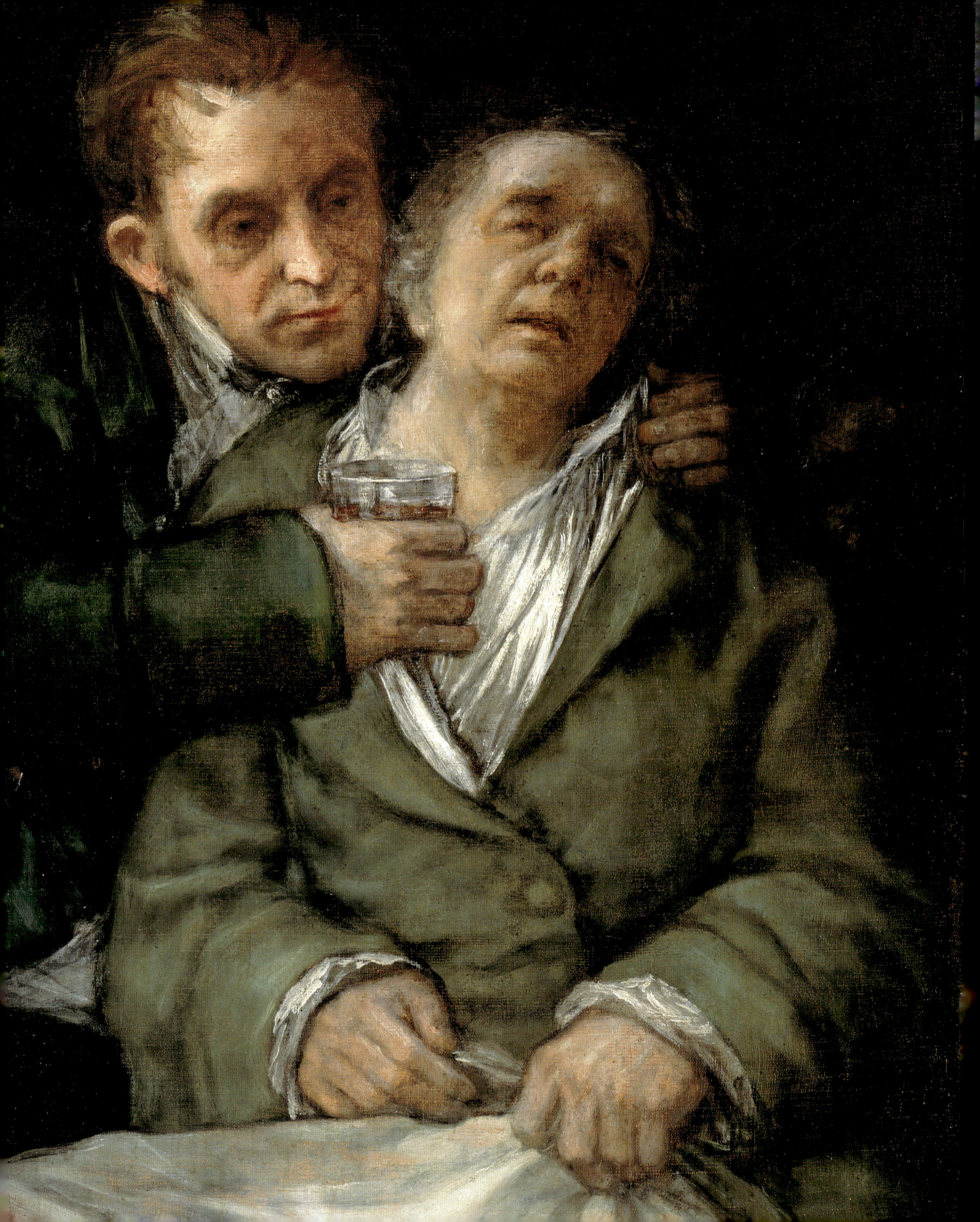

Goya's Self-Portraits and Portrait of His Son

GOYA'S SELF-PORTRAITS ARE OFTEN COMPARED to those of Rembrandt, although they are fewer in number. Like the Dutch painter, the Spaniard represented himself in a variety of guises and media—paintings, drawings, and prints. This is not the place to discuss the self-portraits or to interpret them as reflections of the artist's biography.[1] Instead the focus is on two works of a kind not found in any of Goya's predecessors that represent the artist's brushes with death.

The first crisis occurred in 1792–93, and its physical and emotional toll can be evaluated by looking at portraits executed before and after the illness. A small drawing in pen and ink (cat. no. 1), thought to have been done no later than 1792, although it has been dated as early as 1780, shows Goya as he looked in his mid-thirties or early forties, in the prime of life. Goya emphasizes his vigorous, robust health by the use of forceful, vibrant lines and emphatic shadows in the jacket and hat. The stippling employed on the face heightens the liveliness of the image as does the fashionable sausage curl that tumbles down his neck.

The blow to Goya's health fell in late 1792, when he was forty-six. He appears to have detected the first symptoms in October. On the 14th, he signed a lengthy letter to the Royal Academy in a somewhat trembling hand, for which he begged pardon. "If my hand does not govern the pen as I would wish . . . , I beg Your Excellency to pardon it."[2] Soon after he became seriously ill and in late January 1793 went to Seville to further his recuperation. Unfortunately he appears to have suffered a relapse and was taken to the house of his friend Sebastián Martínez in Cádiz. On March 19 Martínez wrote to Martín Zapater, Goya's friend in Zaragoza, describing the painter's condition, which had been grave but was now slowly improving.[3] His eyesight was returning, but deafness and a ringing in the ears were unmitigated. Goya was able to walk without losing balance and could climb up and down stairs. By June he was strong enough to make the journey to Madrid.

Goya's illness has never been conclusively diagnosed, although several hypotheses have been proposed.[4] Over time, Goya's health was restored but not his hearing, and he spent the last third of his life immersed in silence. He could speak, of course, but could receive verbal communications only through sign language and lip reading. His recovery otherwise was slow. As he wrote to Zapater on April 23, 1794, "I am much the same insofar as my health, sometimes raving with a mood that I myself cannot stand, other times more tempered, as now when I take up the pen to write to you, and I am already tired."[5] In April 1797 he was compelled to resign his post as director of painting at the Royal Academy as a result of his poor state of health, which prevented him from fulfilling his pedagogical duties.[6]

A self-portrait made with a brush and gray wash ink (cat. no. 2) movingly expresses the physical and psychological impact of his illness.[7] The eyes are compelling; they seem to be staring inward, implying his isolation from the sounds of the world. His signature

Goya año 1824

is written in an odd way, upside down on a medallion worn on his chest, facing the painter not the viewer, as if he constantly required a reminder of his identity. Yet Goya is by no means finished; his morbid face is framed by unruly locks of hair that indicate hidden reserves of energy. Goya has been battered but he is not beaten. Although not dated, the drawing has plausibly been assigned to the period 1795–97. It has been remarked more than once that the portrait evokes a famous contemporary, Ludwig van Beethoven, whose loss of hearing began in 1801 and who died in 1827, a year before Goya.

The next brush with death occurred late in 1819 and was commemorated with Goya's most singular self-portrait, the *Self-Portrait with Dr. Arrieta* (cat. no. 3). Nothing is known of this attack on his health except for the cryptic data recorded in the inscription: "Goya, in gratitude to his friend Arrieta: for the skill and care with which he saved his life in his acute and dangerous illness, suffered at the end of the year 1819, at the age of seventy-three. He painted it in 1820."[8] Goya's "thanksgiving" piece shows the artist at death's door, being pulled back from the abyss by the ministrations of his physician. It is hard to believe, looking at the half-closed eyes, the open mouth, the hands clutching the bed linen, the body barely able to support its own weight, that Goya, far from being exhausted, had in front of him the Black Paintings and the richly creative years at Bordeaux.

Goya turned the same unflinching eye on his son in an extraordinary drawing of 1824 (cat. no. 4). Despite his great affection for Javier, Goya did not delude himself about his son's lack of ambition and energy.

JB

NOTES

1 For comprehensive studies of the self-portraits, see Gállego 1978 and Ciofalo 2001.

2 Canellas López 1981, p. 312, no. 184.

3 Ibid., p. 455, no. LXIX. For the chronology of Goya's illness, see Baticle in Lille 1998–99, pp. 111–12.

4 For a history of psychological and pathological interpretations of Goya's sickness, see Glendinning 1977, pp. 165–74. The most recent hypothesis advances the theory doubted by Baticle that Goya suffered from lead poisoning, the consequence of using this metal in some of his pigments; see Rodríguez Torres 1993.

5 Canellas López 1981, p. 317, no. 192; translation Tomlinson 1994, p. 94.

6 Ibid., pp. 323–24, no. 204.

7 Equally haunting is the small self-portrait in oil in the Museo Nacional del Prado, Madrid; see Wilson-Bareau and Mena Marqués 1994, p. 259.

8 Translation Tomlinson 1994, p. 252. The small pen-and-ink drawing of Goya in profile wearing a cloth cap (Museo Nacional del Prado, Madrid, no. 483; GW no. 1658) is now thought to be the work of Rosario. The precise, delicate technique makes this attribution plausible.

facing page Javier Goya *(Francisco Javier Pedro Goya y Bayeu)* (detail of cat. no. 4; reproduced larger than actual size)

I

Self-Portrait with Three-Cornered Hat

c. 1780–92
Pen and brown ink, with framing line in black chalk, on paper, $3^7/_8 \times 3^7/_{16}$ (9.8 × 8.8)
The Metropolitan Museum of Art, New York, Robert Lehman Collection, 1975

Annotated on a separate piece of paper, probably in eighteenth-century script: *D. Francisco Goya y Lucientes, Pintor de Camara de S.M: Dibujado por el mismo.*

PROVENANCE: Juan Agustín Ceán Bermúdez, Madrid; Paul Lefort, Paris; his sale, Hôtel des Commissaires-priseurs, Paris, January 28–29, 1869, lot 105; Charles Yriarte, Paris; Mrs. Jay, Frankfurt am Main; Philip Hofer, Cambridge, Massachusetts; Robert Lehman, New York, 1948; The Metropolitan Museum of Art, 1975.

PRINCIPAL REFERENCES: Gassier and Wilson 1971, no. 332; Gassier 1975, no. 319; Tomlinson 2002, pp. 13–16.

This self-portrait has been dated over a fairly wide spectrum of time, from as early as 1780 to as late as 1795, although the latter date, which falls after Goya's serious illness of 1793, is improbable.[1] In any event, the image depicts Goya in the prime of his life. It is true that in November 1787, he wrote to his friend Martín Zapater, observing the passing of his youth: "I have turned old and with many wrinkles, so that you would not recognize me except for the snub nose and the deep-set eyes. What is certain is that I note greatly my 41 years. . . ."[2] Perhaps he was indulging in self-pity, for there is no conspicuous trace of aging to be seen. Rather, the drawing shows Goya as he would have appeared before his critical illness of 1793, which surely robbed him of the vestiges of his youth (see cat. no. 2).

The vigorous linear technique and the stylish hat enhance the impression of vitality. And the three-cornered hat, usually worn by *majos*, imparts a raffish air onto the portrait.

The drawing has a distinguished provenance and was owned by several early writers on Goya, commencing with his supporter and close friend Juan Agustín Ceán Bermúdez and including the French critics Paul Lefort (1824–1904) and Charles Yriarte (1832–1898). In 1876 it was used as the frontispiece for the third edition of the Tauromaquia.

JB

1   Gassier 1975, p. 448, no. 319, assigns a date of 1785–95; Tomlinson 2002, pp. 15–16, proposes a date of c. 1780.
2   Canellas López 1981, p. 287, no. 140.

I

Self-Portrait after Illness of 1792–93

c. 1795–97
Brush and gray wash on paper, 6 × 3⁹/₁₆ (15.3 × 9.1)
The Metropolitan Museum of Art, New York, Harris Brisbane Dick Fund, 1935

Signed with point of brush on medallion pinned to lapel: *Goya*; numbered in pen and brown ink at upper right: *I*.

PROVENANCE: Javier Goya, 1828; Mariano Goya, 1854; Román Garreta y Huerta, agent for Federico Madrazo, Madrid; Mariano Fortuny y Madrazo, Venice; purchased by The Metropolitan Museum of Art, 1935.

PRINCIPAL REFERENCES: Wehle 1941, pp. 7–8; Bean 1964, no. 92; Gassier and Wilson 1971, no. 666; Gassier 1975, no. 331; Wilson-Bareau 2001, pp. 24–25.

This moving self-portrait is one of five executed after Goya's serious illness of 1792–93 and before 1800. The best known is the frontispiece of Los Caprichos, securely datable to 1797–98 (a preparatory drawing is in The Metropolitan Museum of Art). Another is a small full-length portrait of the artist at his easel, holding a palette and paintbrush (Real Academia de Bellas Artes de San Fernando, Madrid). The last two are the most expressive, a tiny oil in the Museo Nacional del Prado, Madrid (fig. 29) and the present drawing, both of which show Goya sunk in thought or meditation. In all five, the artist wears the bushy sideburns that he grew after his illness.

In the drawing, made with a pointed brush and gray wash, Goya depicts himself with an intense inward gaze that appears to cut him off from the world. His deafness seems palpable; hence the frequent comparison of this image to those made of Beethoven after his loss of hearing.[1] Nevertheless, this portrait is hardly devoid of energy, which is implied by the unruly locks of hair that cover the artist's head and continue along his cheeks and chin. It has been suggested that this motif may have been derived from an etched self-portrait of the young Rembrandt (*Self-Portrait with Curly Hair*, 1630) and that it may be understood as a metaphor for the "wildly creative thought processes" of the painter.[2] This latter interpretation may be stretching the point, but it is apparent that Goya has created a contrast between his introspective expression and the bursts of energy implied by the restless movement of his hair, so different from the carefully coiffed sausage curl in the earlier drawing.

The portrait was inherited by Javier Goya, who used it as the frontispiece of one of the three albums he assembled of his father's drawings.[3] This explains the Roman numeral "I" in the upper-right corner. After Javier's death, the albums and other works by Goya were inherited by his son, Mariano, who began to sell them. The album drawings were acquired by Federico Madrazo, director of the Museo del Prado, via the intermediary of his brother-in-law, and were then widely dispersed by gifts and sales. In 1894 a group of fifty was inherited by Madrazo's grandson Mariano Fortuny y Madrazo, who sold them to The Metropolitan Museum of Art. This *Self-Portrait* is among the group.

JB

Fig. 29 *Self-Portrait*, c. 1795–97, oil on canvas, 7¹/₁₆ × 4³/₄ (18 × 12.2), Museo Nacional del Prado, Madrid

1   For example, see the portraits of Beethoven done in 1818 by August von Klober, in Comini 1987, figs. 11–12.
2   See Symmons 1998, pp. 18 and 23. It has also been suggested that the self-portrait was influenced by the engraving *Leonine Head*, illustrated in the 1781–86 French edition of Lavater's *Essays on Physiognomy*; see Stoichita and Coderch 1999, pp. 71–73.
3   For the provenance of the albums, see Wilson-Bareau 2001, p. 24.

2

3

Self-Portrait with Dr. Arrieta

1820
Oil on canvas, $45^1/_2 \times 31^1/_8$ (115.7 × 79.1)
The Minneapolis Institute of Arts, The Ethel Morrison Van Derlip Fund

Signed at bottom margin: *Goya agradecido, á su amigo Arrieta: por el acierto y esmero con qe la salvo la vida en su aguda y peligrosa enfermedad, padecida á fines del año 1819, a los setenta y tres de su edad. Lo pintó en 1820.* (Goya, in gratitude to his friend Arrieta: for the skill and care with which he saved his life in his acute and dangerous illness, suffered at the end of the year 1819, at the age of seventy-three. He painted it in 1820.)

PROVENANCE: Collection of the sitter, Madrid; J. J. Martínez Espinosa, Madrid; M. A. de Ajuria Temple, Paris and Mexico; Dr. Eduardo Lucas-Moreno, Paris; Germain Seligman, Paris; Otto Weinberger, Paris; M. Knoedler & Co., New York; purchased by The Minneapolis Institute of Arts, 1952.

PRINCIPAL REFERENCES: Carderera y Solano 1835; Royo Villanova 1927, pp. 15–16; Trapier 1964, pp. 42–43; Gassier and Wilson 1971, no. 1629; Gudiol 1971, I, no. 697; New York 1971, p. 503, no. 269; Licht 2001, pp. 160–64; Camón Aznar 1980–82, IV, p. 126; Moffitt 1981–82; Baldwin 1985; Pérez Sánchez and Sayre 1989, no. 121; Morales y Marín 1994, no. 497; Alcalá Flecha 1997; Ciofalo 2001, pp. 96–110; Portús 2004, pp. 364–65, no. 66.

This memorable work is a masterpiece of self-portraiture. Little is known of the circumstances that inspired the artist to paint it, except for the information provided in the lengthy inscription. The portrait is above all a thanksgiving offering to Dr. Eugenio García Arrieta and a tribute to his skill in saving Goya's life from the "acute and dangerous illness, suffered at the end of the year 1819."[1] Goya's enfeebled body is cradled in the arms of his physician, who proffers a healing medication to his patient. Goya has painted himself with unflinching candor. He seems at death's door, his eyes half shut, his lips barely parted; with his left hand, he clutches at the bedclothes.[2] The doctor and the patient fill the foreground and are dramatically lit against a black backdrop. Lurking in the shadows are the heads of three figures; the one at the left holds what seems to be a long-stemmed drinking vessel.

The significance of the picture was well understood by Valentín Carderera, a painter and early biographer and collector of the master's works. Writing in 1835, he responded to the composition with a few sentences that still seem relevant.

Not all the works of his final period began to give way to his diminishing physical forces. The canvas in which he portrayed himself as moribund, at the moment in which the distinguished Professor Arrieta gives him a drink that restored him to his native land and to his numerous admirers, is a work that recalls all the vigor and valor of his best period. His portrait of himself in agony [death throes] and the physiognomy of the doctor, animated with the most benign expression, are drawn and colored with the greatest mastery, and in the entire work it seems that Goya wanted to rejuvenate his genius to show the complete scope of his gratitude.[3]

Despite the transparent significance of the painting, there have been attempts to tease out other resonances or levels of meaning, which have focused on three elements—the inscription, the poses of the protagonists, and the shadowy figures in

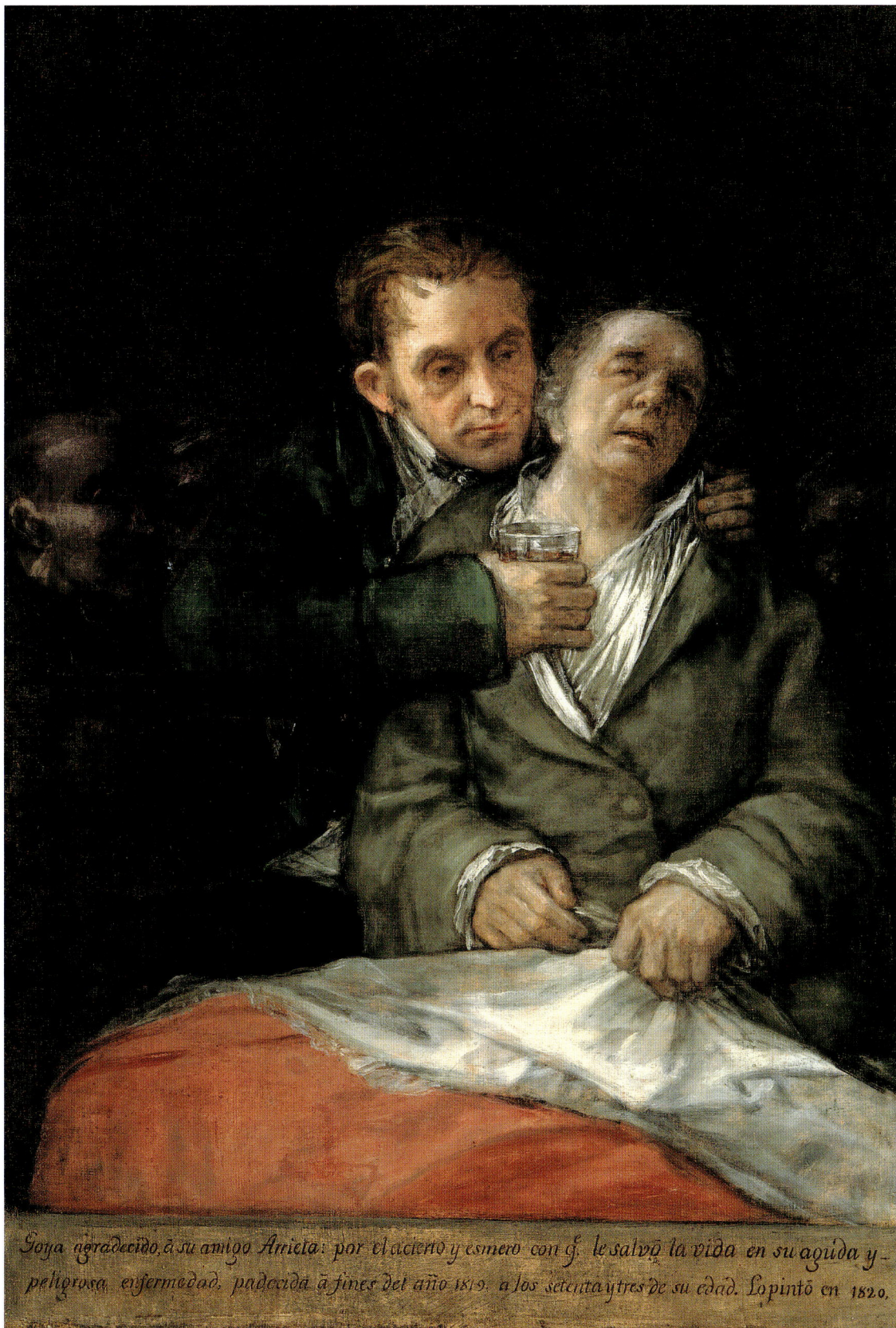

Goya agradecido, á su amigo Arrieta: por el acierto y esmero con q. le salvó la vida en su aguda y peligrosa enfermedad, padecida á fines del año 1819. a los setenta y tres de su edad. Lo pintó en 1820.

the background. There is no difficulty in accepting that the two-line narrative inscription was inspired by ex-voto images, religious works, often crudely painted, offered in gratitude by beneficiaries of divine intervention. The use of this format can plausibly be explained by Goya's wish to glorify Dr. Arrieta by casting him in a saintly role. This formula inevitably has led to a search for more specific religious significances. For example, it has been suggested that the poses of Arrieta and Goya paraphrase the traditional composition of the *Pietà*, the scene in which the Virgin Mary holds her dead son in her lap and mourns his death.[4] Although in this picture Goya is alive, if barely so, the pose is reminiscent of this venerable religious composition.

Another line of inquiry posits that the painting is situated in the Christian tradition of *Ars moriendi* (the art of dying), a spiritual guide to a "good death" that pits angels against demons in a deathbed struggle for a man's soul.[5] This argument casts Arrieta as the Good Angel and the three background figures as demons, waiting to snatch Goya's soul and transport it to Hell. However, the identification of the background figures as devils is not sustainable.[6] The figure at the left is unmistakably human; he seems to have his hand clutched around the stem of a glass or chalice which, as has been suggested, might represent a priest or monk poised to administer the last rites. This identification would be consistent with the idea that a conventional deathbed scene is represented and would

emphasize the very closeness of Goya's brush with death.

Next to this figure, wedged into a tight space defined by Arrieta's upper arm, is a sketchy head, of which only an eye and the top of the head can be seen. With so little visual data, it is impossible to determine the man's identity or function. At the extreme right is a third man's head, which can be readily discerned despite the murky shadows. These forms can be interpreted unequivocally as human beings by comparing them to some of the Bordeaux miniatures, especially the one now in Princeton (cat. no. 14). Once these demons are converted into mere mortals, this interpretation of the *Self-Portrait with Dr. Arrieta* vanishes with them.

While there are undeniable echoes of religious art in this striking composition, the struggle represented here takes place on a secular stage.[7] Goya's wish to live yet a while longer had been granted by a physician wearing a coat of green, the color of hope. (Goya's coat is the same color.) At the age of seventy-three, Goya realized that his medical salvation would be transitory; thus the unmistakable references to imminent death imparted by the poses of the protagonists and the man with a chalice. He was again living on borrowed time and, as this great picture tells us, was determined to make the most of it.[8] In the very year it was painted, Goya moved to the Quinta del Sordo and commenced the murals known as the Black Paintings.

JB

1 For the little that is known of Arrieta's life, see Royo Villanovo 1927, pp. 15–16. He was born in Cuéllar (Segovia) and cared for aristocratic patients in Madrid. In 1820 he was appointed by royal decree to a commission charged with studying an outbreak of plague in North Africa.

2 As Baldwin 1985, pp. 71–72, points out, this motif was commonly used by Goya's contemporaries in paintings and in theatrical representations of deathbed scenes.

3 Carderera y Solano 1835, pp. 253–55; cited in Centellas Salomera 1996, pp. 32–33. For reasons unknown, the painting was twice copied by Goya's assistant Asensi Juliá; see Gil 1990, p. 82, no. 8.

4 Ciofalo 2001, pp. 106–8, develops this argument, testing several hypotheses.

5 Moffitt 1981–82, pp. 37–49.

6 Licht 2001, pp. 207–9, was also misled by this identification. The suggestion by Alcalá Flecha 1997, pp. 347–48, that the figures represent the Three Fates is highly speculative and not supported by the comparative material he adduces.

7 For the possible impact of contemporary plays, see Portús 2004–5, pp. 364–65, no. 66.

8 As the above text makes clear, we share Baldwin's optimistic interpretation (1985); Goya is being liberated from the clutches of death and not delivered unto them.

right   *Self-Portrait with Dr. Arrieta* (details of cat. no. 3)

73

4

Javier Goya (Francisco Javier Pedro Goya y Bayeu)

1824
Graphite on paper, $5^{7}/_{8} \times 4^{15}/_{16}$ (14.9 × 12.5)
Private collection, courtesy The Metropolitan Museum of Art, New York

Signed in lower center, immediately below figure: *Pr Goya año 1824*; and immediately below first signature, in larger script: *Pr Goya año 1824*.

PROVENANCE: Javier Goya?; Félix Boix, Madrid; Philip Hofer, Cambridge, Massachusetts; Robert Lehman, New York; private collection.

PRINCIPAL REFERENCES: Mayer 1924, 195, no. 691; Gassier and Wilson 1971, no. 1636; Gassier 1975, no. 377.

Javier Goya was born on December 2, 1784.[1] As sole survivor of the six children born to Goya and Josefa Bayeu, he was a focal point of their life and the recipient of their material bounty. In 1803 he was assigned an annual pension of 12,000 reales, obtained by the sale to the crown of the plates and unsold sets of Los Caprichos. Two years later Javier made an advantageous marriage to Gumersinda Goicoechea, daughter of the wealthy merchant Martín de Goicoechea and his wife, Juana Galarza. Both families bestowed handsome dowries on the fortunate couple. It was on the occasion of the marriage that Goya painted a set of portrait miniatures on copper of Javier and his new relatives.[2] Javier, then twenty-one years old, looks young and handsome, although more like his mother than his father (see fig. 6).

In 1812, following the death of his wife, Goya, in accordance with their joint will, divided their common property and possessions with his son.[3] The total estate was appraised at about 350,000 reales, a small fortune. Goya kept some household furnishings, a valuable collection of jewelry, and cash, while the remainder, which included paintings by Goya and others and a house on the calle de Valverde, went to Javier. In other words, Goya, given his age, kept the liquid and near-liquid assets, giving Javier real property that

might appreciate over time. Javier would appear to have been set for life.

On the negative side of the ledger, however, is the fact that Goya's son had neither job nor vocation. It is true that from time to time he was called a "painter," which has recently fired speculation that he was the author of some of Goya's most renowned works, or, at a minimum, a skilled imitator of his father's later style.[4] As yet, however, no work has been conclusively attributed to him. His vocation, if such it may be called, was as a rentier.

This circumstance seems to have made him feel both insecure and entitled. The only time he is known to have acted decisively was when he prevented his father from altering his will in favor of Leocadia Weiss in the belief, not entirely misguided, that he was his father's only legitimate heir. Although he lingered in Madrid too long to see his father before he died, he soon traveled to Bordeaux to take possession of his belongings and ensure that Leocadia would have nothing but the pittance he granted her. On his return to Madrid and until his death in 1854, Javier lived off his investments, supplementing his income by the sale of his father's pictures.[5]

When Goya drew this small portrait, perhaps to take with him into exile, he no longer harbored illusions about his son. The image is pitiless, drawn as if

there were no relationship between the two men. One need only compare the drawing to the portrait miniature of 1805. In less than twenty years, Javier had become fat, as seen in the slack fold of heavy skin that droops over his collar. More telling still is Javier's vacant stare, imbued with the melancholy of a man who has abandoned his ambitions. Javier inherited Goya's wealth but, if his father is to be believed, little of his energy or spirit.

JB

1 For Javier's biography, see Lafuente Ferrari 1947, pp. 291–94.
2 Reproduced and discussed in Wilson-Bareau and Mena Marqués 1994, pp. 266–69, figs. 67–73, and pp. 365–66.
3 For this transaction, see Sánchez Cantón 1946, pp. 103–7, and Cruz Valdovinos 1987, pp. 133–53.
4 For Javier's putative activities as a painter, see Wilson-Bareau 1996(a); Junquera 2003(a), pp. 353–70, esp. 368–70; and Glendinning 2004, pp. 244–45.
5 Wilson-Bareau 1996(a).

4

Portraits on Canvas

From 1820 through 1827, Goya continued to paint portraits of his friends and family. The standard catalogue lists eleven of men and three of women.[1] Most of his pre-1820 portraits (more than 200 in number, about one-third of his output in painting) were commissioned works that proclaimed the status and power of his royal, aristocratic, or wealthy upper-class subjects, though Goya also produced private informal likenesses of his friends. The late portraits, however, are mainly intimate pieces created for his own pleasure as tokens of friendship, affection, or gratitude. His sitters were for the most part members of his own professional class—doctors, lawyers, bankers, educators, and merchants.

Portraits play a special role in Goya's late work. In contrast to his drawings, prints, and miniatures, they provided him with a particularly grounded occasion and challenge. They are the product of an intense encounter—a two-way exchange with a significant person, often carried out in a single session. In several of his late portraits, Goya included his age in inscriptions to his sitters, suggesting that they were as much important markers in his painting life as they were likenesses of particular individuals captured in a specific moment in time. One of Goya's early biographers, Laurent Matheron, who found his late painting "feeble and slack," made an exception for the portraits, noting that "before the living model, a double *binocle* on his nose, he found himself again for a brief space."[2]

The late portraits represent a process of breaking through convention and decorum to reach a simpler form of representation and deeper psychological insight. They are not so much a departure from Goya's earlier work as an assertion of his fundamental belief in artistic freedom and instinct, which he put forth in his famous address on the curriculum of the Royal Academy of San Fernando in 1792. "There are no rules in painting," he asserted, observing that the painter cannot explain "why he has been happier perhaps with a work where less care has been taken, than with one of greater finish."[3] In his late work Goya permitted himself to experiment yet more freely with the convention-bound genre of portraiture on which his reputation and livelihood had largely rested, and to take greater risks. He left behind the polish and refinements of his earlier work for a more stripped down, expressive, sometimes crude vocabulary of form to capture the essence of his sitter by the simplest means possible. These are works of extraordinary directness and feeling, which seem to anticipate modern art, yet which echo his own earlier canvases and those of his artistic forebears. As Goya's son, Javier, noted in a brief biography of his father published shortly after his death, "He observed with veneration Velázquez and Rembrandt, and neither studied, nor observed, anything but nature, that he claimed as his master. . . ."[4]

Facing page   Joaquín María de Ferrer (detail of cat. no. 8)

*   *   *

Fig. 30 *Ramón Satué*, 1823, oil on canvas,
42$^1/_8$ × 32$^7/_8$ (107 × 83.5), Copyright
© Rijksmuseum Amsterdam

The first in the series of canvases of his late years is the *Self-Portrait with Dr. Arrieta* of
1820 (cat. no. 3), which, though unique in composition and style, establishes the tone
for the rest. The palpable bond between two persons, expressed in the painter's interac-
tion with his doctor in this great canvas, is also present between the artist and the sitter in the portraits of single figures that follow. Goya's portrait of Don Tiburcio Pérez y
Cuervo (cat. no. 5), also of 1820, is generally seen as the first in which his late portrait
style is fully manifest. Here he uses a traditional portrait format—a single figure standing against a neutral ground—but proceeds to pare away all that is extraneous to elicit
the character and vitality of his young friend. In its dark tonality, neutral ground, and
free and direct manner of painting, the work pays homage to Velázquez. At the same
time it breaks new ground, not simply through a reinvigorated manner of painting but
also by means of an informality of presentation: Pérez has broken out of a staged pose

and stands in a characteristic natural manner, arms crossed and shirtsleeves rolled up.
Through the substitution of a spontaneous for a more formal pose, Goya unsettles the
viewer's expectations and increases the sense of liveliness of his sitter. Pérez appears as
vivid to us today as when he stood before Goya.

In his portrait of 1823 of another young friend, Ramón Satué (fig. 30), a judge of the
supreme court in Madrid,[5] Goya pushes his more informal and abbreviated manner further. Standing in front of a dark ground, Satué fills the canvas with his powerful, sensual presence. The jauntiness of his attire—a black topcoat with tails and trousers,
enlivened with a flamboyant red waistcoat and white shirt with a frilled inset—is com-
plemented by the casualness of his stance and his slightly ironic expression. The radical
simplifications of Goya's late style may be best appreciated through a comparison of this
portrait with an earlier one of another fashionable young man, Bartolomé Sureda y

Miserol, whom he had painted twenty years earlier (fig. 31). In both, the figures are standing and three-quarter length, the backgrounds are neutral, and a flash of red stands out in a generally subdued palette. Sureda emerges from a dark atmospheric space in a self-conscious, contrapposto pose with an almost baroque torsion, while Goya's virtuoso brushwork underlines his sitter's nonchalance and glamour. In the Satué portrait, light focuses on the sitter's carefully rendered volumetric head, while the rest of the bulky figure is reduced to a simple flattened black silhouette shot through with a slash of red at the waist that indicates his girth. Goya skims over detail and enlists the viewer's participation to fill in the rest. "I don't count the hairs of the beard of the man who passes [my way], and the buttonholes of his suit do not stop my eye. My paintbrush should not see better than I do," Goya is reported to have said to his young friend the painter Antonio de Brugada.[6] Satué is represented in the frontal plane of the picture, up close to the viewer. He faces us matter-of-factly, with his collar open and his hands thrust into the pockets of his trousers; the studied casualness of the earlier portrait gives way to a new simplicity of means and pose. Arrogance is replaced by a more ironic "make-of-me-what-you-will" self-presentation. In the portraits of both Tiburcio Pérez y Cuervo and Ramón Satué, Goya appears to have been challenged by the youth and vigor of his friends to find a more immediate, unencumbered language of representation in which to capture them in their world—a new social order, with mores and manners distinct from his own.

Goya adopts a similar format to those of Pérez and Satué in his 1824 portrait of a woman thought to be María Martínez de Puga (cat. no. 7): in all three the figure is facing left, standing but cropped above the knee, and attention is concentrated on the essential expressive elements of head, arm, and hand. The body is diagonal and the head in three-quarter view, the eyes facing left or front. Like Pérez and Satué, the subject is dressed in black, up-to-date fashion. Here Goya pushes further some of the audacious formal characteristics of the previous two works: a condensed range of somber neutral tones, compressed space, and a variety of animated brushwork—small precise strokes for the face and broad, sweeping ones for her costume. As compared with the portraits of Pérez and Satué, this one is somewhat more formal, perhaps a reflection of the sitter's personality or gender. Or was it a commissioned work? (As the figure's identity is not secure, there is no way of knowing what Goya's relationship with her might have been.) Her stance and gestures are more dignified than casual, the composition is somewhat more elaborate, and Goya uses certain portrait conventions, such as the gloves and fan. The figure dominates the space and, although smaller than life size, has, as de Salas has noted, a sense of monumentality.[7]

The pair of portraits of Joaquín María de Ferrer and his wife, Manuela de Álvarez Coiñas y Thomas de Ferrer (cat. nos. 8 and 9), painted in Paris in 1824, are the first of his late works in which Goya added a place of execution to the date and signature.[8] A

facing page Portrait of a Lady (Maria Martinez de Puga?) (detail of cat. no. 7)

80

wealthy and powerful couple who were staunch Liberals, the Ferrers were at the center of the Spanish expatriate community in Paris and became Goya's friends during his two-month stay in the capital in the summer of 1824.[9] Many of the aspects of Goya's portraits before his departure are here intensified: the dark palette, emphasis on silhouette, and vigorous brush strokes, which become even sketchier. The lively character of the portraits of Pérez and Satué is replaced by a more static arrangement of the half-length figures within the frame; in fact the term "primitive" has been applied to them.[10] The portrait of Joaquín de Ferrer recalls aspects of the nearly monochromatic portrait of José Duaso y Latre (cat. no. 6), a priest and scholar, whom Goya painted shortly before his departure for France. In both the Duaso and Ferrer portraits, Goya concentrates on his sitters' intellectual power, to which all else is subordinated. Each holds a small crimson book, and while the priest is portrayed in a moment of deep absorption in the act of reading, Ferrer appears to be lost in contemplation of what he has just read. The portrait of Manuela de Ferrer shares aspects with that of María Martínez de Puga; both subjects are depicted in fashionable black dresses of similar style, face left, and hold a fan in one hand, and in both paintings a fine gold watch chain flows over the bust of the figure defining its contour. A comparison with Jean-August-Dominique Ingres's portrait of one year earlier of Mme Leblanc (fig. 32), also dressed in a fashionable black dress and wearing a long gold chain with a watch tucked into her waistband—a masterpiece of meticulous illusionism by an artist who was more than thirty years younger than Goya—sets off the dramatic simplicity of the Spaniard's late style. The sense of formality noted above in the Puga portrait is also evident in the image of Manuela de Ferrer, which Gudiol describes as "hieratic," a trait he commonly finds in Goya's representations of women.[11]

Distance is obliterated in Goya's first Bordeaux portrait, where he was reunited with one of his closest comrades, the poet and playwright Leandro Fernández de Moratín (cat. no. 10). Shortly after settling in his new home in September 1824, the painter took the measure of his old friend in a half-length portrait, an affirmation of their renewed friendship. A slight sense of resistance to the painter's scrutiny is registered in the face of the sixty-five-year-old writer. Twenty-five years earlier, when both artist and playwright were at the height of their careers in Madrid, the playwright had sat for one of Goya's most beautiful portraits, in which the writer appears as the personification of artistic sensibility (see fig. 39). Goya rarely painted his friends more than once; the second portrait of Moratín points to the intimacy of their relationship and their mutual trust.

As in the Ferrer portrait, Goya adopts a pyramidal composition and depicts the poet in a moment of reflection; his slightly ironic expression, however, conveys the paradoxical character of a man whose physical appearance has coarsened over time, but whose spirit has remained undimmed. A few leaves of white paper scattered on a wooden desk

Fig. 32 Jean-August-Dominique Ingres (1780–1867), *Madame Jacques-Louis Leblanc*, 1823, oil on canvas, 47 × 36¹/₂ in. (119.4 × 92.7 cm), The Metropolitan Museum of Art, New York, Catharine Lorillard Wolfe Collection, Wolfe Fund, 1918

suffice to give a minimal sense of context and to set off the hand. We feel the presence of Goya in this portrait, as if he were seated on the other side of the table, and though cut off from the sound of Moratín's voice, reacquainting himself with him through his brush. The poet's solitariness seems to reflect that of the painter's—for both are now old and in exile.

Whether Goya painted Moratín's close friend Manuel Silvela (cat. no. 11) in Bordeaux or earlier in Madrid during the French occupation is not known for certain. The fact that the portrait is unfinished adds to the problem of dating it. Opportunity and motive, as discussed in the entry, argue for placing it in the Bordeaux years. But can this work be held to the standards of his late portraits discussed so far? Perhaps it was a commission, which may account for the fact that it is larger in scale and more complex in composition than most of the late portraits, and that he appears to have turned back to some of his earlier formats and repertoire of gestures. Whether the composition presented difficulties for the aging artist or the busy schoolmaster was too impatient to sit is not known, yet even in its unfinished state, the work shares characteristics of the late portraits in its muted tones, broadness of form, architectonic quality, and focus on the personality of the sitter, as revealed through his tense, upright posture and meditative expression.

83

The last three portraits from Goya's hand were carried out in 1826 and 1827, in the last year and a half of his life—two in Bordeaux and one on a brief trip back to Madrid. In them, Goya appears to be driven by even greater determination to break down the barriers between himself and his sitters and to continue to experiment with portrait conventions and take new risks. Goya drew inspiration from the energy of his last sitters, two of them young or middle-aged men who played vital roles in his late life, one a beloved family member. In these final works, his brush stroke is looser and somewhat tremulous as a result of failing eyesight and some loss of motor control, as several writers have noted, though long experience, discipline, and instinct continue to guide his hand. Formally and emotionally, these portraits are close-ups.

If we can imagine the painter sitting across a table from Moratín, the self-made magnate Jacques Galos—one of the leading entrepreneurs in Bordeaux and Goya's banker, financial manager, and steadfast friend—appears to be knee-to-knee with the artist (fig. 33). (Goya undoubtedly had to paint him at close range to compensate for his diminished eyesight.)[12] Seated on a wooden chair against a luminous gray ground, this dapper entrepreneur is dressed in a dark blue jacket with brass buttons and a white shirt with a high collar and white cravat, which Goya lays in with free, broad strokes. The odd cropping of the figure, longer than bust-length but not half-length, and its tilt in the frame, enliven the composition and are vaguely unsettling for the viewer. Energy flows from the alert handsome face, with its rugged planes, sleeked-back graying hair, and intensely focused eyes, and is directly channeled through the vitality and sureness of Goya's hand and concentration on essentials. The uncontrived pose, broad handling of form, tension between figure and space, and powerful evocation of personality make this portrait one of his most innovative and compelling late works. With evident pride and affection for the sitter, the painter added an inscription on the chair: D.n.Santiago Galos / pintado por Goya, de / edad de 80 años / en 1826.[13]

Whether the Galos portrait was executed before or after the painter's first return trip to Madrid in May to June 1826 is not known. While there, Goya obliged his monarch, Ferdinand VII, by sitting for a formal, life-sized portrait by Vicente López y Portaña (1772–1850), who was appointed first court painter in 1815 (see fig. 13).[14] Though the king recognized Goya's genius, he preferred López's highly detailed realistic style.[15] After two sittings, Goya proclaimed the portrait finished, telling his friend that further work with "his niggling brush" would be detrimental; the resulting canvas is López's masterpiece and a tour-de-force of illusionism.[16] The contrast between Goya's young successor's precise academic realism and the direction of his own late work could not be greater.

On his final trip to Madrid in the following summer (probably from July to September 20, 1827), Goya recorded the image of his beloved grandson and heir, Mariano, in a likeness of great tenderness (see fig. 14), demonstrating the range of emo-

Fig. 33 *Jacques (Santiago) Galos*, 1826, oil on canvas, 21⅝ × 18⅛ (55 × 46), The Barnes Foundation, Merion, Pennsylvania, BF #5, Gallery VI

D.ᶰ Santiago Galos,
pintado por Goya, de
edad de 40 años
en 1826

Fig. 34   *Juan de Muguiro*, 1827, oil on canvas, 40⅛ × 33½ (102 × 85), Museo Nacional del Prado, Madrid

Fig. 35   *Sebastián Martínez*, 1792, oil on canvas, 36⅝ × 26⅝ (92.9 × 67.6), The Metropolitan Museum of Art, New York, Rogers Fund, 1906

tion he was capable of eliciting in his final years. He had painted two previous portraits of him as a boy;[17] here he is twenty-one, on the threshold of manhood. With a few strokes, Goya sketched in Mariano's fashionable formal attire, marking his entry into adulthood and society. The head, however, painted in a softer, almost caressing brush stroke, is that of a cherubic adolescent. The pure oval of the face framed in wispy black curls, the large, brown eyes and pursed lips have an almost feminine softness. The callow young man presents himself impassively to the penetrating scrutiny of the old artist, whose fortune he would eventually squander.

Before leaving for Madrid in May 1827, Goya had painted one of the largest and most ambitious portraits of his final period, a work that has acquired an almost iconic status in his oeuvre (fig. 34). The subject, Juan de Muguiro, a successful businessman and banker, whose brother had married the younger sister of Gumersinda Goicoechea, the wife of Goya's son, Javier, was another friend of the artist's in Bordeaux (and, in fact, accompanied Goya on his final trip to Madrid not long after sitting for the portrait).[18] As in his portrait of Silvela, Goya depicts his subject seated with legs cropped below the knee. Wearing a dark blue suit, white shirt with a frilled inset, and a soft black foulard, Muguiro is seated on a fine wooden chair with a yellow seat, holding a document or letter. To the right of the figure is a table with papers and writing implements. He looks out at the viewer with a forthright gaze and an air of authority—an *homme d'affaires* in command of his world. Here Goya brings back some of the familiar codes of official portraiture—the commanding staged pose, frontal face, formal attire, and fine appointments—within the simplified syntax of his late work. Was it the sitter who required this more elaborate treatment? Or could it have been Goya's experience of the previous summer of sitting for an official commissioned portrait himself that goaded him to create a final masterpiece in this genre, and to reinvigorate it?

Looking back from the portrait of Muguiro to the magnificent likeness of the 1790s of Sebastián Martínez, another powerful Spanish merchant (fig. 35), we see the distance Goya traveled in what might be described as an excavation down to the foundation of representation. The three-dimensional figure in space of the earlier portrait is replaced by a comparatively flattened form; a harmonious combination of pleasing pastel colors and virtuoso display of precise and animated brushwork is substituted by a reduced spectrum of dark and light tones and an impetuous laying in of broad strokes of paint, thickened in places with the addition of sand. Though pushed close to the picture plane, the image of this refined late eighteenth-century merchant aesthete remains behind an imaginary transparent pane; that of his brash nineteenth-century counterpart, however, seems to lie on the surface, aggressively confronting the viewer. The earlier painting is a unified whole, in which the relation of each part to the others is clearly articulated. The later portrait is a composite of expressive elements—the masklike frontal face, the fleshy hand on the thigh, the letter midway between the two, the large back of the wooden chair, the disproportionately small desk. A harmonious integration of parts gives way to a rawness and immediacy of expression.

Goya's elaborate inscription on the side panel of the desk, which reads "D. Juan de Muguiro, por su amigo Goya a los 81 años, en Burdeos, Mayo de 1827," expresses his affection for the last sitter of his small circle of friends. It also appears to be something of a valedictory salute. Over a period of forty years, Goya produced portraits that linked the rococo period to the dawning romantic era and anticipated the modern in certain respects. Édouard Manet, an ardent admirer of Goya's, would not have known the artist's last portraits, many of which remained in private hands until the early decades of the twentieth century. Yet in his radical works of the late 1860s, such as his *Portrait of Émile Zola* of 1868, Manet seems to pick up in the process of simplification of painting where Goya had left off four decades earlier. Goya's late portraits are penetrating analyses of the character of his subjects and a distillation of his life's experience as a painter. In Enriqueta Harris's words, they made his reputation "as the greatest master of his age, and the first of the moderns."[19]

SGG

NOTES

1   See Gassier and Wilson 1971, nos. 1629–35 and 1659–66. The portrait of Manuel Silvela, which is included in this survey of late portraits, is dated to an earlier period in the 1971 publication (see GW no. 891). Since that catalogue was published, the attribution of the portrait of José Pío de Molina (Oskar Reinhart Collection, Winterthur, Switzerland) has been questioned as has that of the *Portrait of a Woman*, The National Gallery of Ireland, Dublin. For the purposes of this essay, the painting of Tio Paquete (Museo Thyssen-Bornemisza, Madrid) is not included here.

2   Translation Harris(a) 1975, p. 14.

3   Address of October 14, 1792, translation Tomlinson 1994, p. 306, Appendix I.

4   Javier Goya, originally published in 1831 by Pedro Beroquí, translation Tomlinson 1994, p. 307, Appendix II.

5   The Rijksmuseum's Web site gives this as Satué's title; Gassier and Wilson 1971, p. 323, no. 1632, list his former office as city councilor.

6   Matheron 1996, p. 168.

7   De Salas 1979, p. 156.

8   The portrait of Joaquín de Ferrer bears an inscription that reads "Goya Paris 1824." The portrait of Manuela de Ferrer is signed "Goya 1824."

9   Camón Aznar 1980–82, IV, p. 194, notes that they were commissioned works.

10   Gudiol 1971, p. 348.

11   Ibid.

12   For biographical information on Galos (1774–1830), see Trapier 1964, p. 46, and Fauqué and Villanueva Etcheverría 1982, pp. 586–87 and 593.

13   Information provided in a curatorial report by Wilson-Bareau to The Barnes Foundation, Merion, Pennsylvania, in 2003.

14   Díez 2004, p. 266.

15   Ibid.

16   Calvert 1908, p. 116.

17   GW nos. 885 and 1553.

18   For a recent discussion of this work, see Portús 2004, p. 366, cat. no. 67.

19   Harris(a) 1975, p. 14.

5

Don Tiburcio Pérez y Cuervo, the Architect

1820
Oil on canvas, 40¼ × 32 (102.2 × 81.3)
The Metropolitan Museum of Art, New York, Theodore M. Davis Collection,
Bequest of Theodore M. Davis, 1915

Signed and dated, lower left, with an inscription to the sitter: *A Tiburcio Perez / Goya. 1.820*

PROVENANCE: Collection of the sitter, Madrid; Francisco Durán y Cuervo, nephew of the sitter, Madrid, by 1900–3; purchased by Durand Ruel, Paris, February 1903; Theodore M. Davis, Newport, June 1903; bequeathed to The Metropolitan Museum of Art, 1915.

PRINCIPAL REFERENCES: Desparmet Fitz-Gerald 1928–50, II, p. 222, no. 511; Gassier and Wilson 1971, no. 1630, description and illus., p. 304; Gudiol 1971, I, no. 698; De Angelis 1974, p. 620; Camón Aznar 1980–82, IV, p. 139; Baticle 1992, pp. 446–47; Morales y Marin 1994, no. 498; Stein 1995, pp. 39, 45.

Following his near-fatal illness at the end of 1819, Goya produced two intimate portraits dedicated to the sitters: his *Self-Portrait with Dr. Arrieta* (cat. no. 3) and a portrait of Tiburcio Pérez y Cuervo, both of 1820. They have been associated with the artist's process of recuperation and his restoration to full health.

An early source refers to the subject of this portrait as a *torero*, and his stance and physical robustness could perhaps suggest a bullfighter.[1] The sitter, however, was a classically trained architect. Tiburcio Pérez y Cuervo was born in Oviedo, Asturias, in 1786. His uncle, Juan Antonio Cuervo, was a leading neoclassical architect of the turn of the century.[2] Juan Antonio was appointed director of the Royal Academy of San Fernando in Madrid in 1815 and four years later sat for a portrait by his friend Goya (fig. 36).[3] The artist portrayed him in the sumptuous black jacket trimmed in silver braid of a royal academician over a red vest, seated at a desk with the plans for one of his projects spread out

Fig. 36 *Juan Antonio Cuervo*, 1819, oil on canvas, 47¼ × 34¼ (120 × 87), © The Cleveland Museum of Art, Mr. and Mrs. William H. Marlatt Fund, 1943.90

A. Tiburcio Perez.
Goya. 1820.

5

before him.[4] As has been noted, Goya appears to have had a special affinity for architects and painted portraits of five of them over his lifetime.[5]

Following in his uncle's footsteps, Tiburcio Pérez enrolled as a student at the Royal Academy in December 1801, at age fifteen, and seven years later received a prize for his design for a monument to be erected on the battlefield of Bailén to commemorate the Spaniards' heroic victory over the French in 1808.[6] Pérez was received as a member by merit of the Academy in 1818 and went on to design a number of important commissions: with Francisco Javier de Mariátegui (the future father-in-law of Goya's grandson, Mariano) he oversaw the construction of the Royal College of Medicine in Madrid in 1831 and designed a gymnasium on the Paseo del Prado.[7]

At the time of his portrait, Pérez was thirty-four, about the same age as Goya's companion, Leocadia Weiss. The two men appear to have had a close friendship. When he left Madrid for Bordeaux in June 1824, Goya entrusted the care of Leocadia's ten-year-old daughter, Rosario, to Pérez.[8] (In September, Leocadia and her two children followed Goya to Bordeaux to resume their lives together.)

In contrast to the official portrait of Juan Antonio Cuervo, Goya's likeness of Pérez is emphatically informal. Every element, from the subject's stance and attire to the artist's technique, contributes to a sense of naturalness and vivid presence. Pérez emerges from a dark ground facing left and diagonal to the picture plane, his legs cropped above the knee. His head turns slightly to the front, with eyes looking alertly into the distance and fleshy red lips upturned in a slight smile. His thick black hair mounds up around his head, conveying a sense of vitality and power.

Pérez stands at ease, with his arms folded around his chest and hand tucked into the crook of his elbow. His body seems to rotate gently in space around the pivot of his projecting right elbow, enhancing the liveliness of the image. The neutral ground surrounding the figure is bisected from the upper right corner of the canvas to the lower left into subtly different shades of black. His head is set against the lighter area at the left. Light floods in from the upper left, drawing out the figure from the surrounding darkness in bold relief.

Pérez wears a simple black vest over a voluminous white shirt with a frilled inset, loose black trousers or pantaloons with a woven sash or cummerbund with touches of color and a fringed end wound around his waist.[9] His shirtsleeves are rolled back, and he holds his glasses in his hand. Without an outer coat—either a frock coat or tails—however, it is difficult to tell whether the architect is dressed for day or night.[10] The black suit with a white shirt was standard attire for men of the professional class and aristocracy alike by 1820. After the French Revolution, as Aileen Ribeiro has noted, men's dress "becomes plain in design and sober in colour. . . . It symbolizes gravitas and an indifference to luxury—essential elements of republican austerity; its virtual uniformity emphasizes the revolutionary ideal of equality."[11] Pérez stood for his portrait in the year of the reestablishment of a constitutional government over the absolutism of Ferdinand VII—a moment of triumph for Liberals and the middle class and of jubilant though short-lived optimism. In his assertiveness and studied disarray, Goya's young friend personifies the new professional man as well as a person of artistic temperament.[12] Pérez's robust good looks, sensuality, and allegedly tempestuous nature—which may have reminded Goya of his own youthful self—appear to have challenged the aging artist to push beyond the limits of his previous portraits to capture his sitter's image in as direct and unmediated a means as possible.

The portrait appears to have been painted rapidly, with great assurance; x-radiographs reveal no pentimenti.[13] Thin layers of black paint are applied over a pink-orange ground that is visible through the inscription, signature, and date, which Goya scraped through the still-wet paint with the handle of a brush or reed in the lower left-hand corner. The areas of white in the shirt are underpainted in black, creating an illusion of depth in the fabric and intensifying the contrast of light and dark.[14] With a brush or palette knife, Goya conjured up the wrinkled, translucent white cloth in swift long strokes—a sort of free improvisation set off by the careful treatment of the hand and face. (Similarly vigorous passages appear in The Frick Collection's *Forge* of 1815–20, for example, in the socks of the man in the foreground.) The portrait has also been connected through its dark palette with Goya's Black Paintings, carried out around this time at the Quinta del Sordo.[15] The simplicity of means and naturalism that characterize this portrait—freely executed with a minimum of paint, using a strictly limited palette—open the way to the informal portraits of members of his circle of his last years.

SGG

1   Tild 1921, p. 121.
2   On Cuervo's career, see Sambricio 1986, pp. 319–22. He worked on plans for the Renta de Correos (post office) and two churches in Madrid. See also Caveda y Nava 1867, pp. 37–38.
3   GW no. 1561.
4   Cleveland 1982, p. 484.
5   Sánchez Cantón 1964, p. 111. Goya's portraits of architects also include those of Juan de Villanueva (GW no. 803); Ventura Rodríguez (GW no. 214); and Isidro González Velázquez (GW no. 859). See also Trapier 1964, pp. 41–42.
6   On Tiburcio Pérez y Cuervo's biography and career, see Caveda y Nava, 1867, pp. 37–38; Baticle 1992, pp. 446–47; *Guía de arquitectura y urbanismo de Madrid* 1982–83, pp. 1, 3, 43, and 171.
7   The Royal College of Medicine was designed by González Velázquez; Baticle 1992, pp. 446–47.
8   For some details of her stay with Pérez, see a biography of Rosario Weiss (originally published in *Semanario Pintoresco Español*, November 24, 1843—a year after her death), printed in Lafuente Ferrari 1947, p. 22. The author notes that she continued her training in drawing at casa Pérez, copying some of Goya's Caprichos with amazing likeness. See also Sánchez Cantón 1951, p. 124.
9   On men's dress of the period, see Tortora and Eubank 1998, p. 270. Trousers became prevalent after 1807, replacing knee breeches. They could be cut close or, as they appear to be in this portrait, full.
10 Shirts with frilled insets were usually worn in the evening, pleated in the daytime.
11 Ribeiro 1988, cited in Tortora and Eubank 1998, p. 263.
12 Vallentín 1951, pp. 373–74, refers to Pérez as a "new type of man of the generation of tomorrow."
13 Notes from an examination in the Paintings Conservation Laboratory at The Metropolitan Museum of Art conducted by Dorothy Mahon on January 20, 2005. The authors express their thanks to Ms. Mahon for observations on the technique of this painting.
14 Ibid.
15 Wilson Bareau 1996(a), p. 101.

6

José Duaso y Latre

1824
Oil on canvas, $29^{3}/_{8} \times 23^{1}/_{4}$ (74.5 × 59)
Museo de Bellas Artes, Seville

Signed, lower right corner: *D. Jose Duaso/ Por Goya de 78 años*

PROVENANCE: Collection of the sitter, Madrid; by descent to the Rodríguez Bavé family; acquired by the Spanish state for the Museo de Bellas Artes, Seville, 1969.

PRINCIPAL REFERENCES: Sánchez Cantón 1954, pp. 130–35; Gudiol 1971, 1, p. 345; Pardo Canalís 1968; Gassier and Wilson 1971, pp. 323, 329, no. 1633; Ansón Navarro 1995, pp. 234–38; García Guatas 1996, pp. 326–30.

José Duaso y Latre (1775–1849), like Goya, was a native of Aragon. Born in the village of Campol del Valle de Solana (Huesca), he moved to Zaragoza and in 1788 initiated his studies at the university, obtaining several degrees, the highest of which was doctor of canon law in 1801.[1] In order to subsidize his education, he became a member of the clergy in 1794 and was ordained in 1799. Duaso's scholarly interests were not confined to theology: he was a keen student of mathematics, economics, political science, and agriculture, which he studied in the schools of the Real Sociedad Económica Aragonesa. In 1802 he was appointed to the chair of mathematics at the Sociedad.

Three years later, Duaso moved to Madrid in search of a wider arena in which to deploy his talents. In 1805 he applied for and won the position of Capellán de Honor de Su Majestad (his majesty's chaplain of honor), the first of many offices and honors bestowed on him. During the Peninsular War, Duaso joined the fight against the French and acted with bravery to safeguard the precious liturgical furnishings of the chapel from the depredation of the French, for which he was decorated with the Real Orden de Carlos III.

In addition to his intellectual gifts, Duaso was a nimble politician. His political posture has been described as that of a "moderate reformer," a

judicious stance that enabled him to enjoy the favor of Ferdinand VII without alienating his Liberal friends. In the years following the restoration of the monarchy in 1814, Duaso occupied numerous positions, both administrative and honorific, including administrator of the Church and Hospital del Buen Suceso, Madrid.

Duaso and Goya not only shared Aragonese origins; they were friends or at least acquaintances. Thus when Goya decided to seek refuge from the purge of Liberals launched by Ferdinand VII in November 1823, he sought help from Duaso. Soon after Duaso's death, a short biography was published by Vicente de la Fuente, which reports how, heedless of his safety, he succored his countryman.

> In the meanwhile, his house served as a refuge for several of his friends and countrymen, who were compromised by their liberalism, whom he hid or protected as they needed. Among them we can count the celebrated Goya, his countryman and friend, who, for the space of three months, he had in his house.[2]

The exact date of Goya's retreat to Duaso's quarters in the Hospital del Buen Suceso is not certain, although it is generally thought to have commenced in January 1824, when the king began to clamp down on his Liberal enemies.

The date and signature inscribed on the canvas offer some confirmation. Goya celebrated his seventy-eighth birthday on March 30. If it can be assumed that he painted the portrait on returning to his own house, then he would indeed have gone into hiding during the first month of the year.[3] In any event, the inscribed date fixes the execution of the portrait after March 30 and before early June, when the painter departed for France.

Duaso's biographer provides a curious anecdote about the creation of the portrait:

> With this motive [taking refuge in Duaso's house], that famous artist proposed to make his portrait, and it was shocking to him that, despite his undeniable dexterity and having begun the portrait up to four times, he did not succeed in producing a full likeness, which caused no little anger in that celebrated artist, whose violent nature and temper are well known.[4]

The portrait shows no signs of this struggle. It may be the most somber of the late portraits, but it is superb nonetheless. The overall black tonality, of course, was dictated by the sitter's priestly vocation. His voluminous garment seems to fuse with the background, although upon scrutiny and under good light, the outline of the figure is discernible. Goya took a chance by painting black on black, and it worked. Two medals or decorations punctuate the cleric's garb. The largest is the golden insignia of the Order of Charles III; the smaller has not been identified. Evidently Goya wished to draw attention to the distinction of the sitter in the secular world and to his bravery. On his head, the priest wears a skullcap, pushed back to reveal dark brown hair, flecked with strands of gray.

Goya concentrates his firepower on the face and left hand, which holds a book, perhaps a prayerbook, bound in crimson. Duaso has been captured in a private moment, his eyes focused intently on the text in front of him. The face looks as if it is sculpted in malleable clay, the result of the subtle interplay of thick, impastoed touches of reddish and yellow colors. In Goya's eyes, Duaso was a quiet hero and a rock-solid friend.

J B

1   This biographical sketch is based on Pardo Canalís 1968.
2   Cited by Sánchez Cantón 1954, p. 131.
3   Goya made a tiny drawing in black chalk of Duaso's nephew Francisco Otín, signed and dated 1824, presumably executed while the artist was in hiding (GW no. 1634). It is now owned by Belén and Rafael Moneo. Baticle 1992, p. 48, dates Goya's stay with Duaso to February–April 1824.
4   Sánchez Cantón 1954, p. 132.

7

Portrait of a Lady (María Martínez de Puga?)

1824
Oil on canvas, 31$\frac{1}{2}$ × 23 (80 × 58.4)
The Frick Collection, New York

Signed, lower left corner: *Goya, 1824*

PROVENANCE: Aureliano de Beruete y Moret, Madrid; Sir Hugh Lane, London; J. H. Dunn, London; Colnaghi and Knoedler, London and New York; purchased by Henry Clay Frick, 1914.

PRINCIPAL REFERENCES: Beruete y Moret 1924, p. 328 (text of lecture delivered in Madrid in 1915); Desparmet Fitz-Gerald 1928–50, II, p. 228, as *Portrait de jeune femme inconnue*; New York 1968, pp. 300–2; Gudiol 1971, I, pp. 334–45, no. 720; Gassier and Wilson 1971, pp. 336, 338, no. 1635; Morales y Marín 1994, pp. 302–3, no. 389.

Although the identification of the sitter as María Martínez de Puga is generally accepted, there is little supporting documentation. The name was introduced into the Goya literature by Aureliano Beruete y Moret, former director of the Museo del Prado, who owned the work in the early years of the twentieth century.[1] Beruete offered no evidence for applying this name to the portrait. However, in 1956 Sambricio published a document that at least confirmed that a person with this surname, if not the sitter, was in contact with the painter in 1824, the date inscribed on the picture.[2] The document in question, signed by Goya and dated February 19, 1824, grants power of attorney to a certain Gabriel Ramiro to collect the painter's salary from the crown. One of the witnesses was Dionisio Antonio de Puga, presumably the husband of the sitter.

From time to time, the identification has been questioned. For instance, Desparmet Fitz-Gerald opined that she might be Rosario Weiss, despite the fact that Rosario was only ten years old in 1824.[3] Gudiol, a mild dissenter, noted that there is no trace of this individual in any contemporary reference to Goya.[4] As the catalogue of The Frick Collection judiciously notes, "This identification [as Martínez de Puga] has never been verified."[5]

The problem is compounded by the fact that in 1824 Goya spent time in Madrid, Paris, and Bordeaux, and in each place painted portraits (*Duaso*, Madrid; *Joaquín de Ferrer* and *Manuela de Álvarez*, Paris; and *Moratín*, Bordeaux). The only internal clue to the place of origin is the sitter's costume, but this is not conclusive. According to information generously provided by Aileen Ribeiro, French fashion had been adopted in Spain by the 1820s.[6] The sitter's "hairstyle and dress, the watch pinned to her belt, are versions of French fashion, as is the handkerchief she holds." Other details point to a modified French costume of a kind worn in Spain. Ribeiro concludes, "all says she's Spanish to me and possibly a resident of Bordeaux, although one can't be sure." Implied in this opinion is the possibility that the sitter is a Spanish woman living in Madrid or possibly in Bordeaux, although wearing a garment and accessories acquired in her native land. In fact, a somewhat similar costume is worn by Manuela de Álvarez Coíñas y Thomas de Ferrer (see cat. no. 9).

The prevailing identification of the sitter raises another question. All the extant portraits done between 1820 and Goya's death were of members of the artist's inner circle, with the exception of the Ferrers, who were prospective

97

Fig. 37 *Manuela Goicoechea*, 1805, oil on copper, diameter: 3³/₁₆ (8.1), Museo Nacional del Prado, Madrid

patrons. It is puzzling that this portrait, one of the most impressive of the group, should represent the wife of a person who, as far as is known, was an incidental acquaintance. But if not María Martínez de Puga, then who might this woman be?

At present, only a list of candidates can be assembled. Leocadia Weiss can almost certainly be struck from this list. She was born in 1788 and would therefore have been thirty-six, older than the sitter, who looks to be in her twenties. Javier Goya's wife, Gumersinda, is another child of 1788 and thus can be removed from consideration. Among Gumersinda's three sisters, Manuela, Gerónima, and Cesárea, there are certain physiognomic resemblances to the Frick portrait. Manuela (fig. 37) bears the closest resemblance and is known to have been in touch with Goya in 1824.[7] They were briefly together in Paris and returned to Bordeaux in the same coach on September 1. However, she was born in 1785 and would have been nearly forty in 1824.

The Frick portrait has long inspired praise from writers on Goya, who hail the painting as a precursor of Manet. Certainly the bold construction of flattened space and the fluid, remarkably concise brush strokes invite this comparison. Goya began by applying a light ground of whitish olive-green, which never disappears from view. Then he worked mainly with translucent tones of black and ochre, vigorously applied with a stiff brush and subtly modulated by the priming. The wall behind the sitter is divided into two zones of unequal dimensions. The

lower section is painted in black, the upper in ochre, and they are separated by a thin band of green that varies in width before petering out at the left.

The figure, except for the face and neck, was created with a similar economy. Goya rearranged the pose by altering the position of the shoulder, as can easily be seen along the sitter's right shoulder. For the dress, the painter resorted to the same black pigment used in the background, which is heightened with an admixture of lead white to render the folds and highlights. Upon scrutiny, the coiffure can be seen to be painted with short, curved strokes, into which are integrated sliver-like touches of orange, matching the headband. Especially deft is the lace collar, which Goya executed with a pliable reed. Another small detail confirms Goya's inventive use of the medium (fig. 38). The translucent shadow that falls just below the neck, on the sitter's right, is created by scratching the surface with a pointed instrument, the same technique Goya employed in the Bordeaux miniatures, lithographs, and drawings.[8]

Where Goya and Manet part ways is in the treatment of the face and neck, which Goya meticulously painted with smooth, opaque brushstrokes. In this area Goya pulls back from the threshold of the revolutionary style of Manet, but he does come close indeed.

JB

1   Beruete y Moret 1924, p. 328. It is noteworthy that Beruete produced a specific name for a sitter otherwise unknown.
2   Sambricio 1956, pp. CLVII–CLVIII, no. 250. Forty-one years later, a notary of Madrid named Antonio Puga compiled a postmortem inventory of the count of Yumuri (November 22, 1865, and first half of 1866), which included still lifes by Goya. See Vischer 1997, pp. 121–23.
3   Desparmet Fitz-Gerald 1928–50, vol. III, p. 228, no. 517.
4   Gudiol 1971, p. 197.
5   New York 1968, p. 300.
6   Undated letter (2004) to Susan Grace Galassi.
7   For Goya's miniature portraits of the Goicoechea sisters, done in 1805, see Wilson-Bareau and Mena Marqués 1994, pp. 266–69, figs. 70–73.
8   We thank Dorothy Mahon for conducting a technical examination of the painting in January 2005 and for sharing her observations with us.

Fig. 38 *Portrait of a Lady (María Martínez de Puga?)* (detail of cat. no. 7)

8

Joaquín María de Ferrer

1824
Oil on canvas, $28^{3}/_{4} \times 23^{1}/_{4}$ (73 × 59)
Private collection

Signed: *Goya, Paris, 1824*

PROVENANCE: Collection of the sitter, Paris and Madrid; by descent to Marqués de Baroja, Madrid; Marquesa de Gándara, Rome; private collection.

PRINCIPAL REFERENCES: Von Loga 1921, pp. 143–44; Beruete y Moret 1924, p. 331; Desparmet Fitz-Gerald 1928–50, II, p. 227, no. 516; Gassier and Wilson 1971, no. 1659; Gudiol 1971, I, pp. 347–48, no. 735; Camón Aznar 1980–82, IV, p. 194; Fauqué and Villanueva Etcheverría 1982, p. 554–55, 560–62; Morales y Marin 1994, no. 519; Ribemont and Garcia 1998, pp. 84, 191; Madrid 2002, no. 113; Berlin 2005, no. 139.

Joaquín María de Ferrer y Cafranga was born on December 7, 1777, at Pasajes de San Pedro in the Basque province of Guipúzcoa on the northeastern coast of Spain. A self-made man, he became wealthy in the Latin American trade and eventually rose to the highest post in the Spanish government, prime minister. Accounts of his early life differ. According to one source, he started out at age twelve in a business establishment in nearby San Sebastián and by seventeen moved to Cádiz to join his older brother, Francisco Javier, a banker involved in commercial ventures in Latin America.[1] From there he went on to Peru (and possibly Argentina) and amassed a fortune. By 1815 or 1816 he was back in Spain and living in Madrid, where he married Manuela de Álvarez Coiñas y Thomas (see cat. no. 9).

Ferrer was named deputy for Guipúzcoa in 1822 and served on the council of administration of the Banco de San Carlos.[2] He supported the constitution of 1820 and vociferously called for the removal of Ferdinand VII; with the king's return to power in 1823, he was a marked man. He escaped to London, however, and then to France, and settled in Paris, where he had ties with the Spanish colony of bankers and businessmen as well as members of the wealthy community of exiled Liberals, among them Vicente González Arnao,

the marquis of Pontejos, and the duke of San Carlos. By the beginning of May 1824 he was living in a grand house at 15, rue Bleue, in what is now the ninth arrondissement, and his wife joined him shortly thereafter. Because of his political connections, the French police considered him a "dangerous revolutionary" and kept him under close surveillance. An official report sent from Spain describes him unflatteringly as a "man of mediocre ability, his only talent seems to be for hatching plots . . . he has constantly exhibited revolutionary ideas and has managed to buy national property for more than a million francs."[3]

While in Paris, however, Ferrer devoted himself to cultural activities, investing in artistic and publishing ventures. He brought out illustrated books, such as *Don Quixote en Miniatura* (1827), for which he provided an introduction.[4] With Ferdinand's death in 1833, amnesty was granted to political exiles, and the Ferrers returned to Madrid. Joaquín María de Ferrer resumed his post as deputy for Guipúzcoa and swiftly ascended the ministerial ladder in the new government. In 1841 he was named presidente del consejo de ministros (prime minister).[5] He died in Santa Águeda in Andalucia in 1861 at age eighty-four.

Goya's connection with Ferrer began during his stay in Paris, from the first week of July through the end of August 1824. Goya probably met the couple through the jurist Vicente González Arnao, to whom Leandro Fernández de Moratín had sent him with a letter of introduction.[6] As discussed elsewhere in this catalogue, Goya hoped to secure Ferrer's help in establishing a market for his work in France. The Ferrers offered Goya their warm hospitality while in Paris, and the artist painted their portraits. The artist also painted a bullfight, the *Suerte de Varas* (see cat. no. 22), though whether on commission or as a gift is not known. Once he was settled in Bordeaux in September, Goya remained in contact with Ferrer, soliciting his assistance in selling his lithographs (the Bulls of Bordeaux, see cat nos. 23–26), as well as in securing training in miniature painting in Paris for Leocadia Weiss's young daughter, Rosario. Although Ferrer was less than helpful in these matters, Goya's letters to him provide valuable insight into his activities in lithography and his paintings on ivory during his first two winters in Bordeaux.[7]

Ferrer was forty-seven years old when Goya made his portrait. He is represented half-length and standing. He turns to the right, with his face in three-quarter view, and his left arm is bent and held close to his body, with a small crimson bound book held half open in his hand. Ferrer's attire is simple and elegant: a dark brown redingote with a large white *cravatte à jabot* wound around his neck,[8] and his black hair is cropped short and slightly tousled in a romantic fashion. His lean face, thin nose, slightly compressed lips, and the inward expression of his eyes create an austere demeanor . While the face is painted in fine brush strokes, the figure, set off by a luminous gray-green ground, is very broadly brushed, with areas of impasto in the neckwear. Goya signed his portrait of Joaquín María de Ferrer, "Goya, Paris, 1824." The addition of "Paris" to the date and signature suggests the special importance Goya gave to the place of execution, suggesting that it was the first work he painted in France. The only other possibility is the portrait of María Martínez de Puga, signed and dated 1824, which could have been painted in Paris, or in Madrid or Bordeaux.

Goya painted three half-length portraits of men in 1824, all in different locales: José Duaso y Latre in Madrid; Ferrer in Paris, and Moratín in Bordeaux. They are approximately the same size, painted in subdued tones, with an emphasis on silhouette. In all three, the figures face right and hold, or rest a hand on, a book or papers that refer to their spiritual or intellectual interest, or political beliefs.[9] Simplicity and directness mark all three portraits, as well as a strong sense of characterization of the sitter. As compared with the other two, however, the Ferrer portrait is simpler, and the figure, while remarkably fresh and expressive, is more enclosed within himself. This may reflect Goya's more distant relationship with Ferrer, a new powerful friend, whose patronage he hoped to secure in his home in exile.

SGG

1   Fauqué and Villanueva Etcheverría 1982, pp. 554–55, 560–62; For other biographical accounts, see Nuñez de Arenas 1950, pp. 238–40; Morales y Marin 1994, p. 358, no. 519; Baticle 1998(b), pp. 83–84; and Madrid 2002, p. 222.
2   See Baticle 1998(a), p. 43, and Baticle 1998(b), p. 84.
3   For the political agitators with whom Ferrer was said to be in touch and an English translation of the extract from an official report sent from Spain, see Fauqué and Villanueva Etcheverría 1982, p. 555; for the original Spanish version of the police report extract, see Nuñez de Arenas 1950, p. 239.
4   Sánchez Cantón 1951, p. 125, noted two editions, 1827 and 1832; Gassier 1971, p. 249, noted that he also brought out the *Recuerdos* of Antomarchi on Napoleon.
5   For his various governmental posts between 1833 and 1841, see Madrid 2002, p. 222.
6   Fauqué and Villanueva Etcheverría 1982, pp. 550–51.
7   For Goya's letters to Ferrer, see Canellas López 1981, p. 386, no. 268, and pp. 389–90, no. 273.
8   Desparmet Fitz-Gerald 1928–50, p. 227.
9   See Berlin 2005, p. 314 and note 4. Manuela Mena Marqués speculates that the book that Ferrer holds in his portrait might well be the Spanish constitution of 1812, which was published in small format in red leather in Madrid in 1820. The book would thus serve to underline Ferrer's deep allegiance to Liberal principles, a bond he shared with Goya and fellow Spanish exiles.

8

9

9

Manuela de Álvarez Coiñas y Thomas de Ferrer

1824
Oil on canvas, $28^3/_4 \times 23^5/_8$ (73 × 60)
Private collection

Signed: *Goya 1824*

PROVENANCE: Collection of the sitter, Paris and Madrid; by descent to Marqués de Baroja, Madrid; Marquesa de Gándara, Rome; private collection.

PRINCIPAL REFERENCES: Von Loga 1921, pp. 143–44; Beruete y Moret 1924, p. 331; Desparmet Fitz-Gerald 1928–50, II, p. 229, no. 518; Gassier and Wilson 1971, no. 1660; Gudiol 1971, I, pp. 347–48, no. 736; Camón Aznar 1980–82, IV, p. 194; Fauqué and Villanueva Etcheverría 1982, pp. 560–61; Morales y Marín 1994, no. 520; Ribemont and Garcia 1998, pp. 84, 191; Madrid 2002, no. 118; Berlin 2005, no. 140

.Goya painted fewer portraits of women than of men during his period of exile and the years just before his departure from Madrid. Two of them date from 1824: that of the woman presumed to be María Martínez de Puga (see cat. no. 7) and the present portrait of Manuela de Álvarez Coiñas y Thomas de Ferrer, the companion piece to that of her husband, Joaquín María de Ferrer (see cat. no. 8). The Ferrer portraits were painted in Paris during Goya's stay from early July through the end of August, probably at the couple's house at 15 rue Bleue, where a temporary studio would have been set up.[1]

Less is known of Manuela de Ferrer than of her husband. Her family had land holdings in Peru, and it must have been through the world of Spanish bankers and investors involved in Latin American commerce that Joaquín María de Ferrer came to know them. She was much younger than he and probably from a higher social class; by the time they had married, however, he had acquired great wealth and was on his way to a prominent political career.

After her husband escaped to France in the spring of 1824, a death sentence over his head, Manuela and her twenty-seven-year-old brother, José de Álvarez, joined him in Paris in early May.[2] The Ferrers were at the center of the Spanish expatriate community in the French capital and entertained in grand style at their house on rue Bleue. Manuela gave birth to their first child, Flora, on February 20, 1825. In a letter to Joaquín de Ferrer of December 1825 from Bordeaux, Goya sent greetings to "your good wife Doña Manuela and the beautiful daughter which heaven has given you."[3] In fact, she would have been in the early stages of pregnancy with the child when she sat for her portrait. In the summer of 1826, the family moved to the fashionable suburb of Montmorency on the outskirts of Paris, where two other daughters were born.

The portrait of Manuela de Ferrer is closely related to the Frick portrait. Both are signed and dated "Goya 1824," though the order in which he painted them is not known for certain. The Puga portrait is slightly taller ($31^1/_4$ inches compared to $28^1/_2$ inches), and the background is divided into lighter and darker rectangles, as opposed to the simpler monochromatic tone of the Ferrer portrait that corresponds with that of her husband. The female subjects are standing, facing left, and wearing dark dresses of a similar style, with long gold chains and a watch or medal around their necks.

Manuela is dressed in the current French Romantic style. Emphasis is now placed on the shoulders to set off a narrow waist, which has dropped from just below the bust in the Empire period to a few inches above the natural waistline.[4] Her gown has the characteristic *gigot* or *demi-gigot* sleeve (puffed at the shoulder, tapering to the cuff), with a horizontal or elliptical neckline, and she wears a belt with a golden buckle that accentuates her not-so-narrow waist. The neckline is filled with a pleated *chemisette* or tucker made of white linen or tulle, a separate, changeable piece worn in daytime, and her hair is arranged in Romantic fashion with curls around her forehead and temples and the back in a knot or chignon.[5] The long gold chain (*genre sautoir*) outlines her ample bust and separates the figure from the dark background. A similar gold chain is seen in Ingres's portrait of Mme LeBlanc (see fig. 32), painted in 1823, which is also worn over a black dress of comparable style. Manuela's closed gold-tipped fan, held in her bare right hand, forms part of an artful arrangement with the gold chain, square belt buckle, and medal, which draws the eye down to the lower part of the canvas.

Manuela's portrait was painted as one of a pair: husband and wife face each other—although she acknowledges the viewer with one eye—and are connected through pose, palette, and arm gesture. Her youthful plump face and figure, luxurious, though simple attire, and

discreet display of wealth in the form of her cascading gold chain and watch cover complement the more austere image of her lean middle-aged husband, with his abstracted air.[6] Both portraits are remarkably simple in composition, objective in style, and relatively flat, and as Beruete has noted, unlike any other work produced in France by the most celebrated artists of the time—Gros, Prud'hon, Ingres, and Delacroix.[7] The work has suffered some abrasion, as seen in the face, yet like the portrait of the husband has a strong sense of natualism

SGG

1 Fauqué and Villanueva Etcheverría 1982, p. 561.
2 Nuñez de Arenas 1950, p. 239. He notes that her escape route took her from Cádiz to England and to France. See also Fauqué and Villanueva Etcheverría 1982, p. 555.
3 Letter of December 6, 1825: Canellas López 1981, p. 389, no. 272; translation in Fauqué and Villanueva Etcheverría 1982, pp. 561–62.
4 On women's fashion of the Romantic period, see Tortora and Eubank 1998, pp. 280–88.
5 Ibid., pp. 283–84.
6 See Berlin 2005, p. 314, for Manuela Mena Marqués's interesting reading of the watch as possibly conveying a meaning more specific here than that of the traditional memento mori and alluding to the transience of all things, including political systems, and to the necessary passage of time of Spanish exiles before returning home.
7 Beruete y Moret 1924, p. 331.

10

Leandro Fernández de Moratín

1824
Oil on canvas, 23⅝ × 19½ (60 × 49.5)
Museo de Bellas Artes, Bilbao

Signed in lower center of canvas, upside-down on corner of a sheet of paper: *Goya*

PROVENANCE: Collection of the sitter, Bordeaux and Paris; bequeathed to Victoria Silvela, 1828; Francisco Silvela; Museo de Bellas Artes, Bilbao, 1932.

PRINCIPAL REFERENCES: Beruete y Moret 1916–18, no. 286 (or 277); Mayer 1924, no. 359; Desparmet Fitz-Gerald 1928–50, no. 523; Gudiol 1971, I, p. 216, IV, no. 1231 (or no. 707); De Angelis 1974, no. 658; Gassier and Wilson 1971, no. 1661; Camón Aznar, 1980–82, IV, pp. 199, 326; Luna 1989, pp. 90–91; Morales y Marín 1994, no. 521; Gállego 1996, pp. 186–87; Budapest 1996, pp. 132–34; Ribemont and Garcia 1998, no. 3; Bilbao 1999.

The poet, playwright, and critic Leandro Fernández de Moratín (1760–1828) was one of Goya's closest friends, and it was in part because of him that the painter settled in Bordeaux. Their friendship stretched back some thirty years. This portrait is the second Goya painted of Moratín; the first, in the Real Academia de Bellas Artes de San Fernando, Madrid, dates from twenty-five years earlier.

Moratín, who has been called the Spanish Molière, is considered the most important dramatist since the *Siglo de oro* and the renovator of Spanish theater; he was as eminent in the theatrical world as Goya was in art.[1] Their work has some affinities, particularly in their biting satires on social customs and mores of the time.

Born in Madrid on March 10, 1760, in the calle de San Juan, Leandro Fernández de Moratín was of aristocratic Asturian origin.[2] His father, Nicolás, was a lawyer, a professor of poetry at the Imperial College, and also a playwright. Leandro was the only one of four children to survive. At the age of four he contracted smallpox—an often fatal disease at the time—but he was nursed back to health by his grandparents.[3] According to his close friend and biographer, Manuel Silvela (1781–1832) (see cat. no. 11), the disease

left his face deeply scarred and his personality transformed. The lively, impetuous child became argumentative and timid; he would "abandon his reserve and reveal his rich comic side only to his close friends."[4]

Nicolás Fernández de Moratín educated his son in the Greek and Roman classics at home and encouraged him to pursue a career in the arts. The young Leandro won prizes for poems from the Spanish Academy and soon earned recognition from some of the leading *ilustrados* of the day. Through the statesman Gaspar Melchor de Jovellanos (a friend and patron of Goya's), he obtained a post as secretary to the Conde de Caburrús, founder of the National Bank of San Carlos in Madrid, and in 1787 accompanied him on a yearlong economic mission to Paris. During this time, he wrote his first two plays, *The Old Man and the Young Girl* (*El viejo y la niña*) and *The Baron* (*El barón*), commissioned by Caburrús as a *zarzuela* (musical) and later converted into a comedy. A third, *The Defeat of the Pedants (La derrota de los pedantes)*, in which he ridiculed the bad poetry of the time in the mode of Cervantes's *Voyage to Parnassus* (*El viaje al Parnaso*), followed soon thereafter.[5]

In 1790 Moratín gained the patronage of the favorite of Charles IV

Fig. 39 *Leandro Fernández de Moratín*,
1799, oil on canvas, 28³/₄ × 22 (73 × 56),
The Museum of the Royal Academy of Fine
Arts of San Fernando, Madrid

and María Luisa, Manuel Godoy, who would be appointed prime minister in 1795. Through him he obtained the necessary license to bring out his plays previously denied him by the ecclesiastical authorities. In 1792 he set off on a three-year tour of Europe with a generous pension from Godoy to study theater and complete his education.[6] Moratín returned to Spain in December 1796, landing in Algeciras, and on Christmas day called on Goya, who was staying in Cádiz as a guest of his friend and patron Sebastián Martínez, and visited him frequently in January.[7] Most likely they had met before 1792, but their friendship blossomed between 1797 and the turn of the century, as the numerous references to Goya in Moratín's diary attest.[8] Scholars have pointed to affinities in the work of the two men in the late 1790s, when they were particularly close, noting a similarity of motifs that run through Goya's Caprichos and Moratín's plays: mismatched marriages, the upbringing of children, superstition, and common vices, such as avarice and hypocrisy.[9]

During this period of close friendship, Moratín sat for Goya, noting in his diary on July 16, 1799: "chez Goya: portrait."[10] Here, the thirty-nine-year-old rising star of the theater is depicted half-length against a dark ground, looking directly out at his friend (and the spectator) with an unguarded expression (fig. 39). Goya captured his image in fluid strokes, using a subdued palette of rich, glowing neutral tones. The poet wears a *casaca* and a black cravat with a white shirt, and his unpowdered hair is parted in the middle.[11] Details of dress, however, are downplayed, drawing attention to the sensitive face and almost speaking expression. Moratín thanked Goya with a reciprocal work, his *Verses for Francisco*

Goya, Distinguished Painter, in which he expresses his wish that posterity will forever associate his name with that of the celebrated artist.[12] That same year, Goya was named First Painter to Charles IV, and Moratín soon went on to produce several new plays, reaching the height of his fame with the last of his five classic comedies, *A Daughter's Consent* (*El sí de las niñas*) of 1806, one of the major theatrical successes of the time, which was published in many languages.[13]

With the fall of the prime minister in 1808, Moratín, who was regarded as "Godoy's creature,"[14] fled from Madrid and then returned and accepted the post of first librarian of the Royal Library under Joseph Bonaparte in 1811. With the withdrawal of the French army from the capital in August 1812, Moratín was forced into exile. As a suspected *afrancesado* (French sympathizer), his property and assets were seized by the government of Ferdinand VII. His reputation, however, was eventually cleared and most of his property returned to him in 1814, although he was ordered to remain at least twenty leagues from Madrid.[15] After a period in Barcelona, where his plays were performed to great acclaim, Moratín left Spain in 1816, infuriated with the Inquisition's ongoing interference with his work, and eventually settled in Bordeaux, arriving in October 1821. A year later he moved in with his close friend Manuel Silvela, a former judge in the court of Joseph Bonaparte, and his family and lived contentedly with them in the former governor's palace in the center of town, near the Grand Théâtre, helping Silvela

run his school and indulging his passions for chocolate and the theater "without which man cannot live."[16]

It was soon after Goya settled in Bordeaux in September 1824 that he painted a second portrait of his friend. The approximate period of this work— fall of 1824—is known from a reference that Moratín made in a letter to Melón dated September 20, 1824: "He wants to do my portrait, and from that I infer how pretty I am when such skilled paintbrushes aspire to multiply my copies."[17] And on September 30 he noted, "Goya follows me around everywhere and never leaves me alone for a moment."[18]

In this portrait, smaller than the previous one of Moratín, the sitter is represented not quite half-length, seated at the corner of a wooden table or desk. His body is turned slightly to the right at an angle to the table, and his head is in three-quarter view, facing right. His eyes look off in the distance, and his lips form the ironic smile of someone, as Françoise Garcia notes, "in amicable complicity with the painter."[19] His short curly hair has remained dark, though age has blunted his once delicate features. He wears a black dressing gown flecked with brown, trimmed at the collar and cuffs with black velvet plush or fur. An anonymous portrait print of Moratín shows him in similar attire (fig. 40).[20]

Under his robe he wears a white shirt open at the neck with a prominent pointed collar that frames his face and the fleshy folds of his neck and upper chest. His right arm, bent at the elbow, rests on loosely scattered papers on his desk. In the corner of one of them,

Fig. 40   Artist unknown, *Portrait of Leandro Fernández de Moratín*, engraving, frontispiece of *Comedias de Don Leandro Fernández de Moratín*, Paris, 1838

Fig. 41 X-radiograph of cat. no. 10
(*Leandro Fernández de Moratín*)

green, white—is something which seduces through the power of suggestion, sensual and refined at same time. . . ."[21]

Recent x-rays carried out for the Museo de Bellas Artes de Bilbao reveal changes that occurred in the laying out of the composition (fig. 41).[22] In an earlier stage, the subject's face was turned further to the right, almost in profile. Both eyes were visible, but the edge of the proper left side of the face was lost. The face appears thinner and the eyes look off to the sitter's left. The x-ray also shows that the sitter appears to have held a pen in his hand. By eliminating the pen, and turning his gaze back toward (but not directly at) the viewer, Goya emphasized the contemplative mood of his friend and the warm connection between them. The face is built up in careful, dense brush strokes, though he painted the robe more freely.[23]

Moratín left Bordeaux reluctantly in October 1827 to follow the Silvelas to Paris, where they had founded a new school.[24] He wrote to a friend on December 11, 1827, that there he led the "most insipid life and had only been to the theater twice since his arrival."[25] Goya died in Bordeaux the following spring, on April 16, 1828. In a letter of May 16, 1828, to his old friend Manuel Garcia de la Prada, Moratín notes that "in September I will leave this place for good, making my way little by little to Bordeaux. . . ."[26] And in his last letter, dated June 4, 1828, he spoke of returning "to my Bordeaux, in which I want to live and die."[27] He died in Paris, however, on June 21, 1828, little more than two months after Goya.

oriented to the sitter's point of view, is written "Goya." The warm flesh tones of the hand, enlivened with strokes of red, is set off by the whiteness of the papers, as is the head by the angled collar of the white shirt, while the figure as a whole is placed within a luminous green ground. As Lasterra notes, "these subtle color harmonies so knowingly combined—red, green, black, black

Silvela "closed his eyes" and paid for the poet's sepulcher in Père Lachaise cemetery, which was just steps away from that of Molière.[28] His remains were later transferred to Spain, and in 1900 they were interred, along with those of Goya and the poet and politician Juan de Meléndez Valdés, in the Pantheon in Madrid.

SGG

1 Deacon 1995, pp. v–xi, provides an excellent summary of the reform movement in eighteenth- and early nineteenth-century Spanish theater.

2 On Moratín's life, see Andioc 1973; Fernández de Moratín 1871 and 1968; Paris 1838; Silvela(b) 1845; and Tréverret 1882.

3 Silvela(b) 1845, p. 10.

4 Ibid., p. 11.

5 Paris 1838, p. vi.

6 See Silvela(b) 1845, p. 26–31.

7 Fernández de Moratín 1968, p. 175.

8 Andioc 1998, pp. 24–25.

9 See Helman 1959, pp. 110–11, for her discussion of the possible influence of Moratín's edition of the *Auto de fe celebrado en la cuidad de Logroño, en los días 6 y 7 de noviembre de 1610* (which he published in 1811 or 1812) on Goya's images of witches in the Caprichos. For a response to Helman's argument, see Andioc 1982 and 1998, pp. 27–28. See also Levitine n.d., pp. 135–36. (My thanks to Silvina Leone for providing this article.) Janis Tomlinson also offered some valuable insight on this topic at a lecture given at the Institute of Fine Arts, New York University, on November 18, 2004.

10 Cited in Helman 1959, p. 103.

11 Viñaza 1887, p. 250, describes the costume as a *casaca lisa*, buttoned with three buttons, with a high double collar and no lapels (*solapas*), as was worn by people in the Directory in France in the last days of the century.

12 For an English translation of the poem, see Fauqué and Villanueva Etcheverría 1982, pp. 662–63.

13 On the critical reception of this play, see Deacon 1995, pp. lxii–lxvii. Two other plays were produced: *El barón* in 1803 and *La mojigata (The Female Hypocrite)* in 1804. After *El sí de las niñas*, his theatrical activity was limited to two translations or adaptations of plays by Molière: *La escuela de los maridos* and *El medico a palos*, and his *Orígenes del teatro español*, which he completed in Bordeaux in 1825.

14 Silvela(b) 1845, p. 45.

15 Tréverret 1882, p. 193, cites two letters by Moratín dating from October 18 and 30, 1814, in which he recounts the difficulties he had suffered since 1812.

16 Silvela(b) 1867–68, II, p. 416, cited in Tréverret 1882, p. 419.

17 Ibid., p. 594, no. 307. (See also Canellas López 1981, p. 498, no. CLII.)

18 Ibid., p. 596, no. 308.

19 Ribemont and Garcia 1998, p. 191.

20 The print appears as the frontispiece of *Comedias de Moratín*, 1838. Lasterra 1967, pp. 95–96, calls his coat a *casaca* (defined as a long fitted jacket). However, this description seems to fit his costume in the 1799 painting better than in this painting. On the *casaca*, see Herranz Rodríguez 1996, p. 209. For a comparative garment to Moratín's in the 1824 portrait, see José de Madrazo's portrait of Manuel Godoy of 1812 (private collection), illustrated in Portús 2004, p. 268.

21 Lasterra 1967, p. 96.

22 A complete conservation study of the painting was carried out in 2002 by Maite Rodríguez Torres. The unpublished report is in the files of the Museo de Bellas Artes de Bilbao and was sent to the authors by Sra. Ana Sánchez-Lassa de los Santos, Curator and Head of Conservation. To both we extend our warm thanks.

23 Gaya Nuño 1964, p. 284; see also Bilbao 1999, p. 142.

24 Fauqué and Villanueva Etcheverría 1982, p. 662, note that on September 13, 1827, he requested a passport, which was granted by the police because of his "excellent conduct."

25 Andioc 1973, p. 695, no. 383, translation Fauqué and Villanueva Etcheverría 1982, p. 662.

26 Ibid., p. 701, no. 388.

27 Ibid., p. 704, no. 389.

28 Silvela(a) 1845, p. xxxv.

11

Manuel Silvela

1824–27
Oil on canvas, 37⅜ × 26¾ (95 × 68)
Museo Nacional del Prado, Madrid

PROVENANCE: Collection of the sitter; his descendents; sold by his great grandson, Jorge Silvela, to the Ministerio de Instruccíon Pública, June 1931; acquired for the Museo Nacional del Prado, 1931.[1]

PRINCIPAL REFERENCES: Lafond 1907(a), pp. 129–30; Beruete 1916, no. 278; Mayer 1921, no. 421; Desparmet Fitz-Gerald 1928–50, no. 505; Llanos de Torriglia 1946, p. 69; Núñez de Arenas 1950, p. 233; Sánchez-Cantón 1951, pp. 100, 126; Gassier and Wilson 1971, no. 891; Gudiol 1971, I, no. 567; De Angelis 1974, no. 539; Camón Aznar 1980–82, III, p. 171; Pérez Sánchez, 1987, p. 317; Morales 1994, no. 39; Luna and Moreno de las Heras 1996, no. 168; Moreno de las Heras 1997, no. 122; Ribemont and Garcia 1998, no. 4.

Manuel Silvela y García de Aragón was born on October 31, 1781, in Valladolid. Having spent part of his childhood in Avila, he returned to Valladolid to study philosophy and law and received his law degree in 1808.[2] At that time there were no vacancies in the Colegio de Abogados (bar), and he sought help in obtaining a license to practice from the new administration of Joseph Bonaparte. According to his son and biographer, Francisco Agustín Silvela, the reputation of the distinguished young lawyer and professor of law at the University of Valladolid, who was fluent in French and sympathetic to liberal ideas, attracted the attention of members of Joseph's court, and he was offered the position of royal judge (Alcalde de Corte y Casa) in 1809 and sat on the criminal tribunal (junta criminal).[3] Silvela said he accepted the position in the French administration with ambivalence but was determined to make use of his post on the "monstrous tribunal" to rescue his countrymen from summary execution; this he performed in exemplary fashion.[4]

During the French occupation he met the playwright Leandro Fernández de Moratín (see cat. no. 10), who sought his help on several occasions on behalf of friends who had run afoul of the French authorities. Moratín was twenty-one years his senior, but the two men established a deep rapport, and their relationship developed, in Silvela's words, from "a truly fraternal tenderness, to all the idolatry of friendship."[5] Goya's acquaintance with Silvela—perhaps through Moratín—is thought to date from these years.[6]

In 1813, a year after the departure of the French army from Madrid, the thirty-two-year-old Silvela, with his wife, mother, three small children, and a stepchild, moved to Bordeaux with a large wave of afrancesados (sympathizers with the regime of Joseph Bonaparte). His departure was voluntary; in fact, he had been asked to stay by members of the new regime because of his benevolent behavior on the junta criminal.[7] Like many émigrés, Silvela began supporting his family in Bordeaux by giving Spanish lessons and by 1816 had enough of a following to found a school for the children of Spanish and Latin American émigrés.[8] With the establishment of the constitutional government in Spain in 1820, the afrancesados had the possibility of returning to their homeland. Silvela, however, chose to remain in France because of his responsibilities to his school.[9] Nonetheless, he expressed his passionate support for the new government in a series of published letters and in a play.[10]

II

In October 1821 Moratín joined Silvela in Bordeaux and a year later settled into his home in the elegant eighteenth-century Hôtel Barada on the Allée de Noyers (now rue David Johnston), where the school was established. He remained with the family for the rest of his life. The poet's letters tell us much about Silvela's school, which played an important role in preserving and promoting Spanish language and culture in the wealthy expatriate community.[11] The Silvelas, their students, and Moratín moved in 1823 into the palatial Hôtel du Gouvernement in the Tourny district in the center of town. The school flourished, and Silvela amassed a sizable fortune and was one of the most prominent figures in the Spanish exile community. By 1826, however, Ferdinand VII began to deny passports to prospective students, and in August 1827 Silvela and his family, soon followed by Moratín, moved to Paris, where there was a larger pool of potential applicants, and opened a new school on the rue de Montreuil.[12] According to his son, Manuel Silvela's constant hard work and the climate in Paris, combined with his frail health, contributed to his early death on May 9, 1832, at age fifty-one.[13]

Manuel Silvela is remembered today largely through Goya's portrait. The date of the work is not documented. There are two possible periods, separated by about a dozen years, in which it could have been painted: during the French occupation from 1809 to 1813, when both sitter and artist lived in Madrid, and during their overlapping years in Bordeaux from September 1824

Fig. 42 *Andrés del Peral*, 1797–98, oil on poplar, 37⅜ × 25⅞ (95 × 65.7), © National Gallery, London

to August 1827. Goya was thirty-six years Silvela's senior, and there is no direct evidence of a close relationship between them. During the Bordeaux years, however, they would have had greater opportunity to see each other through their common friendship with Moratín. Writing from Madrid on August 13, 1827, to Leocadia in Bordeaux, Goya mentions the "matter of Silvela and Moratín," evidently alluding to their move to Paris, but there is no other reference to him in the artist's published correspondence.[14]

Silvela is depicted seated, facing right, his legs cropped at the knees. Light falls on the left side of the face and figure, set against an opaque black ground. His

head is in three-quarter view, facing right, and his gaze is fixed on something beyond the border of the picture. A handsome man of indeterminate age, he has a long nose, prominent eyebrows, a pale complexion, and grayish-brown hair, parted in the middle. As in his portraits of Moratín (see cat. no. 10 and fig. 39), Goya omitted the smallpox scars on Silvela's face.[15]

The subject sits on a simple wooden ladder-back chair, with his body turned diagonally to it; his right elbow is akimbo, and his hand, directly below his head, is turned under and rests on his thigh. This expressive backward turn of the hand appears in some of Goya's finest earlier works, such as his portrait of Ferdinand Guillemardet (1798), while the composition as a whole is reminiscent of his images of Sebastián Martínez (1792) (see fig. 35) and Andrés del Peral (1797–98) (fig. 42).[16] Silvela is elegantly attired in a close-fitting taupe redingote with a high collar, trimmed in leather, with wide lapels and narrow sleeves. It falls open over his legs, showing his yellow britches or trousers. Under his jacket he wears a yellow silk vest and a pleated white shirt; a blue and white patterned foulard is wound around his neck. Details of the coat are minimized (although there appear to be faint suggestions of a place for a button at his waist and a pocket near his elbow), and he wears no decorations or insignia. Light focuses attention on his face and meditative expression. The work is thinly painted, with the red ground showing through in places and some impasto in the scarf. There is an unevenness of finish from the top to the bottom of the canvas. The head

Fig. 43   J. A. López, *Portrait of D. Manuel Silvela*, engraving, frontispiece of Francisco Agustín Silvela, *Obras Póstumas de D. Manuel Silvela*, Madrid: Establecimiento Tipográfico de don Francisco de Paula Mellado, 1845

and upper body are clearly delineated, though the right hand and cuff are less finished; the thighs are oddly elongated, and the left arm, in shadow, is spatially unresolved. The painting appears to have been left unfinished, which contributes to the difficulty of placing it securely within either the period of the French occupation or the Bordeaux years.

The portrait was first exhibited in the major Goya exhibition in Madrid of 1900. It was then in the hands of the sitter's grandson, Francisco Silvela (1845–1905), a well-known politician and writer, who lent the work along with Goya's Bordeaux portrait of Moratín, which he also owned. (The names of the sitters were switched by error in the exhibition catalogue, leading to confusion in some of the reviews as to which portrait was actually being referred to.)[17] In a review of the exhibition in *La época*, May 11, 1900, the author notes that Don Francisco Silvela, presidente del Consejo de Ministros, contributed two works to the exhibition that are "a reminder of the close fraternal friendship that united the three illustrious Spaniards in exile," adding that perhaps both were painted when "the distinguished writer and immortal artist stayed in the house of Manuel Silvela . . . united in art and friendship."[18] Might this information have been passed on by the lender, whose father was with the three men in Bordeaux and would have known about the portrait's origin? In his 1907 article on Goya's years in Bordeaux, Paul Lafond asserted (without stating a source) that the Silvela portrait "was painted after the portrait of Jacques Galos [1826] and in the same year as the *Milkmaid of Bordeaux* [c. 1827]."[19] Both the Moratín and Silvela portraits were still in the Silvela family in 1924, when Aureliano de Beruete y Moret illustrated them side by side in his *Conferencias de arte*, in which he placed them in the Bordeaux years.[20]

In 1928, however, when the work was shown in an exhibition of Goya's paintings at the Prado, Allende Salazar and Lafuente Ferrari noted that neither the sitter's clothing nor the painter's technique is compatible with the Bordeaux period.[21] Subsequently, most scholars continued to date the work to the French occupation, some with reservations about the sitter's apparent age.[22] Then, in 1996 Margarita Moreno de las Heras argued for placing the work in Goya's Bordeaux period. The age of the sitter, she notes, is closer to forty than thirty, and the context of Goya's renewed friendship in exile with Moratín, who lived with Silvela, makes the Bordeaux years the more reasonable moment for the painting of the portrait. Furthermore, she argues, the picture's intimate character, which does not allude to the position Silvela would have held in 1810, and its subdued palette are consistent with the portraits of the last years.[23]

To Moreno de las Heras's arguments may be added that the reflective, slightly melancholic spirit of the sitter, which seems more characteristic of a man in middle age who had endured hardships than of one embarking on a career in his early thirties, also suggests a later date. (In comparing Goya's portrait with a print by J. A. López depicting Silvela in profile [fig. 43], in which he is clearly a mature man, we see that the features are softer in the painting, but not dramatically different. Silvela died before growing old, and his appearance may not have changed greatly over time.)

In my view the painting does indeed fit better with the Bordeaux years than the period of the French occupation. Still, the painting remains something of an anomaly. It is somewhat larger and more complex in composition than the other Goya Bordeaux portraits. Though the painting is not fully resolved, parts are painted with remarkable skill and sensitivity, such as the head and facial expression, which convey Silvela's strong and sympathetic character. Yet the portrait does not appear to have been greatly esteemed by Silvela or his family. Was it perhaps a commission that fell short of the sitter's expectations, or considered not to be a good likeness by his family? According to the reviewer of the Goya retrospective of 1900, Silvela's grandson, the lender, "especially esteemed the portrait of the *poet* which he kept in his office."[24] Silvela's son, who would have known the painter in Bordeaux, makes no mention of the portrait in his biography of his father, nor does he mention Goya, though he listed the notable men of the time who "honored [his father] with their friendship."[25] Nor does Manuel Silvela mention the portrait in his biography of Moratín, in which he gives a fair amount of detail about their shared life in Bordeaux. In fact, he does not mention Goya at all and makes the perplexing remark that "if he [Moratín] had not become a poet, he would have certainly become the major painter of the century."[26] What is clear is that whatever the nature of Silvela's relationship with the aged artist who gave him immortality, it paled in comparison to his adoration for the poet.

SGG

1   Provenance information from Luna and Moreno de las Heras 1996, p. 434, no. 168.
2   See Silvela(a) 1845 for a biography of Manuel Silvela. This account, written by his son Francisco Agustín Silvela (1790?–1850?), accompanied an edition of Manuel's collected writings.
3   Ibid., pp. xiii–xiv.

4   Silvela(b) 1845, p. 40. See also his son's account, Silvela(a) 1845, p. xv, on the wrenching toll of the position on his father.
5   Silvela(b) 1845, p. 40.
6   Glendinning 1989, p. lxxii, notes that Silvela's daily exposure to summary execution orders issued under the French during the occupation may have alerted Goya to the arbitrariness of justice in wartime, so powerfully portrayed in the Disasters of War.
7   Silvela(a) 1845, p. xvii, cites an account in the *Gaceta de Madrid* of August 25, 1812, which praises the humanity of his father on the tribunal.
8   See López Tabar 2001 on the Spanish community in Bordeaux. In 1819 Silvela published his *Library of Spanish Literature (Biblioteca selecta de literatura española)*, a four-volume anthology of Spanish literary texts from the fifteenth century to his contemporaries for use in his school.
9   Silvela(a) 1845, p. xxiii.
10 The five letters, known as *Correspondencia de un refugiado con un amigo suyo de Madrid*, published in Vitoria as in Bordeaux in May 1820, are reproduced in Silvela(b) 1845, pp. 269–326. The play, *El reconciliator* (1820), was never performed. See Silvela(b) 1845, pp. 65–145.
11 Andioc 1973, p. 492, note 2, informs us that the program of study at the school took seven years and that in order to be admitted, students had to be vaccinated against smallpox. Both Moratín and Silvela had suffered from it in childhood; the vaccine was developed by Edward Jenner in 1796. Andioc draws his information on the school from a prospectus Silvela published in 1828. According to Sánchez Cantón 1951, p. 100, note 23, some pamphlets on the school are preserved in the Prado; see also Luna and Moreno de las Heras 1996, p. 436, note 5.
12 Núñez de Arenas 1950, pp. 233–34, note 3; see also Luna and Moreno de las Heras 1996, p. 434, note 6.
13 Silvela(a) 1845, p. xxxxi.
14 Young 1972. In a postscript to a letter to Moratín in Paris after Goya's death, Leocadia Weiss expresses her thanks to the Señores

Silvela for their help (Canellas López 1981, p. 515, no. CLXXXIII). The authenticity of a portrait once considered to represent Silvela's daughter Victoria (GW no. 1665), now lost, has been questioned with regard to its attribution to Goya and the identity of the sitter. See Núñez de Arenas 1950, p. 254.
15 Silvela(a) 1845, p. viii, comments on the smallpox marks, noting that his physiognomy remained handsome.
16 For the portrait of Guillemardet, see GW no. 677.
17 See Madrid 1900(a), p. 18, nos. 44 and 45, and Vega 2002, II, pp. 96–97.
18 Madrid 1900(b). The article, which is unsigned, is cited in Vega 2002, II, p. 98, though the reference is dated incorrectly as May 10. My thanks to Iraida Rodríguez-Negrón for finding it.
19 Lafond 1907(a), pp. 129–30. Much of the information for Lafond's article came from Matheron via Goya's very close friend the young marine painter Antonio de Brugada.
20 Beruete y Moret 1924, p. 332; illustrations facing page.
21 Madrid 1928, pp. 62–63, no. 60, which cites the earlier opinion of Tormo y Monzó 1902, pp. 217, 223, who places the work between 1800 and 1809. For further clarification, see Moreno de las Heras 1997, p. 340, note 7.
22 See, for example, Sánchez Cantón 1951, p. 100; GW no. 891; de Salas 1979, p. 105; and Pérez Sánchez and Sayre 1989, no. 72.
23 Luna and Moreno de las Heras 1996, pp. 434–35, no. 168; see also Moreno de las Heras 1997, p. 340, no. 122; Ribemont and Garcia 1998, p. 191, no. 4, which states that undoubtedly the painting was executed at the same time as that of Moratín. For a response to Moreno de la Heras's redating, see Glendinning 1996, p. 74; he believes the earlier dating is correct on the basis of the artist's style and the costume.
24 Madrid 1900(b).
25 Silvela(a) 1845, pp. xxvi–vii
26 Silvela(b) 1845, pp. 12–13.

12

Milkmaid of Bordeaux

c. 1827
Oil on canvas, 29$\frac{1}{8}$ × 26$\frac{3}{4}$ (74 × 68)
Museo Nacional del Prado, Madrid

Signed in lower left: *Goya*

PROVENANCE: Leocadia Zorrilla y Weiss; purchased by Juan de Muguiro, c. 1830; his descendants; bequeathed to the Museo Nacional del Prado, 1945.

PRINCIPAL REFERENCES: Beruete y Moret 1924, pp. 369–70; Madrid 1928, no. 89; Desparmet Fitz-Gerald 1928–50, no. 277; Gudiol 1971, no. 767; Gassier and Wilson 1971, no. 1667; De Salas 1978, p. 46; Pérez Sánchez and Sayre 1989, no. 124; Morales y Marín 1994, no. 529; Luna and Moreno de las Heras 1996, no. 124; Moreno de las Heras 1997, no. 124; Ribemont and Garcia 1998, no. 6; Vega 2002, no. 79; Glendinning 2002; Wilson-Bareau 2002.

The *Milkmaid of Bordeaux* has long been considered one of Goya's most evocative works. Admired for the pensive, wistful expression and the loose, sketchy technique, the *Milkmaid* has been interpreted as both an autumnal masterpiece and a harbinger of French Impressionism. Catalogue entries from commemorative exhibitions at the Prado epitomize the received opinion about the painting. The first dates from the 100th anniversary of the artist's death (1928), the second from the 250th anniversary of his birth (1996).

> It is one of the most surprising works of the artist's old age. In his final period, Goya, always renewing himself, uses a technique of small brush strokes that is a prelude to what would later be French Impressionism. Perhaps in no other work does this divisionist technique stand out more strongly, both in the background as in the chest of the young girl, whose corporeality is admirably achieved by the new technique of the old master.[1]

> But where his genius shines with special splendor is in a painting that passes for a masterpiece, which is in the Prado and was completed months before his death. In it, as in the fourth movement of Beethoven's Choral Symphony, Goya seems to recover from the bitterness and crises that emerge from the most intimate part of his spirit and crowns an entire life dedicated to art, a life without whose creations the history of universal painting would have been different: this is the *Milkmaid of Bordeaux*, painted in 1827, the year before his death.[2]

The painting is signed in the lower left by incising into the wet paint with a sharp instrument, in a way that is similar to the signatures on *Don Tiburcio Pérez y Cuervo* and *María Martínez de Puga* (see cat. nos. 5 and 7). It is also documented in a letter written on December 9, 1829, from Leocadia Weiss to Juan de Muguiro, a friend whom Goya had portrayed in May 1827 (see fig. 34). (The letter was not posted until January 13, 1830.) By this time, Leocadia was experiencing serious financial difficulty, which compelled her to offer to sell the *Milkmaid* to Muguiro. The relevant part of her letter reads as follows:

> My dear Sir, Although I am a woman, I have character and [keep my] word. You urged me frequently to give you the *Milkmaid* and that I was to tell you how much I wanted for it. I responded that I wasn't thinking of selling and that if one day I were to sell it, it would be for

12

reasons of need and that you would have preference.

Today, much to the sadness of Rosario, we are in that situation. The deceased [Goya] used to tell me not to give it for less than an ounce [of gold]. If you still have the same desire, tell me if you want me to send it to your friend Don Ignacio García in Bayonne and, if not, let it be as if nothing was said.[3]

Evidently Muguiro accepted the offer because the painting remained in the possession of his descendants until it was bequeathed to the Prado in 1945, together with his portrait.

Given the apparent certainty of authorship established by the document and provenance, the authenticity has been taken for granted since the painting appeared in 1900, and it is often considered to be Goya's final work, although that date of execution has to have been earlier than July 1827, when Muguiro left for Madrid. Recently, however, the noted Goya specialist Juliet Wilson-Bareau has cautiously suggested that the attribution may be problematic. Her suspicions were first reported in the Spanish press in 2001 in connection with a public lecture at the Prado. To judge from these reports, Wilson-Bareau had suggested that the true author was Rosario Weiss. A year later she revised and published her views in detail, raising questions but only hinting at answers or conclusions. In the main, her arguments seem intended to undermine old verities rather than to establish new ones.[4]

After summarizing the conventional appreciations of the picture—noting in passing that she does not share them—Wilson-Bareau draws attention to the unusual motifs that are visible just beneath the paint film. Even with the naked eye, a number of disconnected shapes and forms can be seen. The most prominent is located immediately to the left of the milkmaid and looks like the large head of a man in profile, wearing a turban. Just above and to the right of the figure is the faint impression of a wall pierced by an arch or portal. Beneath this architectural motif and visible only in x-radiographs is the small figure of a woman who appears to lean her arms on a balcony.[5]

According to Wilson-Bareau, these random out-of-scale underdrawings, over which the composition has been painted, are unprecedented in Goya's art and uncharacteristic of his practice. Goya, she states, only reused canvases during the Peninsular War, when "new material was scarce."[6] Equally problematic is the pose. Depictions of milkmaids were published in sets of prints at the time, and in at least one (1818–19) by the Bordeaux engraver Gustave de Galard, we can see the milkmaid seated on a donkey that carries baskets on his flanks, filled with milk jugs.[7] It is usually supposed that the *Milkmaid* depicts a similar scene, although the donkey is not visible and a milk jug is only notionally represented at the left. The picture seems to be cut down at the bottom, but it is reported to be intact. As Wilson-Bareau observes, "the resulting lack of clarity in the pose and action of the figure is absolutely atypical of Goya."[8]

Wilson-Bareau further notes that even the most enthusiastic admirers have expressed reservations about one or another of its features. In 1917, for example, Aureliano de Beruete suggested that Goya, having run out of inspiration, was prompted to paint the picture by catching sight of a milkmaid who passed his way every day. Wilson-Bareau takes exception to this observation by pointing out that, as seen in the lithographs and miniatures, Goya was not in need of such mundane events to fire his imagination. Despite his infirmities, Goya continued to be an original artist, full of energy and ideas. His friend Moratín wrote in June 1825 that Goya, having recovered from a serious illness, was painting frenetically.[9]

The only way to judge the quality of the picture, she avers, is to compare it to works securely attributed to Goya in his Bordeaux years, which unfortunately are few in number. It may be that other pictures from this period were purposely destroyed or lost. Although Brugada observes that Goya painted incessantly, the surviving output is small even if disputed pieces are counted. Hence, the benchmarks for evaluating works attributed to Goya's final years are the miniatures and lithographs. The former are characterized by the "energy and decision of the figures that assure that, however free and sketchy they may appear, in looking at them there is not the slightest doubt about the structure and movement of the bodies and clothes they wear."[10] These qualities, she implies, are absent from the *Milkmaid*.

In the next stage of her argument, Wilson-Bareau wonders if it may be possible to find closer formal ties between the *Milkmaid* and works executed in Madrid just prior to the departure to France, such as the lithographs known as *El Sueño (The Dream)* (see fig. 91) and *La Lectura (Woman Reading)* (see fig. 47), and the drawings of the Black Border Album (Album E). Also to be noted is that Goya's paintings over the last ten years of his life move away from strong bright colors (*Duchess of Abrantes*, 1818, Museo Nacional del Prado, Madrid) toward a restricted palette, dominated by blacks and blues and a few touches of muted colors (*María Martínez de Puga*, 1824, cat. no. 7). Implied is the notion that the higher-keyed palette of the *Milkmaid* is not consistent with the pictures painted in France.[11]

The next question concerns the authorship of the underdrawings, assuming that they are not by Goya. These are attributed to Rosario on the basis of two groups of her juvenile drawings.[12] These drawings, which are Goyesque, are accepted by scholars as having been executed under Goya's tutelage in 1820–23. By inference, Rosario's hand is evident in these inchoate sketches seen beneath the figure of the milkmaid and perhaps even on the surface.

To sum up, it is possible, if not probable, that the *Milkmaid* was started and possibly finished before Goya went to France. The fact that Javier did not remove it from Goya's apartment may imply that he did not believe that it had been done by his father. Leocadia's decision to sell it was taken, "much to Rosario's sadness" at the removal of her (their?) picture. And the monetary value placed on it by Goya is only a reflection of his unbounded admiration for Rosario's artistic talent. Having thus

cast doubt on some of the reasons for supporting the attribution to Goya, Wilson-Bareau hints that the work may be a collaboration between Goya and Rosario who, upon achieving maturity as an artist, worked for a time as a copyist, although she never became more than mediocre. Wilson-Bareau concludes by calling for further study of the question.

This reasoned argument merits a reasoned response.[13] Wilson-Bareau's analysis will be broken down into two categories: textual/documentary and artistic. A further criterion will be employed, as seeming to be helpful in analyzing the problem. This is Occam's Razor, defined in the *Shorter Oxford English Dictionary* as "the principle that in explaining a thing no more assumptions should be made than are necessary." The letter from Leocadia to Muguiro is the most important piece of documentary evidence and is the cutting edge of the razor. While it may be argued that the *Milkmaid* was not taken by Javier when he removed the contents of Goya's apartment, and while it is true that Goya's name is not mentioned in the letter, the data provided by Leocadia are reasonably clear. Muguiro, as a distant relation and friend of Goya's (his brother had married the sister of Javier's wife, Gumersinda, and was the sitter in the portrait of 1827), had admired the painting in Goya's home, was correctly informed about the master's authorship, and had left a standing offer to purchase the work if it became available. Goya is not named as the author of the *Milkmaid* because his authorship was a given; it would have made sense to

identify the author only if it had been another person. The reference to Rosario's *sentimiento* at the proposed sale to Muguiro, implying that the picture had some special meaning for her and that she was sad to see it go, is a misreading of the document. Leocadia is referring to Rosario's sadness at their parlous financial situation. As to why Javier did not take the picture to Madrid, there are many possible explanations—it was not on the premises; Leocadia persuaded him that she owned it; it might have been, as some of have suggested, a portrait of Rosario and thus of no interest to Goya's son. Although Leocadia's text can be deconstructed to advance the argument against the attribution to Goya, it is reasonable to take it at face value.

The other piece of textual evidence concerns the testimony of Moratín and Brugada (via Matheron) about Goya's slapdash working methods in his final years. Brugada is the first witness. Goya painted until the end, he says, but with increasing carelessness. Sometimes he did not even use brushes, seizing whatever came to hand—a palette knife, a piece of cloth, anything at all. "Each day brought its work. He often covered in the morning what he had painted the night before."[14] In considering the reliability of Brugada's observation, Wilson-Bareau notes that Matheron was prone to make errors of detail. However, Moratín provides corroboration for Goya's almost frenetic artistic activity. In June 1825 he wrote to a correspondent that the artist, having survived a close call with death, was painting "like nobody's business, without ever wishing to correct anything he paints."[15]

This brings us to the artistic argument and the heart of the debate— the style, the technique, the place in Goya's evolution.[16] For Wilson-Bareau's argument to be valid, it must be accepted that Goya maintained a consistent level of draftsmanship and artistry until he could no longer work, despite the testimony of Brugada and Moratín. As she writes about the miniatures, they are characterized by the "energy and decision of the figures that assure that, however free and sketchy they may appear, in looking at them there is the not the slightest doubt about the structure and movement of the bodies and the clothes they wear."[17] This criterion implies that he was an unfailingly correct painter. As will be seen, this is not the case. Nor does this notion seem to fit the execution of the Bulls of Bordeaux. The crowds in the background of the prints can be described as schematic notations and masses of undifferentiated forms. This is especially true of the unpublished plate in the Musée des Beaux-Arts de Bordeaux (see fig. 54). In addition, the problematic etchings with aquatint are further evidence of an unsteady hand (see cat no. 45). It should be remembered that the Milkmaid could have been produced at a date even later than the miniatures (winter 1824–25) or the Bulls of Bordeaux (autumn 1825). During 1826 and some of 1827, Goya continued to work even as his condition deteriorated. The portrait of Juan de Muguiro, dated May 1827, is considered by Wilson-Bareau to be of superior quality to the Milkmaid.

That may be so, but this does not mean that the Milkmaid is a failure or uncharacteristic of Goya. The ambiguous pose, which seems to be unresolved in the lower part of the figure, can be found in earlier portraits such as Francisco Bayeu of 1795 (Museo Nacional del Prado) and Isidoro Máiquez of 1807 (Museo Nacional del Prado). In other ways, however, the pose of the milkmaid is subtle; the young girl is seen from below and set against a sky of changing blue. Goya worked at positioning the figure in the composition, improvising as he went along and making adjustments, visible on the surface, to the contour of the milkmaid. By modulating the color, from dark blue in the upper right to light blue at the left (carefully achieved by allowing the ground to be seen), Goya animates the composition and sets the figure apart from the background. As for the apparently anomalous use of lighter, more varied tones, these can be explained by the fact that the scene is set out-of-doors instead of in an interior space appropriate to portraits. (See Woman with Clothes Blowing in the Wind, cat. no. 20, for a comparable exception to the dark-background criterion.)

As critics have often remarked, the execution of the shawl, the kerchief, and the dress involves a complex blending of colors and brush strokes that is typical of Goya's technique in his mature years. The highlights on the shawl and kerchief are deftly applied. Of course the technique is tremulous: Goya's eyesight was failing, his hand was unsteady, he was not painting for a patron, he had good days and bad.

Yet a residual mastery is apparent; the knowledge of technique remains as strong as ever, but the touch falters.

Finally, the facial expression is evocative of a certain pensive melancholy. In fact, this register of emotion is seen in earlier works, especially in the Albums—C. 25 (Piénsalo bien); C. 107 (El tiempo hablará); E. 40 (Déjalo a la providencia); and F. 32. As in many other cases, Goya has reached back into his repertory of inventions, which he recycles in new ways.

If this review of the textual and biographical evidence and the analysis of the picture's formal characteristics is credible, then the attribution of the Milkmaid to Goya is secure. As for the underdrawings, here Wilson-Bareau's case for an attribution to the young Rosario does carry weight. Is it not plausible, even possible, that Goya painted the Milkmaid of Bordeaux on a canvas that Rosario was using to practice? The opportunity offered by this exhibition to study the Milkmaid in the context of a sizable and representative number of works from the Bordeaux period may bring us closer to an answer.

JB

1 Madrid 1928, p. 83.
2 Juan J. Luna in Luna and Moreno de las Heras 1996, p. 34.
3 "Muy Señor mío: Aunque soy muger tengo caracter y palabra. Me instó Vstd mucho para que le diera 'la Lechera' y que le dijera lo que quería por ella; le respondía a Vstd que no pensava benderla, y que si algun día la bendía sería por necesidad, y seria Vsted preferido. En el día, con mucho sentimiento de Rosario, estamos en ese caso; el difunto me decía que no la tenía que dar menos de una

onza; si Vsted está con los mismos deseos, me dirá si quiere se la dirija a su amigo Don Ignacio García a Bayona, y si no, como si no hubiera dicho nada." Canellas López 1981, p. 515, no. CLXXXIV.

4 Wilson-Bareau 2002, pp. 349–67.

5 The x-radiographs are discussed in some detail (but not published). Upon examination, they seem to add little to what can be seen with the naked eye.

6 This is not correct. See Garrido 2003 for a particularly striking example of a portrait painted over two earlier compositions. On page 53, Garrido makes the following observation: "La reutilización de los lienzos es frecuente en las obras de Goya, como se puede ver en numerosos retratos y escenas."

7 Reproduced in Ribemont and Garcia, p. 73, fig. 13.

8 Wilson-Bareau 2002, p. 355.

9 Canellas López 1981, p. 503, no. CLXIV.

10 Wilson-Bareau 2002, p. 358.

11 Wilson-Bareau also mentions in passing that the canvas and stretcher "appear to be of Spanish origin," but no technical data are provided to confirm this observation.

12 Gómez-Moreno 1941 and López-Rey 1956(b).

13 Some of the arguments presented here coincide with the ones adduced by Glendinning 2002, especially pp. 334–45. Glendinning's observations are based on articles in the Spanish daily press that antedate Wilson-Bareau's study of 2002 cited here. A close analysis and vigorous rejection of her speculations are found in Álvarez Lopera 2001, pp. 50–51. It should be noted that this short essay also appeared before the publication of Wilson-Bareau's article of 2002. Her initial public statements appear to have been more conclusive about Rosario's authorship than the discussion in her publication of 2002.

14 Matheron 1996, p. 256.

15 Canellas López 1981, p. 503, no. CLXIV.

16 We are grateful to Carmen Garrido, chief of the Gabinete de Documentación Técnica, Museo Nacional del Prado, for sharing the results of her examinations of paintings by Goya in the collection.

17 Wilson-Bareau 2002, p. 358.

Miniatures on Ivory

URING THE WINTER MONTHS OF 1824–25, Goya, then approaching seventy-nine years of age, created a number of innovative miniatures. These tiny paintings, executed on slivers of ivory, measuring either about 5.5 centimeters or 9.5 centimeters square, are grand in conception and imagination. On December 20, 1825, Goya mentioned them to his contact in Paris, Joaquín María de Ferrer; this is the same letter in which he responded to Ferrer's lack of interest in the Bulls of Bordeaux. It appears that Ferrer, in a communication now lost, had made reference to the miniatures, perhaps thinking that they might be salable in Paris. With undisguised pride, Goya acknowledged their existence and briefly described them:

> It is true that last winter I painted on ivory, and I have a collection of nearly forty exercises, but they are original miniatures which I never seen the like of before, because the whole is made up of points and things which look more like Velázquez' brushwork than that of Mengs.[1]

Goya's reference to the mini-pictures as "original miniatures" may mean that he considered them to be novel or may imply that he wanted to assure Ferrer that they were paintings not prints and therefore might not be of interest. He supplies some information about the technique by referring to two painters who had long been the protagonists of his artistic thought—the revered Velázquez, master of freely brushed, "naturalistic" painting, and Anton Raphael Mengs, court painter of Charles III, whose linear style and polished technique were anathema to Goya.

Goya's interest in this format probably was piqued by his plans for Rosario to study miniature painting. However, with his eyesight failing and his hand unsteady, he had to change the rules of the game. Conventional miniature painting was precise and painstaking. Miniatures were executed by a stipple technique in which tiny touches of color were applied with a fine-tipped brush until they coalesced into the desired image. Most often, they were used for portraits. Although Goya provided only a laconic and somewhat contradictory description of his miniatures and said nothing about how he actually painted them, there was a well-qualified witness who watched the master as he worked. This was Antonio de Brugada, the young painter from Madrid who was Goya's "right-hand man" in Bordeaux. In this passage, he describes Goya's extraordinarily inventive procedure.

> His miniatures bore no resemblance to fine Italian miniatures nor even those of [Jean Baptiste] Isabey. . . . Goya had never been able to imitate anyone, and he was too old to begin. He blackened the ivory plaque and let fall on it a drop of water which removed part of the black ground as it spread out, tracing random light areas. Goya took advantage of these traces and always turned them into something original and unexpected. These little works were still in the vein of the *Caprichos*; today they

facing page Maja and Celestina (detail of cat. no. 16; reproduced larger than actual size)

Fig. 44 *Boy Staring at an Apparition*, 1824–25, carbon black and watercolor on ivory, $2^5/_{16} \times 2^3/_8$ (5.9 × 6.0), Museum of Fine Arts, Boston, Gift of Eleanor Sayre, 1992

would be very much sought after, if the dear man had not wiped off many of them in order to economize on the ivory. Those that remained at his death were, I believe, taken to Madrid by his son.[2]

Brugada describes the most innovative characteristic of the process—the improvised creation of visual images—which is illustrated in a miniature that appears to have been left unfinished (fig. 44). In order to transform the stains of water into recognizable forms, Goya devised an ingenious method.[3] Accents were added by scratching the surface with a sharp pointed instrument, exactly as in the Bulls of Bordeaux; touches of watercolor were deftly applied; outlines were reinforced in black; and small patches of the surface were wiped to produce a range of shadows and highlights. With their broad execution and caricature-like figures, these ivory plaquettes are startling works of art.

Brugada's comparison of the ivories to the Caprichos seems apposite at first; the visual language is certainly similar. But on reflection the miniatures are different in that they have no overt satirical purpose. However, if *capricho* is defined, as it was in Goya's time, as a product of the imagination unfettered by the rules of art, then it begins to make sense, with one qualification. Many of the pictures conjured up by the aged Goya have an air of familiarity to those acquainted with his previous production. Fantasy is at play, but memory is also at work. Images that appeared in earlier creations make a comeback, summoned by the unpredictable faculty of long-term memory that, as we grow older, displaces the remembrance of things recently past.

Sometimes the self-borrowing is tantamount to a virtual copy, as in the *Woman with Clothes Blowing in the Wind* (see cat. no. 20), the first incarnation of which is plate 33 of Los Caprichos. Two of the small ivories represent literary texts, for instance, the apocryphal story of *Susanna and the Two Elders*; for another, see cat. no. 21. Goya had exploited the erotic possibilities of this narrative in two of his earlier album drawings, Album A. d and Album F. 32. In the miniature he simply reworks the traditional poses and positions of the actors in the drama.

Several are genre scenes, depicting the mundane side of life. *Maja and Celestina* (cat. no. 16) makes a final appearance as one of the leitmotifs of Goya's art; another in this vein is *Seated Majo and Maja* (see fig. 8). The act of delousing (cat. no. 17), a mundane activity if ever there was one, is encountered in Album F. 22 (see fig. 48) and is the subject of two other drawings (Album B. 85 and 87). Even miniatures with no identifiable theme can be linked to poses and compositions that earlier appeared in paintings, prints, and drawings, as seen in the *Reclining Nude* (cat. no. 13) which, as discussed in the entry, can claim several ancestors.

Another category includes miniatures that depict emotions or states of mind, a continual preoccupation of Goya's art after 1808. *Heads of a Child and an Old Woman* (cat. no. 18) demonstrates Mirth; *Monk and Old Woman* (cat. no. 14), Fear mixed with Horror; *Two Children Looking at a Book* (cat. no. 15), Absorption or Concentration.

It is not surprising that Goya's improvised miniatures reflect what he had seen, thought, and experienced; these are the ingredients of artistic creation. His achievement was to find a pictorial equivalent for free associations and fleeting reminiscences. Equally daring was the chance he took to create these compositions without a previous plan. On a stage no larger than an ivory microchip and using shards of memory for the narrative, Goya produced an exhilarating drama of artistic invention.

JB

NOTES

1 Letter of December 20, 1825; Canellas López 1981, pp. 389–90; translation Wilson-Bareau and Mena Marqués 1994, p. 324.

2 Matheron 1996, p. 262; translation Wilson-Bareau and Mena Marqués 1994, p. 324.

3 The Bordeaux miniatures were little studied until the article of Sayre 1966, which remains the standard work. Thirteen are briefly catalogued and reproduced in Wilson-Bareau and Mena Marqués 1994, pp. 324–39 and 372–74. Approximately twenty have been located or are known through photographs. The present exhibition comprises the largest group ever shown.

13

Reclining Nude

1824–25
Carbon black and watercolor on ivory, $3^{7}/_{16} \times 3^{3}/_{8}$ (8.8 × 8.6)
Museum of Fine Arts, Boston, Ernest Wadsworth Longfellow Fund, 63.1081

PROVENANCE: Sir William Stirling-Maxwell, Keir?; Archibald Stirling, Keir; Mrs. Stirling, Keir; her sale, Sotheby's, London, July 3, 1963, lot 64; purchased by the Museum of Fine Arts, Boston, 1963.

PRINCIPAL REFERENCES: Soria 1949, no. 8; Sayre 1966, p. 120, no. 18.; Sayre 1979; Camón Aznar 1980–82, IV, pp. 218–19; Wilson-Bareau and Mena Marqués 1994, no. 110.

The subject of this voluptuous composition has not been identified. Although the figure has been compared with the famous *Maja desnuda*, there is no thematic resemblance except for the motif of the naked woman. However, the sensuality shared by the two pictures is evident. The pose of the woman in the ivory most closely approaches Album B. 64 (fig. 45)—*Aguarda que venga (She Is Waiting for Him to Arrive* or *Await, He Is Arriving)*, a scene with unmistakable sexual connotations. Another point of comparison is the ambiguous, enigmatic lithograph of 1819–22 known as *El Sueño (The Dream)* (see fig. 91). That said, no comparisons are needed to elucidate the theme of this miniature.

The ivory is a brilliant example of Goya's innovative technique. After blackening the sliver of ivory and allowing the water stain to suggest the form, he worked with highly transparent green watercolor to model the cape or mantle and outlined the forms with black lines of differing thickness. In a brilliant maneuver of economy, exposed areas of ivory are transmuted into flesh tones. The subtle half-shadows of the rock formation are probably the result of diluting carbon black with water and wiping it over the white ground. With a touch of the traditional miniaturist, Goya indicates the delicate facial features.

Fig. 45 *Aguarda que venga (She Is Waiting for Him to Arrive)*, Album B. 64, 1796–97, indian ink wash on paper, $7^{1}/_{2} \times 5^{1}/_{8}$ (19 × 13), Museo Nacional del Prado, Madrid

JB

13

14

Monk and Old Woman

1824–25
Carbon black and watercolor on ivory, $2\frac{1}{4} \times 2\frac{1}{8}$ (5.7 × 5.4)
Princeton University Art Museum, Museum purchase, Fowler McCormick, Class of 1921, Fund

PROVENANCE: Edward Habich, Kassel; his sale, Gutekunst, Stuttgart, April 27–28, 1899, lot 306; William Rothenstein, London, by 1900; John Quinn, New York, by 1913; his sale, American Art Galleries, New York, February 9–12, 1927, lot 29; P. Lorillard, New York; Mrs. E. John Heidsieck, New York; her sale, Parke-Bernet, New York, February 12–13, 1943, lot 278; Mrs. Robert Maisel, New York; Richard L. Feigen, New York, 1984; purchased by the Princeton Art Museum, 1985.

PRINCIPAL REFERENCES: Soria 1949, no. 5; Sayre 1966, p. 118, no. 13; Sayre 1979; Wilson-Bareau and Mena Marqués 1994, no. 108.

Comparison to the Black Paintings, and specifically to the scene known as *Two Old Men* (fig. 46), is inevitable and appropriate. However, the ivory has even greater intensity of expression and emotion, as if the figures, shown only in bust-length, are being startled by an unexpected horrific sight. The distortions of physiognomy, especially those of the haggle-toothed woman, are epitomes of fear.

The execution is remarkably complex. Two smudgy patches of white provide the point of departure. Slashing strokes of bluish pigment and a translucent white define the woman's head covering. The cheeks of both faces are defined by crude deposits of black interacting with thin parallel striations probably made with a scraper.

JB

Fig. 46   *Two Old Men*, 1820–23, oil transferred to canvas, $56\frac{3}{4} \times 26$ (144 × 66), Museo Nacional del Prado, Madrid

14

15

Two Children Looking at a Book

1824–25
Carbon black, watercolor and ivory, $2^1/_{16} \times 2^1/_{16}$ (5.2 × 5.3)
Museum of Art, Rhode Island School of Design, Providence, Gift of Mrs. Gustav
Radeke

PROVENANCE: Edward Habich; his sale, Gutekunst, Stuttgart, April 27–28, 1899, lot 308; Dr. Gustave
Radeke; gift to the Rhode Island School of Design, 1921.

PRINCIPAL REFERENCES: Soria 1949, no. 10; Sayre 1966, p. 118, no. 15; Sayre 1974, no. 255; Sayre 1979;
Rosenfeld 1991, no. P 82; Wilson-Bareau and Mena Marqués 1994, no. 107.

For Goya, the act of reading had antipodal meanings. Reading could be related to the emphasis placed on education by the *ilustrados*, or books could be interpreted as a source of evil knowledge. One of the scenes in the Black Paintings (*Man Reading*, Museo Nacional del Prado) falls into the first of these categories and represents four men gathered around a fifth, who holds an open book and reads aloud to the satisfaction of his companions. A similar "reading group" is depicted in the Madrid lithograph *La Lectura (Woman Reading)* (fig. 47), which includes two boys paying close attention to what they hear. To judge from the serious rapt attention on their faces, the two boys in the miniature seem to be soaking up what the book has to tell them.

JB

Fig. 47   *La Lectura* (*Woman Reading*), 1819–22, crayon lithograph on paper, $4^1/_2 \times 4^7/_8$ (11.5 × 12.5), Kupferstichkabinett, Staatliche Museen zu Berlin

15

16

Maja and Celestina

1824–25
Carbon black and watercolor on ivory, 2⅛ × 2⅛ (5.4 × 5.4)
Private collection

PROVENANCE: Luis de Portilla, Madrid; his sale, Madrid, February 1880, lot 189; Sir Kenneth (later Lord) Clark, London, by 1963; Sotheby's, May 30, 1991, lot 83; Stanley Moss, Riverdale-on-Hudson, New York; private collection.

PRINCIPAL REFERENCES: Soria 1949, no. 17; London 1963–1964(a), p. 70–71, no. 123; Sayre 1966, p. 115, no. 3; Sayre 1979; Wilson-Bareau and Mena Marqués 1994, no. 100; Symmons 1998, p. 300; Tomlinson 2002, p. 168–69, no. 26.

The subject of a young prostitute and her procuress (called Celestina in Spanish, after a famous literary character) occurs regularly in Goya's art, starting with the tapestry cartoon, *The Pottery Seller* (1779, Museo Nacional del Prado). The duo reappears in Los Caprichos of 1799 (plates 15, *Bellos consejos*, and 31, *Ruega por ella*) and again as the subject of a painting, *Maja and Celestina* (private collection), of c. 1808–12.[1]

The ivory version is the most subtle. The *maja*, with her crooked smile and sideways glance, expresses wry amusement. The Celestina's face, comprising areas of red and black, is alert. The contrast between the white smooth skin of the *maja* and the sagging facial features of the procuress is especially effective. Goya used a pointed instrument to incise thin lines in the washes, a procedure that effectively suggests the stringy white hair of the hag.

It has been suggested that the Celestina is a self–portrait, but this identification is far-fetched and entirely subjective.[2]

JB

1   GW no. 958.
2   Symmons 1998, p. 300.

16

17

Man Looking for Fleas in His Shirt

1824–25
Carbon black and watercolor on ivory, $2^{3}/_{8} \times 2^{5}/_{16}$ (6.0 × 5.9)
Museum of Fine Arts, Boston, M. and M. Karolik Fund, 1973.733

PROVENANCE: Luis de Portilla; his sale, Madrid, February 16, 1880, lot 192; Warwick, Paris; Schidloff, Paris; Baron von Schlumberger, Vienna; Tomás Harris, London, by 1938; Durlacher Brothers, New York, by 1941; Mr. and Mrs. Vincent Price, Los Angeles, by 1956; purchased by the Museum of Fine Arts, 1973.

PRINCIPAL REFERENCES: Soria 1949, no. 6; Sayre 1966, p. 116, no. 6; Sayre 1979; Wilson-Bareau and Mena Marqués 1994, no. 104.

This image of a flea hunt is anticipated in drawing 22 of Album F (1812–20) (fig. 48). Although in certain contexts, lice or fleas could have amatory connotations, the ivory depicts a straightforward exercise of personal hygiene.[1]

This is one of the most abstract and powerful of the ivories, combining the graffito technique, as seen in *María Martínez de Puga* (see cat. no. 7), to imply creases in the shirt and wiping with a cloth to create tones of gray and black. The intricate treatment of the face suggests a concentration on the task at hand by a rough-hewn middle-aged man with strong facial features and a thick mustache.

JB

Fig. 48 *Man Hunting for Lice near a Shack*, Album F. 22, c. 1812–20, sepia wash on paper, $8^{1}/_{8} \times 5^{3}/_{4}$ (20.5 × 14.6), Museo Nacional del Prado, Madrid

1 Wind 1978.

17

18

Heads of a Child and an Old Woman

1824–25
Carbon black and watercolor on ivory, $2^3/_{16} \times 2^3/_{16}$ (5.5 × 5.5)
Private collection

PROVENANCE: Juan de Muguiro, Bordeaux and Madrid; Stanley Moss, Riverdale-on-Hudson, New York; private collection.

PRINCIPAL REFERENCES: De Salas 1973, pp. 169–71; Wilson-Bareau and Mena Marqués 1994, no. 102.

This miniature is said to have belonged to Goya's friend and distant relative by marriage Juan de Muguiro. As noted, Goya painted Muguiro's portrait in 1827, one of the masterpieces of the Bordeaux period (see fig. 34). And Muguiro acquired the *Milkmaid of Bordeaux* (see cat. no. 12) from Leocadia Weiss after the painter's death. Muguiro's death inventory of 1846 lists two additional paintings by Goya, a portrait of a lady and a masked ball (neither identified).[1]

The compositional format is similar to that of cat. nos. 14 and 15, which employ bust-length or half-length figures, with one head elevated above the other. This arrangement permits the artist to focus his attention on the facial expressions, and by comparing them we can see distinctly different emotional registers depicted in each of the ivories. (Most of the extant ivories contain no more than two or three figures.) This picture is more finished than most of the others, and the faces are drawn with greater precision of detail, although the woman's shawl is largely executed by scraping away the black ground. The boy's face is carefully modeled with admixtures of red for the skin and yellow for the hair.

JB

1   See Glendinning in Portús 2004, p. 366, citing Muguiro's death inventory of 1846.

18

19

Head of a Man

1824–25
Carbon black and watercolor on ivory, $2^3/_{16} \times 2^3/_{16}$ (5.5 × 5.5)
Private collection

PROVENANCE: Juan de Muguiro, Bordeaux and Madrid; Stanley Moss, Riverdale-on-Hudson, New York; private collection.

PRINCIPAL REFERENCES: De Salas 1973, p. 170; Wilson-Bareau and Mena Marqués 1994, no. 101.

Like cat. no. 18, this ivory was owned by Juan de Muguiro, the only known contemporary of the artist, outside his family circle, who possessed examples of these miniature paintings.[1] The activity in which the subject is engaged is not recognizable, although the expression is subtly rendered and somewhat dramatic. His eyes are wide open, his lips are parted, and he leans to one side, supporting his head on his hands, and his hands, perhaps, on a rocky ledge. This is among the most highly finished of the ivories, approximating the technique of such late portraits as *Juan de Muguiro* (see fig. 35), and may have been one of the first to be executed.

JB

1 De Salas 1973, p. 170, states but does not document the ownership of Juan de Muguiro. The information is repeated by Glendinning in Portús 2004, p. 366, who appears to be citing Muguiro's death inventory of 1846.

19

20

Woman with Clothes Blowing in the Wind

1824–25
Carbon black and watercolor on ivory, $3\frac{9}{16} \times 3\frac{3}{4}$ (9.0 × 9.5)
Museum of Fine Arts, Boston, Bequest of Pamela Askew, 1998

PROVENANCE: Private collection, Paris; sale, Hôtel Drouot, Paris, February 22, 1937, lot 56–61; Tomás Harris, London, by 1938; Durlacher Bros., New York, by 1941; Mr. and Mrs. R. Kirk Askew, Jr., New York; bequeathed to the Museum of Fine Arts, Boston, 1998.

PRINCIPAL REFERENCES: Soria 1949, no. 7; Sayre 1966, p. 120, no. 20; Wilson-Bareau and Mena Marqués 1994, no. 105.

As has been noted, the composition of this miniature resembles the foreground figure of Capricho plate 36 (fig. 49). The significance of the etching and its two preliminary drawings—Album B. 81 and Sueño No. 22—is adumbrated in contemporary commentaries, which interpret the women as prostitutes whose nightly rounds are being interrupted by a gale.

In the miniature, Goya decontextualizes the subject and renders it less explicit. The woman's dress in the print and drawings rises to her knees and in the Sueño drawing goes still higher. Her counterpart in the miniature stands alone in a less powerful breeze. Her head is bare and is not covered by a wind-swept shawl. To those who do not know the print, the subject may seem a somewhat banal anecdote.

This adjective cannot be applied to the execution of the plaquette. With subtle, spare technique, Goya creates the impression of a heavy cloth shawl being folded this way and that by the wind. Thin vigorous lines incised on her skirt convey the meteorological turmoil of the moment. By varying the transparency of the washes, Goya creates the impression of a dark hillock in the foreground, beyond which stretches a barren gray landscape seen under the chalky light of day.

JB

Fig. 49 *Mala noche (Bad Night)*, Capricho No. 36, 1799, etching and aquatint, $8\frac{5}{8} \times 6$ (21.8 × 15.2), The Metropolitan Museum of Art, New York, Gift of M. Knoedler & Co., 1918

20

21

Judith and Holofernes

1824–25
Carbon black and watercolor on ivory, $3\frac{9}{16} \times 3\frac{5}{16}$ (9.0 × 8.5)
Private collection

Signed: *Goya*

PROVENANCE: Edward Habich, Cassel; his sale, H. G. Gutekunst, Stuttgart, April 27–28, 1889, lot 302; sale, Christie's, New York, January 31, 1997, lot 219; private collection.

PRINCIPAL REFERENCES: Soria 1949, no. 1; Sayre 1966, p. 116, no. 9; Christie's 1997, lot 219.

The story is told in the Book of Judith, an apocryphal book of the Old Testament. Judith, a young and beautiful widow, resides in Bethulia, a Jewish town besieged by Nebuchadnezzar's army, commanded by General Holofernes. As the town is at the point of surrender, Judith promises to deliver her people from the danger. She goes to the camp of Holofernes, plies him with drink, and, after he falls asleep, beheads him with a sword.

Judith returns to Bethulia with the severed head and rallies her people, who defeat the Assyrians.

As Muller points out, the story of Judith enjoyed a certain success in theatrical productions in Madrid in the early 1800s, when there was a taste for plays with bloody denouements.[1] Judith also personified moral strength and fortitude. She makes only one prior appearance in Goya's art, in the Black Paintings of the Quinta del Sordo (1820–23), where its significance remains an unresolved question (fig. 50). Although seemingly a rarity in Goya's art—the Old Testament held little interest for him—the scene can be inscribed within the familiar theme of the "battle of the sexes." Here, as in Album F. 87, a woman is about to strike a mortal blow to a sleeping oppressor.

In the painting for the Quinta, Judith, accompanied by her maid, holds the sword aloft just a moment before she attacks Holofernes, who is barely visible in the scene. (The painting was cut down in this section.) The depiction in the ivory is more explicit. Judith's sword is now embedded in the neck of the horror-struck general, who emits a scream. Goya's version in the ivory is darker than the version in the Black Painting.

JB

Fig. 50 *Judith and Holofernes*, 1820–23, oil transferred to canvas, $57\frac{1}{2} \times 33\frac{1}{8}$ (146 × 84), Museo Nacional del Prado, Madrid

1 Muller 1984, pp. 179–81.

21

The Bordeaux Lithographs

LITHOGRAPHY WAS YOUNG WHEN THE AGED GOYA began to use this new technique, which had been invented by the Bohemian playwright Aloys Senefelder (1771–1834) between 1796 and 1799. Although Senefelder originally conceived of lithography as a cheap way to circulate musical scores and the texts of his plays, its potential as a graphic medium was soon understood. Unlike existing intaglio and relief methods, which involved the laborious process of cutting a design into a hard surface, usually of copper or wood, lithography permitted the artist or artisan to draw with pencil, brush, or crayon directly on a block of prepared limestone. The images never wore out and could be multiplied with less effort and at a lower cost than ever before.

The use of lithography rapidly spread across Europe. Of particular interest for the study of Goya's prints are the developments in France and Spain. The French, in fact, quickly took the lead in the artistic use of the technique, which also had commercial applications. The most innovative printers were two Parisians, Charles Philibert de Lasteyrie, who published works by Carle and Horace Vernet, Jean-Baptiste Isabey, and Baron Antoine Gros, and Godefroy Engelmann, who made great progress in refining the medium.

In Spain the key figure was José María Cardano, who had studied in the workshops of Munich (Senefelder's home) and Paris.[1] In December 1818 he returned to Madrid, and in March of the following year was appointed Litógrafo de Cámara de Grabar en Piedra (loosely translated as Lithographer Royal). Even before his appointment, Cardano had persuaded Goya, Spain's foremost printmaker, to try this new process. Of Goya's eighteen extant lithographs, ten were made in Madrid between February 1819 and July 25, 1822, when Cardano left for Paris on another study trip. Six of the Madrid lithographs are clearly experimental and not entirely successful.[2] Cardano and Goya had much to learn, and the paper stocks available were not of the best quality. The initial prints were made by the so-called transfer process, which is done by drawing the composition with brush, pen, or pencil on paper and then transferring it under pressure to the stone (*Camino de los infiernos*, Biblioteca Nacional, Madrid, estampa 45623). It was only when Goya began to draw directly on the stone with a greasy lithographic crayon that the results improved and he could start to exploit the freedom, spontaneity, and energy inherent in the process (fig. 51). The difficulties of learning a new technique or technology after age sixty, not to mention at seventy-three, cannot be overestimated. Goya deserves much credit for his courage and eventual success.

Goya's experiments with lithography came to a temporary halt when Cardano left for Paris, where he was still in residence when Goya arrived in France. It has been conjectured that Goya's desire to reach Paris as quickly as possible—his initial stay in Bordeaux lasted no more than three days—may be attributed to a desire to meet with Cardano and to see what was going on in the world of Parisian lithography.[3] Cardano could have arranged a tour of the ateliers and introduced him to artists such as Horace

facing page Cyprien Charles Marie Nicolas Gaulon (detail of cat. no. 27; reproduced larger than actual size)

Fig. 51 *Picador Drawing a Bull in Open Country*, 1819–22, crayon lithograph on paper, 9⅞ × 14 (25 × 35.5), Kupferstichkabinett, Staatliche Museen zu Berlin, Inv. 801–1906

Vernet, whom Goya is said to have met. However, Goya may have had other reasons for hastening to Paris because he could have used the services of a superb lithographer in Bordeaux. Cyprien Gaulon had opened his workshop in 1818 and by 1824 was providing high-quality lithography to the burgeoning commercial and artistic markets of the city.[4] Gaulon published views of the town for the art connoisseurs and wine labels for the oenophiles. (For his portrait and biography, see cat. no. 27.) When he returned to Bordeaux, Goya met Gaulon and, with his assistance, was able to devise a new approach to lithography.

Goya produced eight lithographs in Bordeaux, among them several splendid examples of the art.[5] Three are single sheets—the portrait of Gaulon, *El Vito (Andalusian Dance)*, and the *Duel* (figs. 52 and 53), which were produced in very small numbers and, although signed, apparently never were intended for publication. The remaining five pertain to a famous series known as the Bulls of Bordeaux, a term devised by Paul Lefort in 1868, forty years after Goya's death.

Although the chronology of the Bulls of Bordeaux is secure, mysteries remain to be solved. The first of the four sheets that constitute the series (a fifth was printed once but not used) was completed by November 17, 1825, when it was registered by Gaulon with the Dépôt Legal of the Préfecture de la Gironde.[6] The document in question provides the size of the edition—one hundred sets. By December 6 the job was done, as we learn in a letter of that date from Goya to Ferrer. (The third and fourth sheets were registered on December 23.)

When Mr. [Pedro Sáinz] de Baranda was going to Paris, I sent you a trial lithograph that represents a bullfight with young bulls [cat. no. 25] so that you and our friend Cardano could see it, and if some of them are thought worthy of being sent, I'll send whatever you want; I am putting this note with the print and having no news I beg you again to tell me, because I have done three in the same size and on a bullfight theme.[7]

From these words, it can be deduced that Goya had created the set on speculation in the hope that Ferrer would be interested in marketing them. In a letter dated December 20, 1825, Goya reacted to Ferrer's refusal in a letter now lost.

I take note and agree with what you say about the bullfight prints, but as I thought that they should be seen by artistically aware people of whom there are many in that court as well as the large number of people who will already have seen them, I thought it would be easy to give them to a print dealer without saying my name and do so at a low cost.[8]

The tone and substance of this letter are puzzling and self-contradictory, docile to the point of surrender on one hand, proud on the other. He wanted the prints to be seen by "artistically aware people," who would presumably be impressed by what he had accomplished. But he was quick to throw in the towel once Ferrer had turned them down, asking him in effect to dump them onto the market for cheap prints. The suggestion that his name be withheld is equally strange, as all four prints are signed. In fact, Goya had every reason to be proud of them.

Ferrer's rapid decision to reject Goya's overture is hard to explain, at least as far as the subject of the prints is concerned. During his stay in Paris in the summer of 1824, Goya

Fig. 52 (*below left*)   *El Vito (Andalusian Dance)*, 1819–22, crayon lithograph on paper, $7\frac{1}{8} \times 7\frac{1}{8}$ (18 × 18), Biblioteca Nacional, Madrid

Fig. 53 (*below right*)   *Duel*, 1819–22, crayon lithograph on paper, $7\frac{1}{2} \times 7\frac{1}{2}$ (19 × 19), Biblioteca Nacional, Madrid

had painted a bullfight picture which he either gave or sold to Ferrer (see cat. no. 22). It seems likely that Ferrer had expressed admiration for the work, although perhaps more out of politesse than enthusiasm. This would have led Goya to believe that a series of bullfight scenes might meet with his approval. In the event, they did not appeal to Ferrer; he urged Goya to reissue Los Caprichos, an impossible request because the plates were no longer in his possession, and in any event, as he said with bravado, he had better things to do.

Perhaps a factor in Ferrer's decision was the conflictive status of bullfighting.[9] It is true that outside Spain, bullfighting was often regarded as a picturesque, typically Spanish entertainment and that scenes of the *corrida* were in demand. (Goya's personal view on the spectacle and his involvement as an aficionado and even amateur matador are largely irrelevant, because the series was designed to satisfy a perceived market for bullfight prints.) However, in Spain itself, the attitude toward bullfighting was ambivalent. During the late eighteenth century, it had been attacked by certain *ilustrados* (men of the Enlightenment) as a mindless public event that incited the populace to unruly behavior. As a result, bullfighting became a political symbol, damned by the Liberals, defended by the conservatives. It had been outlawed during the Liberal government of 1820–23, only to be reinstated immediately when Ferdinand VII returned to power. Ferrer, of course, was a Liberal in exile, as were many of the Spaniards then residing in Paris. Unless the Bulls of Bordeaux is to be interpreted as a satire or visual manifesto aimed at bullfighting, which is hard to see from looking at the prints, it was ill advised for Goya to have chosen this subject, especially because his earlier series, La Tauromaquia, had enjoyed only modest success.

Another strike against Goya was the very execution of the prints; they are unlike any that had ever been made in the short history of lithography. The majority of Goya's contemporaries approached artistic lithography as if they were painting formal pictures, producing set pieces executed with precision and attention to detail. Goya, by contrast, devised a kind of linear shorthand, abbreviating forms that most artists would have carefully delineated. The heads and bodies of the spectators are abstractly represented by choppy, staccato strokes and touches; heavy use is made of a scraper to carve out rough highlights from the darkness of the oily lithographic crayon. The sheer visual energy is astonishing. Similarly, the construction of pictorial space is unorthodox. Each scene is contained within the *barrera* (the barrier between the arena and the grandstand) and the first few rows of the *tendido*, but the perspective is tilted forward, closing out the sun, the sky, even the upper seats of the stands. However, the qualities that later generations, including our own, have appreciated as brilliant, original, and audacious may have looked to Ferrer as merely crude and unfinished.

These unorthodox effects were achieved by an unorthodox method of working, described in detail by Brugada:

Fig. 54 *Bullfight*, 1825, crayon lithograph on paper, $12\frac{1}{4} \times 16\frac{3}{8}$ (31 × 41.5), Musée des Beaux-Arts de Bordeaux

The artist worked at his lithographs on his easel, the stone placed like a canvas. He handled the crayons like paintbrushes and never sharpened them. He remained standing, walking backward and forward from moment to moment to judge the effect. He usually covered the whole stone with a uniform gray tint, and then removed the areas that were to be light with a scraper; here a head, a figure, there a horse, a bull. The crayon was then brought back into play to reinforce the shadows and accents, or to indicate figures and give them a sense of movement. . . . People will laugh if I said that Goya's lithographs were all executed with a magnifying glass. The fact is that it was not in order to do detailed work, but his eyesight was failing.[10]

Although the Bulls of Bordeaux now comprises four prints, Goya made a fifth, which exists in a unique impression (fig. 54).[11] Evidently this is the initial attempt at working on a stone much larger than any he had previously used. The result is a somewhat unclear but energized composition in which forms overlap and highlights are placed helter-skelter. Goya quickly hit his stride, and soon the "Bulls" were ready for market (cat. nos. 23–26). Two of the prints have titles devised by Goya—*El famoso Americano, Mariano Ceballos* and *Dibersión de España*. A unique set in the Biblioteca Nacional, Madrid, owned by Goya's friend Juan Agustín Ceán Bermúdez, is numbered I–IV in pencil and is assumed to follow the order that Goya intended.[12] The first print in Ceán's set is accompanied by an inscription of authorship, elegantly written in pencil, and added to the bottom margin, which reads, "D. Francisco Goya y Lucientes primer pintor de Camara del Rey de España y Director de la real Academia de San Fernando/ inventó y lithografió estas cuatro estampas en Bourdeaux [*sic*] el año de 1826 [*sic*] a los 80 años de edad." It would appear that the lithographs were now being readied for publication in Spain. Instead they were removed to a warehouse owned by Jacques Galos, presumably to be sold to anyone who chanced to learn of their existence. How these sales happened is unknown.

In one way or another, the prints began to circulate, and it was not long before the modernists caught up to them and understood their importance. Delacroix owned two of the set, which are now in the Biblioteca Nacional, Madrid.[13] Praised by Théophile Gautier in 1842, they received the obligatory blessing from the apostle of modernism, Charles Baudelaire, in 1857:

> At the end of his career, Goya's eyes were so weak that it is said that they had to sharpen his crayons for him. At the same time, however, he made large, very important lithographs, and among other things bullfights full of swarming crowds— admirable plates, vast pictures in miniature.[14]

JB

NOTES

1 For Cardano and his role in the introduction of lithography in Spain, see Vega 1990, pp. 47–53.

2 Here we follow the chronology of Vega 1990, pp. 53–58. The standard reference to Goya's prints is Harris 1964; for the Madrid lithographs, see vol. II, pp. 418–22, nos. 270–79.

3 Florisoone 1966.

4 For Gaulon, see Bouvy 1918, Zaragoza 1983, and cat. no. 27.

5 Harris 1964, II, pp. 424–29, nos. 282–87. The exception is a trial proof for the Bulls of Bordeaux, discussed below.

6 Bouvy 1918, p. 12.

7 Canellas López 1981, p. 389, no. 272.

8 Ibid., pp. 389–90, no. 273; translation Wilson-Bareau and Mena Marqués 1994, p. 332.

9 For a summary of the question, see Martínez-Novillo 1998, p. 121, and Medrano Basanta 2003.

10 Matheron 1996, p. 264; translation Wilson-Bareau and Mena 1994, p. 333.

11 Harris 1964, II, p. 429, no. 287.

12 Madrid 1996, pp. 260–63, nos. 408–12.

13 Wilson-Bareau 2003, p. 428, note 4. He also owned the portrait of Gaulon, received as a gift from Matheron.

14 Cited by Martínez-Novillo 1998, pp. 117 and 129, note 36.

22

Bullfighting Scene, known as Suerte de Varas

1824
Oil on canvas, $19^5/_8 \times 24$ (50 × 61)
The J. Paul Getty Museum, Los Angeles

Inscribed by J. M. de Ferrer on back of original canvas: *Pintado en Paris en Julio de 1824/Por/Dn Fran.co Goya/ JMF.* (now copied on relining).

PROVENANCE: Joaquín María de Ferrer, Paris and Madrid, 1824; by descent to Marqués de Baroja, Madrid, by 1900; by descent to Marquesa de la Gándara, Rome, by 1970; private collection, Switzerland; sale, Sotheby's, London, December 9, 1992, lot 84; purchased by The J. Paul Getty Museum, 1992.

PRINCIPAL REFERENCES: De Salas 1964, p. 38; Baticle 1998, pp. 119–20; Martínez-Novillo 1998, pp. 119–20; Madrid 2002, pp. 234–25.

This small, intense painting is documented by a careful inscription on the verso, which supplies information that it was painted in Paris in July 1824. The inscription is signed with the monogram "JMF," referring to Joaquín María de Ferrer, the original owner, whose rubric is placed just below the initials. Although the inscription was covered when the canvas was relined in 1959, it is recorded in a photograph published in 1964.[1] A copy was placed on the new canvas lining.

As mentioned, Ferrer was a Spanish Liberal who had sought political exile in Paris and was being cultivated by Goya as a possible patron or dealer for his prints. These hopes were to be dashed when Ferrer declined to market the Bulls of Bordeaux (cat. nos. 23–26). Nevertheless, he seems proud to have owned the painting—hence the formal inscription—although he may have esteemed it as the work of a famous painter and not as incentive to sell Goya's depictions of bullfighting.

Scenes of bullfighting recur in Goya's output and appear for the first time in the so-called cabinet paintings exhibited at the Royal Academy in 1794. Six of the eleven pictures were devoted to the bullfight. Goya returned to the subject in 1816, with the publication of the thirty-three etchings known as La Tauromaquia. His final engagement

with the theme is the Bulls of Bordeaux. Goya himself was *aficionado a los toros*—how avid is a matter of debate—which may explain in part his long-term interest in the spectacle.

In composing the Getty picture, Goya appropriated motifs from his earlier renditions of the *fiesta brava*, notably La Tauromaquia.[2] The motif of the *picador* about to lance the bull appears in reverse in plate 27 (fig. 55). Goya repeats this grouping in a painting of roughly the same date, now in the Royal Academy (fig. 56), and in a lithograph of 1819–22 known as *Suerte de vara en el campo*. As for the pose of the bull, it closely follows plate 7 of La Tauromaquia and, again, the *Suerte de vara en el campo*. A year and a half after painting the picture for Ferrer, Goya brought the *picador* back for a return engagement in plate 2 of the Bulls of Bordeaux, which also appropriates the crumpled form of the dead horse in the middle ground. Another element that reappears in the lithographs is the notational treatment of the spectators: their bodies are mere allusions to their corporeality.

Goya's technique is daring and complex. In his account of the years in Bordeaux, Goya's early biographer, Laurent Matheron, describes how he virtually put away his brushes and "replaced them with a [palette] knife, a

Fig. 55 (*below*) *The Celebrated Picador, Fernando del Toro, Draws the Fierce Beast on with His Pique*, Tauromaquia No. 27, 1815–16, etching and aquatint, $9^5/_8 \times 13^3/_4$ (24.5 × 35), Biblioteca Nacional, Madrid

piece of cloth, anything at all."[3] This opportunistic application of paint to the canvas accounts for the churning power of the image; unconventional means produce violent effects. The stage is set by creating a contrast between the thin, delicate prime coat for the background and the rugged impastos of the foreground. The upper section of the canvas, comprising the sandy arena and the phantasmagorical crowd, is schematically rendered on top of the transparent light brown ground, which barely covers the weave of the canvas.

A strange motif is the dead horse, drawn out of scale in a twisted pose, half-floating in the middle distance. Two crouching figures originally flanked the horse but were later covered up.

In the foreground of the composition, Goya used a denser, brighter ground to support the pictorial weight of the figures. Two *picadores* accompanied by four *peones* confront the bull, as a dying horse expires in a puddle of blood. One picador sits astride a badly wounded animal and prepares to launch another strike. Technical examination of the painting has demonstrated that Goya applied the paint in this area with a brush, a palette knife, and his thumb, covered with a rag, thus confirming Matheron's description of his working methods.[4] With these blunt instruments, Goya posed questions about the pictorial representation of the physical world, questions that would not be answered until much later in the century.

J B

1 See Salas 1964, p. 36, fig. 31. The painting is listed in Ferrer's death inventory of 1861; see Blanco Mozo 1998, p. 33.
2 These relationships are pointed out by several writers, e.g. Wilson-Bareau and Mena Marqués 1994, p. 330.
3 Matheron 1996, p. 264.
4 The painting was examined at the Courtauld Institute of Art before the sale at Sotheby's in 1992. The results are reported in the sales catalogue (Sotheby's London, December 9, 1992, lot 84).

Fig. 56 (*left*) *Corrida de toros en un pueblo (Bullfight in a Village)*, 1808–12, oil on canvas, $17^3/_4 \times 28^3/_8$ (45 × 72), The Museum of the Royal Academy of Fine Arts of San Fernando, Madrid

22

23–26

Bulls of Bordeaux

These entries follow the sequence established in the numbered set once owned by Juan Agustín Ceán Bermúdez, now in the Biblioteca Nacional, Madrid.

23

El famoso Americano, Mariano Ceballos

1825
Crayon lithograph with scraper, on white paper, 12 × 15³/₄ (30.5 × 40)
The Metropolitan Museum of Art, New York, Bequest of Mrs. Louis H. Porter, 1946

Signed in stone, lower left corner: *Goya*; printed in lower left margin: *Deposé*; in lower right margin: *Lith de Gaulon.*

PROVENANCE: Mrs. Louis H. Porter, Denver; bequeathed to The Metropolitan Museum of Art, 1946.

PRINCIPAL REFERENCES: Harris 1964, II, p. 425, no. 283; Gassier and Wilson 1971, p. 363, no. 1707; Madrid 1996, p. 260, no. 408.

Fig. 57 *Mariano Ceballos, Alias the Indian, Kills the Bull from His Horse*, Tauromaquia No. 23, 1815–16, etching and aquatint, 9⁷/₈ × 13³/₄ (25.0 × 35.0), Biblioteca Nacional, Madrid

This is one of two prints in the series with a title written in the stone. A unique impression in the Biblioteca Nacional, Madrid, has a lengthy inscription of authorship by a professional calligrapher in pencil in the lower margin.[1]

Little is known of the *mestizo* matador Mariano Ceballos, who, as his sobriquet indicates, was a native of Spanish America. (In the titles of La Tauromaquia, he is referred to as "el indio.") He arrived in Madrid in 1775 and gained a reputation for his ability to fight one bull while mounted on another and for his daring use of a short sword. It was a risky performance and cost him his life in 1780. Goya evidently was impressed by his bravery and cast him in the role of protagonist in two published plates (23 [fig. 57] and 24) and one unpublished proof (J) of La Tauromaquia.

This lithograph demonstrates Goya's freewheeling approach to the medium, which makes extensive use of a scraper to create highlights. The tonal values are dramatically manipulated to achieve maximum energy. In the background, the crowd is pictured as an almost undifferentiated mass of vague dark shapes, while in the foreground, Goya provides a dramatic setting for the lunging move of the matador by leaving the stone behind him almost white, as if he were illuminated by a spotlight. In contrast to the sketchy figures of the spectators, the bullfighter and the bull are drawn with a free, delicate touch. To eyes accustomed to the tidy appearance of most lithographs of the time, *Mariano Ceballos* might have seemed unfinished, if not crude.

JB

1   Madrid 1996, p. 260, no. 408.

El famoso Americano, Mariano Ceballos.

Déposé.   Lith de Gaulon.

23

24

Bravo toro

1825
Crayon lithograph with scraper on white paper; $12\frac{1}{4} \times 16\frac{1}{4}$ (31.2 × 41.2)
The Metropolitan Museum of Art, New York, Rogers Fund, 1920

Signed in stone, lower left corner: *Goya*.
PROVENANCE: Frederick Keppel, New York; purchased by The Metropolitan Museum of Art, 1920.
PRINCIPAL REFERENCES: Harris 1964, II, p. 426, no. 284; Gassier and Wilson 1971, p. 363, no. 1708; Madrid 1996, p. 261, nos. 409–10.

The scene is a composite of earlier bullfight subjects. As Wilson-Bareau has observed, the motif of the *picador* caught on the horns of a bull is found in an unpublished plate from La Tauromaquia (F), although the victim is a matador.[1] The *picador* shielding himself behind a fallen horse and attacking the bull with a lance occurs in plates 26 and 32. And, of course, the *picador* attacking from the left and the fallen horse at the right are among the components of the picture painted for Ferrer. A painted variant of this print in the Prado is now attributed to a follower.[2] The Bulls of Bordeaux inspired a rash of imitators of Goya to paint bullfight scenes in the manner of his late style. The title is a later invention and not original to Goya.

From a technical point of view, this is the least successful of the series. The tonal gradations of the arena are hastily drawn, and the knot of people gathered around the wounded or deceased *picador* at the left background is almost formless. Goya has tried to impose coherence on this section by applying choppy scratches of the scraper but is not successful. Even the foreground figures are weakly delineated and modeled. An uncorrected pentimento corresponds to the snout of the bull. It is possible that this print was the first to be made after the unique impression of the one owned by Matheron and now in the Musée des Beaux-Arts de Bordeaux.

JB

1 Wilson-Bareau 2003, pp. 428–29, no. 43.
2 Whistler 2003, pp. 132–35.

Goya

24

25

Dibersión de España (Spanish Entertainment)

1825
Crayon lithograph with scraper on white paper; $11^{7}/_{8} \times 16^{3}/_{8}$ (30.2 × 41.5)
The Metropolitan Museum of Art, New York, Rogers Fund, 1920

Signed in stone, lower left corner: *Goya*; printed in lower left margin: *Deposé*; in lower right margin: *Lith de Gaulon*; in center: *Dibersión de España*.

PROVENANCE: Frederick Keppel, New York; purchased by The Metropolitan Museum of Art, 1920.

PRINCIPAL REFERENCES: Harris 1964, II, p. 427, no. 285; Gassier and Wilson 1971, p. 363, no. 1709; Madrid 1996, p. 228, no. 325.

This print was sent for approval to Ferrer, as mentioned in Goya's letter of December 6, 1825, and is described as a "*corrida de novillos.*" Goya depicts the moment at the start of a fiesta when the bulls are allowed to run free and are engaged by risk-taking members of the populace. The subject does not appear in La Tauromaquia, probably because the event was frowned upon by authorities eager to protect people from the consequences of poor judgment inflated by bravado. These consequences are predictably apparent in the foreground, where two would-be *toreros* are being trampled underfoot, much to the amusement of a small group of onlookers at the right. Goya has created a convincing impression of the chaotic movement of the crowd. Along the rim of the arena, individuals size up the odds of engaging a bull with their capes; some inch their way into the ring, others begin to retreat. By distorting the size of the animals in relation to the members of the crowd and surrounding them in a brilliant ring of light, Goya magnifies the power of the bulls and the dangers they pose.

A painting in the Ashmolean Museum, Oxford, reproduces the composition in reverse.[1] While the attribution to Goya has sometimes been accepted, those who see the hand of a follower are in the right.

JB

1 Whistler 2003, pp. 127–41.

Dibersion de España!

26

Plaza Partida (Divided Ring)

1825
Crayon lithograph with scraper on white paper, 12 × 16³/₈ (30.6 × 41.6)
The Metropolitan Museum of Art, New York, Rogers Fund, 1920

Signed in stone at lower left: *Goya*.

PROVENANCE: Frederick Keppel, New York; purchased by The Metropolitan Museum of Art, 1920.

PRINCIPAL REFERENCES: Harris 1964, II, p. 428, no. 286; Gassier and Wilson 1971, p. 363, no. 1710; Madrid 1996, p. 289, no. 326.

Bullfights in a divided ring were somewhat infrequent events. Before the Peninsular War, they were organized by towns in which the authorized season was drawing to a close. Fiestas that had been canceled, usually because of poor weather, were made up by scheduling simultaneous *corridas* in the same arena, which was divided in half by a temporary wall. During the war, the *plaza partida* became a way to entertain and provide meat to a hungry populace at one and the same time.

This is perhaps the most brilliant print of the series. (The title is a later invention.) Goya scatters the focal points over the surface, re-creating the visual stimulation that would have been experienced by a witness to the spectacle. The eye first alights on the matador at the right, moving in for the kill, and then skips to the second matador at the left, about to place the *banderillas*. Then it moves deeper into space to the small crowds that watch from inside the rim of the ring, until finally it alights on the spectators in the *tendido*, their heads depicted as small circles of white bounded by zigzag lines. Distances seem to collapse, the scale of the figures arbitrarily changes, the highlights dance on the surfaces. A furious energy infuses every corner of this extraordinary print.[1]

JB

1 The painting in the Ashmolean Museum, Oxford, which shows the composition in reverse, is now considered to be the work of an imitator. See Whistler 2003, pp. 127–41.

Soyol

26

27

Cyprien Charles Marie Nicolas Gaulon

c. 1825
Crayon lithograph with scraper on white paper, $10^5/_8 \times 8^1/_4$ (27.0 × 21.0)
Davison Art Center, Wesleyan University, Middletown, Connecticut

Signed, in lower left corner: *Goya*

PROVENANCE: probably Nicolas Toussaint Charlet (1792–1845), Paris; Davison Art Center.

PRINCIPAL REFERENCES: Bouvy 1918; Beruete 1928, p. 252, no. 285; Harris 1964, II, no. 282; Gassier and Wilson 1971, pp. 345–47, 357, 363, no. 1703; Fauqué and Villanueva Etcheverría 1982, pp. 600–602.

Cyprien Gaulon (1777–1858) was born in Haiti.[1] Orphaned at an early age, he was sent to France when he was six years old and adopted by Bordeaux merchants who were business associates of his father. Having lost his patrimony in the slave rebellion of 1791, he joined the Republican army and served for three years. He returned to Bordeaux and became a professional calligrapher (fig. 58). In 1818 he established a thriving lithographic workshop that catered to the growing market for lithographic prints. Two years later he moved his workshop to a building that still stands on rue Saint Rémi (see fig. 9).

As a master lithographer, Gaulon was the right person to collaborate with Goya in the realization of his unconventional approach to the medium. As a token of gratitude and friendship, Goya made this subtle portrait, which is mentioned by Matheron in his biography, thanks to which the sitter can be identified. The date of execution is probably the same as the Bulls of Bordeaux (1825). After describing Goya's approach to lithography, Matheron writes:

> In this way, using the point of a razor and without any retouching, he once made a a curious portrait emerge from the dark ground tone. This is the portrait of M. Gaulon, lithographer.[2]

The portrait of Gaulon is a masterpiece of the lithographer's art, transferring to the medium the same tonal approach used in the late portraits in oil.[3] Gaulon is posed against a soft grayish background. After drawing the figure on the stone with a crayon, the artist used a scraper to create the highlights on the face. Fine lines are also scratched into the area of the lapels and shoulders, and an even more aggressive scraping on the cravat brings

Fig. 58   Gustave de Galard (1779–1841), *Portrait of Gaulon*, lithograph, Bibliothèque municipale de Bordeaux, Fonds Delpit

this area to life. In a more subtle vein, Goya created the velvety shadows on the face and captured the movement of the studiously unkempt locks of hair. Goya certainly saw his friend and collaborator in a sympathetic light. Gaulon looks more like a Romantic poet than a skilled craftsman. His gaze is alert yet benign. By posing the sitter as if seen from slightly below, Goya bestows a measure of nobility on his personality.

Only three impressions of the print are known, which implies that, like the painted portraits, it was meant for the enjoyment of Gaulon and his inner circle and as a way for Goya to memorialize their fruitful collaboration.[4] This supposition is supported by the fact that the impression in the Museo Lázaro Galdiano, Madrid, was owned by Rosario Weiss.

JB

1   For a brief biography, see Bouvy 1918 and Bériac 1983.
2   Matheron 1996, p. 264.
3   Harris 1964, II, p. 424, and Sayre 1974, p. 309.
4   The other impressions are in the Bibliothèque Nationale, Paris, and the Museo Lázaro Galdiano, Madrid.

27

The Bordeaux Drawings (Albums G and H)

G OYA WAS AN INDEFATIGABLE DRAFTSMAN, and his drawings are among his most compelling creations. Roughly nine hundred sheets are extant and can be divided into two groups—preparatory drawings and the so-called album drawings. For the most part, the preparatory drawings were made for the print series, including Los Caprichos, Los Desastres de la Guerra, La Tauromaquia, and Los Disparates. Their purpose is self-explanatory.

The album drawings, which number about 480–90, are unusual, comprising in their totality a kind of stream of consciousness of the sights he saw and the thoughts he thought during the last third of his life.[1] In all, he created eight albums of different sizes and with varying numbers of pages. These are conventionally identified by the letters A through H, although the alphabetical sequence and the chronological order no longer entirely correspond. (For example, Album F is now dated before Album E.) The term "album" is somewhat misleading, too, if it is understood to be a prefabricated sketchbook of the kind now available in an art-supply store. Some of the albums were bound only after Goya had completed a group of drawings, and some may never have been bound at all until after his death. From the changes in numbering on several of the drawings, it is evident that Goya altered the placement of individual sheets from time to time. (See H. 56 and 57, which originally were in different places.)

It is probably no coincidence that Goya began to compile these albums in 1796, three years after he had lost his hearing in the nearly fatal illness of 1793. Deprived of normal human communication through conversation, he may have used the drawings to "talk to himself" and to find an additional outlet for his thoughts, feelings, and observations. And perhaps they were shown to friends to provide entertainment and provoke comments. Six of the eight albums were made in the twenty-year period between 1808, the date of the French invasion, and 1828, when Goya died. After his death, they were inherited by his son, Javier, who amalgamated them in three large albums, perhaps disturbing the sequences established by his father. The wastrel grandson, Mariano, quickly sold them off after Javier's death in 1854, initiating the farflung dispersal of the sheets.[2] Most of the extant drawings were catalogued in 1973 and reproduced in their original sequences, but it was not until 2001 that a representative number (117) were exhibited together and their qualities could be appreciated by a wider public.[3]

The album drawings, despite the fact that they span some thirty-two years, share many traits. Perhaps the most important is that each drawing is a self-contained, independent composition and resembles a small monochromatic painting. Only a few seem to have been used as preparatory studies for works in other media. The drawings have been likened to entries in a journal or diary, although the analogy is not perfect because, while they have an informal, somewhat private character, they are not usually the records of a day's events. Another salient feature is the cartoon-like style of draftsmanship. Goya's artistic thought was centered on ideas that placed imagination and instinct

facing page   Young Woman Swooning, Surrounded by Witches (detail of cat. no. 51) above academic rules as the basis for artistic endeavor. The classical style of drawing the human figure was not for him. Constrained as he often was by the rules of decorum in his public commissions, Goya sought to create a private world in which to express his thoughts and feelings in a personal idiom. This world comprises small-scale works— paintings, drawings, prints—and is inhabited by somewhat comical types, inspired in part by contemporary English caricatures, who energetically perform diverse activities in a liminal space between fact and fantasy.[4] Their faces are expressive, their gestures, broad, sweeping, and often exaggerated. At times, their shouts of mirth and cries of anguish can almost be heard.

In all but two of the later albums (F and H), Goya wrote pithy inscriptions, usually along the lower margin of the pages, which are a kind of Spanish haiku. These short texts frequently are ironic and initiate a reciprocal relationship between word and image. Nevertheless, the subtitles do not always explain the drawings; sometimes they only deepen the mysteries.

Another characteristic of the albums is the shared thematic repertory. Goya created what might be called a personal iconography consisting of recurrent themes and motifs. The spectrum of these themes is very broad indeed. Some are commonplace, as for instance his censure of the seven deadly sins. Others depict popular superstitions: the frequent representation of witches would be an example. Goya was also fascinated, as were many of his contemporaries in other parts of Europe, with the irrational, especially as evinced in nightmares and insanity. States of mind and emotion held a powerful grip on his imagination. Relations between the sexes, indeed sexuality itself, are a constant preoccupation, although Goya never traversed the forbidden world of pornography. Political satire finds a place, especially in Album C, in which the authority of the Catholic church and especially the nefarious Inquisition are mercilessly attacked. Most extraordinary are the visionary drawings, visionary not in a religious sense but in the depiction of subjects divorced from any discernible connection to mundane reality. Today they would be called surrealistic.

During the years in Bordeaux, Goya worked on two albums, conventionally referred to as G and H. Each of the drawings is numbered in the upper-right corner. The highest number of Album G is number 60, and the whereabouts of all but five are known; Album H is numbered to 63, and only three of these have not turned up. Both are executed on French paper of a greenish hue, now often faded to white. The medium is black crayon in contrast to the pen, brush, and ink employed in the preceding volumes, a choice inspired by Goya's practice of lithography. This softer medium permitted the artist to attain a greater breadth of execution and to compensate for a certain loss of manual dexterity. As in earlier drawings, Goya freely used a scraper to create highlights and modulate tonal values. Nevertheless, the morphology is instantaneously recognizable: the cartoon figures may be more loosely rendered, but their essence is undiluted.

Fig. 59 *Castigo francés (French Punishment)* (Album G. 48), 1824–28, black crayon on paper, $7^1/_2 \times 5^7/_8$ (19.2 × 15) The State Hermitage Museum, St. Petersburg

In general, the subjects of Albums G and H, when they can be understood, differ little from the earlier albums except in one respect. These are scenes observed by Goya as he made the rounds of Paris and Bordeaux and include the ingenious devices used by the less-fortunate members of the populace to make their way through the streets of these cities and two depictions of execution by guillotine, the "French punishment," as he called it (fig. 59).

We cannot be certain whether Goya executed Album H only after Album G had been completed or whether he worked on both simultaneously, although there are differences in execution to suggest that H is slightly later in date. In this group of drawings, the crayon moves quickly over the surface, creating effects that are looser and less detailed and precise. Another difference concerns the scale of the figures, which is larger in H than in G. (See G. 44 and H. 61 [figs. 60 and 61].) In the H drawings, more of the page is left blank than in G, and they often depict a single figure rather than a complex composition. Still, it does not pay to be doctrinaire on this point because it is possible that Goya did not number the drawings until after most or all had been finished, making it possible for a drawing with H characteristics to be included in G and vice-versa.

The major difference between the two Bordeaux albums is literary not visual. In Album G, the drawings are inscribed with short texts, as in most of the earlier albums. As far as Album H is concerned, Goya signed his name to the drawings but wrote inscriptions only on six. This discrepancy is hard to explain. It has been suggested that Album G is the initial stage of a new series of Los Caprichos, a supposition based on

Fig. 60 (*above left*)   *Loco p.r errar (Mad by Error)* (Album G. 44), 1824–28, black crayon on paper, 7$\frac{1}{2}$ × 5$\frac{3}{4}$ (19.2 × 14.6), Museum of Fine Arts, Boston, Arthur Tracey Cabot Fund, 53.2378

Fig. 61 (*above right*)   *Phantom Dancing with Castanets*, Album H. 61, 1824–28, black crayon on paper, 7$\frac{1}{2}$ × 5$\frac{1}{2}$ (18.9 × 13.9), Museo Nacional del Prado, Madrid

Goya's letter to Joaquín María de Ferrer, in which he responds to the latter's lack of interest in the Bulls of Bordeaux and rebuffs the suggestion that he reissue Los Caprichos.[5] As cited above, Goya informed Ferrer that the plates now belonged to the royal chalcography, which collected engraved plates, and that in any case he would not copy them because "I have better ideas that may be sold with greater profit." Goya's wording is ambiguous and has led some to associate the "Nuevos Caprichos" not with the drawings at all but with four etchings with acquatint also made by Goya in Bordeaux. However, for reasons explained below, this is improbable.[6]

On the visual evidence, it does not seem likely that Album G was the first stage in producing a new set of prints modeled on Los Caprichos. In fact, were it not for the letter to Ferrer, the idea of identifying a possible set of "new caprichos" probably would never have occurred. It is true that some drawings fill the satirical bill, such as *Comer mucho (To Eat a Lot)* (cat. no. 40), a critique of gluttony, among other things, or the condemnation of greed in *Del avaro no se espera ningun bien . . . (One Can Expect No Good from a Miser . . .)* (fig. 62). However, the majority of the sheets go off on other tangents. A few depict unusual forms of locomotion seen, according to the inscriptions, in the streets of Paris and Bordeaux (see fig. 72 and cat. no. 31). Another subset depicts the insane and insanity (cat. nos. 41 and 42). And from time to time, Goya would plumb the depths of memory and revive subjects from the distant past, for instance *majos* and *majas* (cat. no. 29). Then there are images summoned from the dark corners

Fig. 62 (*above left*)   *Del avaro no se espera ningun bien . . . (One Can Expect No Good from a Miser . . .)*, Album G. 60, 1824–28, black crayon on paper, 7$\frac{1}{2}$ × 5$\frac{3}{4}$ (19.2 × 14.5) The State Hermitage Museum, St. Petersburg

Fig. 63 (*above right*)   *Gran disparate (Great Folly)*, Album G. 9, 1824–28, black crayon on paper, 7$\frac{1}{2}$ × 6 (19.2 × 15.2), Museo Nacional del Prado, Madrid

of his mind, the meaning of which he seems to have taken to the grave. *Gran disparate (Great Folly)* (fig. 63); *Cómico descubrimiento (Comical Discovery)* (G. 51, Fitzwilliam Museum, Cambridge) and *El perro volante (The Flying Dog)* (cat. no. 44) add up to more than the sum of their recognizable parts, but the identification of their subject and significance has proved to be challenging in the extreme. On balance, it is reasonable to view the drawings of Album G as a thought-provoking mélange of purposely disparate images assembled in a way that permitted Goya to externalize some of his darker thoughts and to entertain and challenge those fortunate enough to see the compositions.

Album H is cast in a similar mold, at least as far as the thematic repertory is concerned. However, in the absence of captions on all but six drawings, the interpretation of intended meanings depends to some extent on familiarity with Goya's repertory of leitmotifs. For instance, the *Procession of Monks* (H. 13; Museo Nacional del Prado) and the brazen *Maja* (cat. no. 29) are known from many earlier works. The satirical barbs launched against the monastic establishment (cat. no. 39), gluttony (fig. 64), and greed (H. 6, Museo Nacional del Prado) are carried over from previous works. Other drawings are unique to this album, such as the four that record odd sights seen at the fair of Bordeaux, including *Serpiente de 4 baras a Bordeaux* (fig. 65). And, once again, we enter the domain of fantasy and encounter a menacing draped figure armed with sword and shield, riding a winged bird (fig. 66); the enigmatic composition of a man awakened by a bear cub (fig. 67); and another of a traveling witch (cat. no. 50).

Fig. 64 (*above left*) *Monk Guzzling from a Large Bowl*, Album H. 63, 1824–28, black crayon on paper, 7½ × 5½ (19 × 14) Museo Nacional del Prado, Madrid

Fig. 65 (*above right*) *Serpiente de 4 baras a Bordeaux (Snake 4 meters long at Bordeaux)*, Album H. 40, 1824–28, black crayon on paper, 7½ × 5¾ (19.1 × 14.7), The State Hermitage Museum, St. Petersburg

The numerical ordering of Albums G and H may seem to imply that the artist had developed an overarching scheme linking the drawings together, but nothing could be further from the truth. In his later years, Goya was not a linear thinker who moved rationally from one set of ideas to the next. He had made an investment in the power of reason during the 1790s, when he associated with the *ilustrados,* and it had failed miserably, but not totally.[7] Thus we see the flashes of satire and mockery that illuminate the pages of the Bordeaux albums. However, Goya came to perceive that other forces were at work: the demons were gaining ground, and he was wary of their destructive power. Yet he did not despair. Fortitude is the attribute that unites the drawings in his final albums and indeed the totality of his final works. At a time when he was compelled to fight against illness and frailty, he never lost his resilience or desire to continue the struggle. He himself confessed that "All I have left is my will," but this power and a compelling desire to make works of art were more than sufficient to keep him going. Seen by Goya, life was absurd and amusing, life was dangerous and frightening, life was worth living until the very last moment. As he moved the black crayon across the fine French paper, distant memories, events of the day, human frailties, and flights of fantasy jostled for space on the pages of his albums.

JB

Fig. 66 (*above left*) *Allegorical Figure*, Album H. 15, 1824–28, black crayon on paper, 7$\frac{1}{2}$ × 5$\frac{7}{8}$ (19 × 15), Museo Nacional del Prado, Madrid

Fig. 67 (*above right*) *Man Awakened by Bear Cub*, Album H. 9, 1824–28, black crayon on paper, 7$\frac{1}{2}$ × 6$\frac{1}{8}$ (19 × 15.5), Museo Nacional del Prado, Madrid

NOTES

1 For general studies of the albums, see Gassier 1973 and Wilson-Bareau 2001.

2 For the fascinating history of the provenance of the album drawings, see Wilson-Bareau 2001, pp. 24–25.

3 These references are to Gassier 1973 and Wilson-Bareau 2001.

4 For Goya's small-scale works, see Wilson-Bareau and Mena Marqués 1994.

5 The suggestion originates with Lafond 1907(b), who reproduces the drawings subsequently acquired by Otto Gerstenberg and now kept at The State Hermitage Museum, St. Petersburg. For a somewhat laundered account of the acquisition by the Russians and a detailed study of this group, see Ilatovskaya 1996, pp. 8–10. The drawings published by Lafond are again reproduced with commentary by Fauqué 1988(b).

6 See Sayre 1971 and cat. no. 45 (*Man on a Swing*) for a discussion of the problem.

7 Tomlinson 1992.

In the entries, the drawings are grouped by theme in this order:

I   Memories of Spain
II   Scenes of Daily Life
III   Social Commentary and Satire
IV   Flights of Imagination

28

Semana Santa en tiempo pasado en España
(Holy Week in a Time Past in Spain)

Album G. 57
1824–28
Black crayon on paper, $7^1/_2 \times 5^3/_4$ (19.1 × 14.6)
National Gallery of Canada, Ottawa, Purchased 1923

PROVENANCE: Javier Goya, 1828; Mariano Goya, 1854; Valentín Carderera and/or Federico de Madrazo, c. 1855–60; John Savile Lumley, 1st Baron Savile of Rufford, 1858–60; by descent to John Savile, 2nd Baron Savile of Rufford, 1896; Colnaghi, London; purchased by the National Gallery of Canada, 1923.

PRINCIPAL REFERENCES: Martin-Méry 1951, no. 11; Stoll 1954, no. 46; London 1963–64(a), no. 201; Popham and Fenwick 1965, p. 211, no. 309; Sayre 1966, p. 87, fig. 12; London 1969, no. 68; Gassier 1973, no. 413; Hofmann 1980, no. 173; Tomlinson 1994, pp. 268, 272, pl. 224; Pérez Sánchez and Sayre 1989, no. 172; Knudsen 2000, p. 81, no. 37; Wilson-Bareau 2001, no. 106.

Religious processions appear with some frequency in Goya's production, as they did in Spanish daily life.[1] Although these processions were enjoyed by the populace, they were regarded with scorn by the enlightened minority, who doubted their piety and suspected their motives. As one Enlightenment critic wrote in 1821, "Certainly in a religion where worship should be all spirit and truth, one cannot explain those trappings and that profusion of finery, those innumerable candles and torches. . . . Instead of a religious act, [the procession is] a wayward insult to God in heaven."[2] Goya's depictions of religious processions share this critique. They always take place in a joyless, menacing atmosphere, which is epitomized by the *Pilgrimage of San Isidro*, one of the Black Paintings. This work is pure invective against the dubious display of piety.

Like the reformers, Goya singled out the Holy Week processions for specific criticism. The most striking aspect of the ritual were the flagellants, who wore tall conical hats known as *corazas*. As they plodded down the dusty streets, they whipped themselves on the back and shoulders, causing rivulets of blood to trickle down their bodies and soak the rough white skirts covering their waists and legs. Ostensibly a dramatic act of penitence, flagellation was dimly viewed by skeptical reformers. As they saw it, the flagellants were rabble who participated in the bloody ritual only to impress female spectators, whom they hoped to seduce. The government agreed and banned flagellation in Holy Week processions on February 20, 1777. Fifteen years later in 1802, the prohibition was decreed for the third time, indicating that the law was not being obeyed.[3]

Fig. 68   *Procession of Flagellants*, c. 1815–19, oil on canvas, $18^1/_8 \times 28^3/_4$ (46.0 × 73.0), The Museum of the Royal Academy of Fine Arts of San Fernando, Madrid

57

Semana S.
En tiempo pasado
en España

28

The drawing in Album G is Goya's third representation of the subject. The first is found in Album B. 80 (1796–97), the second, in a painting of c. 1815–19 (fig. 68). In the drawing of Album G, Goya used compositional elements from both the earlier works. For instance, the pose of the penitent in the middle ground of the drawing in Album G is retrieved from the drawing in Album B. The trumpeter clad in black migrates first to the painting and thence to the version in Album G. Similarly, a banner held above the heads of the crowd appears first in the painting.

Yet for all the common ground shared by these works, the sheet from Album G is more than a collage of motifs appropriated from its predecessors. In the Album G drawing, there is hardly space to breathe. Goya presents the figures in a compact, irregularly shaped mass, broken only by the four *corazas*, creating an illusion of the procession receding into the distance. Rather than framing the composition in straight lines, Goya abruptly stops it in the lower left and, in the triangular space thus created, writes the inscription. This inscription is transparent and opaque at one and the same time. There is no doubt that the first line describes the scene— *Semana Santa*. However, the second part—"in a time past in Spain"—is

mystifying. By casting the action in the "time past," Goya appears to remove the satirical sting. The procession belongs to history and the drawing is an illustration of that history.

But suppose Goya is being ironic. The decrees against flagellant processions had apparently been ineffective, and therefore Goya could be condemning the continuation of the barbarous practice. Beyond this question lies another—why did Goya, now comfortably settled in France, choose to remember this sanguinary Spanish event? Albums G and H contain other flashbacks to Spanish subjects that run a gamut from the bitter to the sweet. Perhaps the answer lies in an exile's nostalgia for his homeland. Or perhaps it lies in the functioning of the brain as we grow old, which causes events remote in time to surface spontaneously from the deep well of memory.

JB

1 This brief account is based on Alcalá Flecha 1988(b), pp. 229–33.
2 Juan Meléndez Valdés, who was portrayed by Goya in 1797 (Barnard Castle, Bowes Museum, County Durham); translation Pérez Sánchez and Sayre 1989, p. 380.
3 See Alcalá Flecha 1988(b), pp. 229–33, for the processions and the critique of the *ilustrados*.

29

Maja

Album H. 22
1824–28
Black crayon on paper, $7^{1}/_{2} \times 5^{3}/_{4}$ (19.2 × 14.7)
Private collection

Signed, lower right: *Goya*

PROVENANCE: Javier Goya, 1828; Mariano Goya, 1854; Valentín Carderera and/or Federico de Madrazo, c. 1855–58; Charles Gasc, Paris and Madrid, 1859; Antonio Santamarina, Buenos Aires, by 1930; his sale, Sotheby's, London, December 13, 1973, lot 46; Colnaghi, London; private collection.

PRINCIPAL REFERENCES: Mayer 1930; Sayre 1971, p. 21; Gassier 1973, no. 439; Wilson-Bareau 2001, no. 111.

Fig. 69   *The Picnic*, 1776, oil on canvas, $107^{1}/_{8} \times 116^{1}/_{8}$ (272 × 295), Museo Nacional del Prado, Madrid

The *maja* was a familiar figure in Madrid during the later eighteenth century and is a recurrent motif of Goya's art.[1] *Majas* often worked as street vendors or fruit sellers, and their brazen manners and reputed availability for sexual encounters made them a conspicuous, colorful presence on the streets and boulevards of the capital. Their costumes, if not their conduct, became fashionable among women of the upper class, including Queen María Luisa herself, who was portrayed by Goya *de maja* in 1799 (Palacio Real, Madrid).

Goya often used the *maja* as the incarnation of female sexuality, notably in Los Caprichos, and fashioned a pose to depict her sensuality and licentiousness. He first deployed this pose in a tapestry cartoon, *The Picnic* (fig. 69), completed by October 30, 1776. In this Spanish version of a *fête galante,* the orange seller assumes a suggestive stance, a hand on her hip and her feet splayed at a right angle.[2] A woman in the same pose and wearing the traditional garb of a *maja* is seen from behind in Album B. 69, where the mise-en-scène, including a dandy and an aged procuress, leaves no doubt about the sexual connotations of the encounter. (A figure in the background of B. 5 also adopts the pose.)

This is one of three drawings in Album H that were reproduced in etchings attributed to Goya (the others are 31 and 58).[3] It has been conjectured that these etchings and possibly the two independent Bordeaux lithographs are the remnants of an abandoned attempt to create a new set of Los Caprichos in response to the suggestion made by Goya's Parisian acquaintance Joaquín María de Ferrer that the first set be

22

reissued.[4] As far as is known, no impressions of these plates were made by Goya; all the extant prints are posthumous.[5]

This bold, impertinent image brims with vitality and sexuality. The *maja* is anchored to the page only by the notional shadows at her feet. Otherwise the figure seems almost to be affixed to the expanse of white paper. The contrast between the lower part of the figure, which is mostly sheathed in a white skirt, and the elaborate, carefully worked jacket and shawl heightens the dramatic effect.

JB

1   For an introduction to the *maja* and her role in Spanish society, see Tomlinson 1989, pp. 33–34, and Gállego 1997, pp. 325–39.

2   For this interpretation, see Tomlinson 1989, pp. 35–36.

3   H. 11 is also associated with an etching known as the *Blind Singer*. Despite a vague similarity of pose, the subject of the drawing is distinctly different from the etching.

4   Sayre 1971. Her thesis that Goya was planning to execute a new series of Los Caprichos is based on a tendentious reading of an ambiguous phrase in Goya's letter to Ferrer, dated December 20, 1825. See cat. no. 45 for a fuller discussion of the question.

5   For the so-called Lumley edition of c. 1859, see Sayre 1971, pp. 37–38, and Harris 1964, pp. 52–59, nos. 30–35. See below, cat. no. 45, for a fuller discussion of the attribution of these plates, in which their authenticity is questioned.

30

*Diligencias nuebas [written over] sillas de moda
(New Stagecoaches [written over] Fashionable Chairs);
o sillas de espaldas (or Shoulder Chairs);
[on the chair] A la Comedia (To the Theater); No. 89*

Album G. 24
1824–28
Black crayon on paper, 7½ × 6 (19.1 × 15.2)
Museum of Fine Arts, Boston, Arthur Tracey Cabot Fund, 53.2376

PROVENANCE: Javier Goya, 1828; Mariano Goya, 1854; Federico de Madrazo, c. 1855–60; private collection, Paris, c. 1934–35; Alfred Strölin, Lausanne; purchased by the Museum of Fine Arts, Boston, 1953.

PRINCIPAL REFERENCES: Gassier 1973, no. 383; Ribemont and Garcia 1998, no. 9.

Fig. 70   *Paseo (Promenade)*, Album G. 26, 1824–28, black crayon on paper, 7½ × 5⅜ (19.2 × 13.8), The State Hermitage Museum, St. Petersburg

A woman seated in a small wooden box just large enough to accommodate one passenger is strapped to the back of a sturdy older man. Facing in opposite directions, this odd couple is about to set off on a journey. He stoops to maintain the box in an upright position with feet planted firmly on the ground and twists his head around to register her directions—"a la Comedia" (to the theater)—which Goya has written on the door of the box along with "No. 89," the vehicle's license number. She looks out the window, smiling and oblivious to his strain. The bearer is dressed in working clothes and a sturdy broad-rimmed hat; the figure on board wears a delicate frilled cap. He is entirely in shadow, while the woman's face and the upper part of the box are in light, emphasizing the disconnection between these temporarily joined figures. (The faint figure of an old woman drinking from a large bowl to the right of the box is a shadow of an earlier drawing.)[1]

Gassier has suggested that the words "a la Comedia" situate the work in Paris, as Goya lived across from the Opéra-Comique (then the Théâtre des Italiens) on the rue Marivaux.[2] The phrase, however, which is written in Spanish, could also refer to the Place de la Comédie in Bordeaux, where the

Grand Théâtre, one of the city's most famous landmarks, stands. Goya lived near the theater during his first year in the city, and his friend Moratín attended the *comedia* every night. All types of conveyances could be hired in the Place de la Comédie. The form of human transport depicted here, which Goya labeled at the bottom of the drawing DILGENCIAS NUEBAS (new stagecoaches) and SILLAS DE MODA (fashionable chairs) to the left of the figure, and O SILLAS DE ESPALDAS (or shoulder chairs) to the right, however, would have been more of an amusement—perhaps connected with a festival or fair—than a common way of getting around, as the sedan chair had been in the previous century.[3]

Goya was evidently intrigued by the shoulder chair, to which he devoted four drawings in Album G, showing the bearer and passenger at different stages of their promenade. In G. 26, *Paseo (Promenade)* (fig. 70), Goya turns the pair in the opposite direction with the stooping man now facing front, his legs spread in the characteristic arch seen in many of his late drawings. The flaps of the box are now down, and the passenger leans out to indicate the direction. As in the present drawing, the artist emphasizes the disparity between the pair through the contrast of light

and shadow, as well as through the differences in their postures and carefully recorded costumes. In the following drawing, *De secreto (The Secret)* (G. 27), a curtain is drawn across the front of the box and the man lumbers forward with his concealed passenger. The final, more loosely sketched drawing in the series, *De todo sirven (They Can Be Used for Anything)* (G. 28), is set in the chair station. Here a porter on his knees staggers up like a beast of burden with his passenger on board, while other laughing women appear to be waiting for their turn in another chair.

In an earlier work, Capricho No. 42 (*Tu que no puedes* [*You Who Cannot*]) (fig. 71), two working-class men strain under the weight of asses riding on their backs. The theme of that work, which has been interpreted as referring to the burden of the leisured class on the poor,[4] may be implicit in this more comical scene drawn from life.

SGG

Fig. 71 *Tu que no puedes (You Who Cannot)*, Capricho No. 42, 1799, etching and aquatint, $8^{1}/_{2} \times 6$ (21.7 × 15.1), The Metropolitan Museum of Art, New York, Gift of M. Knoedler & Co., 1918

Tu que no puedes.

1 Gassier 1973, p. 563.
2 Ibid.
3 Ilatovskaya 1996, p. 29, proposes that shoulder chairs were reintroduced but gives no source for this. Straus 1912, p. 105, notes the decline of the chair in the nineteenth century. On page 107 he writes: "The time, indeed, had come when the sight of a chair was as much a public entertainment as it had been when Buckingham had been borne through the streets 'on men's shoulders.' " See Rèche 1979, p. 30, who notes that in the mid-eighteenth century there was a stand for chairs in the Place St. Project on the Fossés de Chapeaux Rouges. See also Hart 1962, who provides an excellent summary of the subject.
4 Pérez Sánchez and Gállego 1995, p. 57.

A la comedia

N° 89

Mendigos q.ᵉ se lleban solos en Bordeaux
(Beggars Who Get About on Their Own in Bordeaux)

Album G. 29
1824–28
Black crayon on paper, 7¹⁄₂ × 5⁵⁄₈ (19.3 × 14.2)
National Gallery of Art, Washington, D.C., Woodner Collection, 1993

PROVENANCE: Javier Goya, 1828; Mariano Goya, 1854; Federico de Madrazo, c. 1855–60; Jules Boilly, Paris; his sale, Hôtel Drouot, March 19–20, 1869, lot 48 (album), to Leurceau; Hyadès, Bordeaux; private collection, Paris; Alfred Strölin, Lausanne, by 1933; purchased by Ian Woodner, New York, 1987; by descent to Andrea and Dian Woodner, New York, 1990; gift to the National Gallery of Art, 1993.

PRINCIPAL REFERENCES: Mayer 1933, p. 382, 384; Mayer 1934–35, p. 21; Gassier 1973, no. 387; Pérez Sánchez and Sayre 1989, no. 167; Tomlinson 1994, p. 268; Grasselli 1995–96, no. 99; Wilson-Bareau 2001, no. 98.

This work belongs to a group of drawings depicting people moving through the streets in a variety of improvised conveyances—an old woman in a cart pulled by a dog in harness (fig. 72), an old person in a kind of wheelbarrow with mocking figures in the background (G. 25), and, as seen here, a beggar making his way in a wheelchair. As an aged expatriate, deaf, and unable to speak the language of his host country, Goya must have identified with these marginal figures hampered by age, disability, or poverty.

Goya's inscription situates this legless old beggar in his self-propelled wheelchair in Bordeaux and indicates his admiration for his ability to get around on his own. The man sits on a flat platform with a wooden lattice back. Two large spoked wheels are attached to either side of the platform, which is low to the ground, allowing the occupant to lift himself on and off with his arms; a small wheel at the back serves as a rudder. The beggar holds a strap attached to the large wheels, with which he can turn the wheels and propel himself forward, his bag hooked on to the backrest. As Gassier notes, the vehicle would have seemed almost luxurious to Goya, who was used to seeing beggars in Madrid dragging themselves around on crutches or a flat platform on wheels.[1]

The compact pyramidal composition of this powerful image emphasizes the oneness of the man and his car: the figure's torso, arms, and the stumps of his legs—the ends of which are positioned at the center of one of the large wheels—are totally enclosed within its structure. Only the beggar's head at the apex of the pyramid rises above the contraption that restores much of his lost mobility. Goya has taken a viewpoint from slightly above, indicating the man's proximity to the pavement—represented with a few lines of shading under the vehicle—which he shares with pedestrians, though at a lower level.

Most of the man and mechanism are in shadow and are positioned in the center of the sheet of paper. A streak of light enters from the right, however, and cuts a swath across the bridge of the beggar's nose and gaunt cheeks, separating the dark upper portion of his face with his alert eyes and the lower section with his slack mouth, and falls on the precisely drawn wheels.

The truncated body of the beggar—perhaps a war veteran—brings to mind some of Goya's earlier representations of fragmented bodies from his series of etchings the Disasters of War. Here, however, he expresses not outrage but deep sympathy for his subject. One of Bordeaux's outcasts who formed part of the city's colorful spectacle of life, the beggar is lifted out and transformed by Goya to serve as a symbol of resilience, adaptability, and endurance.

SGG

Fig. 72 *Yo lo he visto en Paris (I Saw It in Paris)*, Album G. 31, 1824–28, black crayon on paper, 7.57 × 5.78 (19.4 × 14.8), private collection

1 Gassier 1973, p. 564. See also Manuela Mena Marqués's entry in Pérez Sánchez and Sayre 1989, pp. 372–73.

Mendigos q.e se llevan solos en
Bordeaux

32

Locos patines (Crazy Skates)

Album G. 32
1824–28
Black crayon on paper, $7^{1}/_{2} \times 6$ (19.1 × 15.2)
Museum of Fine Arts, Boston, Arthur Tracey Cabot Fund, 53.2377

Signed, lower left: *Goya*

PROVENANCE: Javier Goya, 1828; Mariano Goya, 1854; Federico Madrazo, c. 1855–60; Hyadès, Bordeaux; Jules Boilly, Paris; his sale, Hôtel Drouot, March 19–20, 1869, lot 48 (album), to Leurceau; private collection, Paris; Alfred Strölin, Lausanne, by 1933; purchased by the Museum of Fine Arts, Boston, 1953.

PRINCIPAL REFERENCES: Mayer 1933, pp. 379, 380; London 1963–64(a), no. 194; Gassier 1973, no. 390; Stuffmann 1981, no. L. 79; Pérez Sánchez and Sayre 1989, pp. 374–75; Wilson–Bareau and Mena Marqués 1994, pp. 40–41; Ribemont and Garcia 1998, no. 12; Wilson-Bareau 2001, no. 100.

Among the sights that intrigued Goya in Bordeaux were people engaged in novel forms of recreation and ways of moving around the city. In *Mendigos q.ᵉ se lleban solos en Bordeaux* (cat. no. 31), Goya depicted a wheelchair-bound beggar with precision and sympathy. In this drawing of a man trying to master the activity of roller-skating, however, all restraint breaks loose, and the figure, with all four limbs extended and mouth open in a shriek, fills up much of the sheet. Diagonals and angles predominate, and Goya's handling of the lithographic crayon in long, free sweeping strokes with forceful accents under the skater's raised leg and across his back underlines the dynamic character of the image.

This drawing is about balance—physical and artistic. From the figure's rounded buttocks at the center of the sheet, all other parts of the body—the right leg and foot on roller-skates touching the ground, the rising left leg, the backward-leaning torso and head, with flying hair, diagonal shoulders, and outflung arms—rotate in a kind of pinwheel. Goya captures the skater at the peak of the cycle, when he is on his way down to the pavement. The gesture of outstretched arms that appears so frequently in Goya's art as an expression of supplication or despair, as seen, for example, in *Fuego (Fire)* (Album G. 22) or *Gimiendo y llorando* (cat. no. 43) is here used for comic effect.

Behind the roller-skater, a more lightly sketched figure on a *celeripede*, an early form of bicycle invented in Paris in 1816, streaks by in the opposite direction. The combination of these activities suggests the setting of a park or amusement area.[1] During Goya's years in Bordeaux, a recreational park known as Vincennes in the Chemin d'Ares, opposite the Chartreuse cemetery, offered roller-skating and cycling races, as well as other activities.[2] It may have been there that Goya

Fig. 73 *The Skaters*, 1824–25, pen and ink on laid paper, $5 \times 7^{3}/_{8}$ (12.8 × 18.6), The State Hermitage Museum, St. Petersburg

encountered the subject of "crazy" skates.

Goya also showed an interest in ice skating, another form of recreation that would have been somewhat unusual for a Spaniard. A pen and ink drawing by Goya in the Gerstenberg collection of the Hermitage in St. Petersburg, thought to have been done in Bordeaux in the winter of 1824–25, represents a group of skaters (fig. 73).[3] Goya's close friend Leandro Fernández de Moratín noted that that particular winter was unusually harsh, and Goya went to see people skating on the frozen marshes near the Garonne.[4] Goya had also devoted a sepia drawing to the subject of ice skating in Album F (no. 30). In both of these group scenes, he focused on the overall pattern made up of the gestures and shapes of the skaters distributed over the surface of the paper. The roller-skater, however, provided the opportunity to freeze-frame a single male figure in a beautifully rendered composition.

As has been frequently pointed out, *Locos patines* does not refer to madness in the sense of mental illness or an existential state of angst, as in the numerous drawings designated "locos" that follow this one in Album G.[5] Here it is a state of exuberance matched by the artist's energy and risk-taking. It is through such figures as the hapless roller-skater, extracted from the everyday life of the city and fixed to paper with his velvety lithographic crayon, that Goya expressed his vital connection to his new home.

SGG

1   Camón Aznar 1980–82, p. 175, suggests a "lugar de deportes."

2   Fauqué and Villanueva Etcheverría 1982, pp. 645–46. The authors cite an announcement advertising these two activities in the *Mémorial* newspaper of November 27, 1824. They also note that Vincennes featured a funfair with a rollercoaster and an open-air café, and that after 1826 nighttime dances were held there.

3   Ilatovskaya 1996, pp. 92–93.

4   Ibid., p. 93.

5   Gassier 1973, p. 565; Pérez Sánchez and Sayre 1989, p. 375.

33

Feria en Bordeaux (Fair in Bordeaux) (The Female Giant)

Album H. 39
c. 1826
Black crayon on paper, $7\frac{5}{8} \times 5\frac{7}{8}$ (19.3 × 15.0)
The Pierpont Morgan Library, New York, Gift of Gertrude Weyhe Dennis in honor
of Felice Stampfle on the occasion of the 75th anniversary of the Morgan Library and
the 50th anniversary of the Association of Fellows, 1999

Signed, lower left: *Goya*

PROVENANCE: Javier Goya, 1828; Mariano Goya, 1854; Erhard Weyhe, New York; by descent to Gertrude
Weyhe Dennis, New York; gift to The Pierpont Morgan Library, 1999.

PRINCIPAL REFERENCES: Pérez Sánchez and Sayre 1989, no. 178; Wilson-Bareau 2001, no. 113.

Fig. 74 Gustave de Galard (1779–1841), *La Foire*, 1832, watercolor with gouache heightening, $7 \times 9\frac{7}{8}$ (17.7 × 25.2), Archives municipales de Bordeaux, © DEC, Bordeaux

At the right, a young woman stands in profile bathed in light, her head turning toward the spectator and eyes looking off into the distance with a dignified though detached expression. Without the faceless crowd to the left, the figure would look normal: the tallest of the men and goggle-eyed children that press in on her reach no higher than her bust. The giantess's upper body and head soar above them, extending to the upper limit of the sheet of paper. Only the slightly contorted position of her left hand, larger than the heads of any of the spectators, betrays her emotion at being on display. (A pentimento shows that the right arm was once lifted over the head of the crowd.) Her "performance" requires no particular skill or even a costume—her mere existence qualifies and condemns her to the role of fairground "freak."

Goya would have seen the subject of this work at one of the major fairs featuring acrobats, menageries, and anomalies that came to Bordeaux twice yearly in October and March and set up in the Place de la Bourse (formerly the Place Royale) bordering the quai.[1] In a letter of November 1824 to the Duchess of San Fernando in Paris, Goya described a drawing (now lost) he had made of three dwarfs, whom he had seen at the fair shortly after settling in Bordeaux.[2] He continued to attend the fairs throughout his stay, often in the company of Leocadia and Rosario, or with the young artist Antonio de Brugada.[3] Along with the present drawing, there are several others in Album H that depict spectacles known to have been on view in the October 1826 fair: a man hoisting a four-yard serpent above his head, a crocodile handler, and an acrobat who imitates the telegraph with his legs.[4] A drawing of an emaciated man known as the

Fig. 75 *Qué sacrificio! (What a Sacrifice!)*,
Capricho No. 14, 1799, etching and
aquatint, $7\frac{7}{8} \times 6$ (20.1 × 15.1), The
Metropolitan Museum of Art, New York,
Gift of M. Knoedler & Co., 1918

"Living Skeleton" was signed by Goya
and dated October 1826.[5] The similar
theme of *The Female Giant*, which has
recently come to light, has placed this
drawing with these others of fairground
subjects carried out in October 1826.[6]

The lively spectacle of the fair drew
the attention of local Bordelais artists as
well as Goya. In a gouache entitled *La
Foire* of 1832 (fig. 74), Gustave de
Galard depicts the colorful booths and
swarming crowds against the backdrop
of a port.[7] In the center, a booth with a
stage well above the spectators' heads
supports a large banner that advertises
its exhibit: LA GRANDE GÉANTE. Goya's
approach, however, is entirely different.
He zeros in on the humanity of the
figure to the exclusion of all else and
emphasizes her connection—but for her
size—with ordinary people. The giant
stands on the same ground as her
viewers, and there is no suggestion of
the ambience of a fun fair. The scene
could as easily take place on the street.
Goya's careful delineation of his subject's
attire also emphasizes similarity rather
than difference. She wears an outsized
version of the well-dressed woman's garb
of the day—a dress with puffed sleeves
at the shoulder, a fichu (scarf) with a
fringed edge that crosses over her bosom
and falls below her waist, a full skirt
with a deep frilled hem, and an
overskirt or an apron tied back in a bow
behind her waist. With a variety of light
strokes of the lithographic crayon, and
darker, sharp accent lines, Goya suggests
the sheen of the cloth and folds of
fabric. (Similar costumes are worn by
spectators in Galard's fair scene.)

The giant's clothing, however, cannot
shield her from the prurience of the

male spectators' and curious children's
gazes, which fall between her genitalia
and bust. They seem to be looking
through her clothing, and the
expressions on some of the faces attest
to what they are "seeing." The
voyeurism of this drawing—a
fundamental theme in Goya's art—
brings to mind another fair scene of a
peepshow (Album G. 2, *Mirar lo q̃ no
ven, They Are Looking at What They
Cannot See*). Here, however, the mood
is more melancholic than comic. The
crude behavior of the crowd sets off the
forbearance of the giant, whom Goya
represents sympathetically as larger than
life rather than an anomaly, a female
variation on the theme of Ecce Homo.
The drawing brings to mind as well one
of the most famous of his Caprichos,
Qué Sacrificio! (What a Sacrifice!) (fig.
75), in which a beautiful young woman
is being sold off in marriage to a rich
old hunchback, who scrutinizes her
with a lascivious expression, while
members of her duplicitous family
look on with pity and greed. The
compositions of the two works are
similar, with the woman standing,
detached and averting her gaze, to the
right and a group of figures pressing
in on her on the left; in the print,
however, it is the leering, deformed
voyeur who is the freak. The towering
giant of Album H also recalls Goya's
representation of Leocadia in his Black
Paintings, where she appears large in
scale and dominating her environment.[8]

In contrast to the delicately shaded
volumetric form of the heroine, the
motley, insignificant crowd is rendered
more two-dimensionally and is cast in
shadow. One man in top hat and tails,

feria en
Bordeaux

39

depicted in profile and at a respectful distance from the giant, however, stands out, perhaps a surrogate for the viewer or the artist himself.

SGG

1   Fauqué and Villanueva Etcheverría 1982, p. 602, note that Charles IX started the tradition of the two two-week-long fairs held in Bordeaux each year in recognition of the loyalty of the people, and that the tradition lasted into Goya's time. In 1853 the fairs were moved to the Place des Quinconces.
2   Cited in Fauqué and Villanueva Etcheverría 1982, p. 603.
3   See Courteault 1908, p. 4, and Wilson-Bareau 2001, p. 203.
4   Album H. 40, 41, and 54.
5   Album H. 45. Fauqué and Villanueva Etcheverría 1982, pp. 603–4, note that the living skeleton, Claude Ambroise Seurat, is known to have been on view in Bordeaux at the time from a notice in *L'Indicateur* of October 17, 1826. See also Wilson-Bareau 2001, p. 203.
6   Wilson-Bareau 2001, p. 203. For a different opinion, see Ilatovskaya, 1996, pp. 71–72.
7   The scene may or may not be set in Bordeaux; the masts in the background suggest Bordeaux's port.
8   GW no. 1622. This connection with the painting of Leocadia was made by Joanna Sheers.

34

*Ni por esas; Que tirania [faintly written]
(Not Even with Those; What Tyranny)*

Album G. 8
1824–28
Black crayon on paper, $7^1/_2 \times 5^7/_8$ (19.0 × 15.0)
Museo Nacional del Prado, Madrid

PROVENANCE: Javier Goya, 1828; Mariano Goya, 1854; Federico de Madrazo and/or Román Garreta y Huerta, c. 1855–60; purchased by the Museo de la Trinidad, 1866; Museo Nacional del Prado, Madrid, 1872.

PRINCIPAL REFERENCES: Gassier 1973, no. 371; Pérez Sanchez and Sayre 1989, no. 166.

Ni por esas exemplifies the deliberate ambiguity encountered in many of the album drawings. The previous interpretations are strangely at odds with one another and with the image and fail to recognize how Goya could open paths that lead to no final destination. In 1973 Pierre Gassier posited that Goya had given a comic "twist" to the "obvious sex symbols of the key and padlock." He correctly recognized that the man is dressed in the costume of an *alguacil*, or constable, and assumed that he was seeking to undo the padlocks worn by the young woman to "attain the object of his desire. Shining with a bright light that may betoken purity, the young woman bends her head sadly toward him and clasps her hands to indicate that he is wasting his time."[1]

In 1989 Michael Armstrong Roche, writing the relevant entry in the catalogue *Goya and the Spirit of Enlightenment,* interpreted the drawing as a political statement.[2] He posited that the female was a personification of the Liberal constitution of 1812 and that the *alguacil* stood for established authority. Citing historical sources, Roche also characterized the *alguacil* as the antithesis of the laws he was meant to enforce. Therefore, he functioned as a useful parallel to Ferdinand VII, who usurped the constitution on his return

to power in 1823. However, this assault on the constitution depicted in Goya's drawing is seen to fail. "The Constitution's moral ruin was impossible, her chastity . . . was unassailable." If Gassier's reading is at once superficial and overly imaginative—the bright, shining light surrounding the female figure cannot be detected—then Roche's is entirely arbitrary and reads into the image a political dimension predetermined by the theme of the exhibition.

To some extent, Goya has left clues to the mystery of the meaning. The most helpful is the original title, which hovers just above the second and is still faintly visible. It reads, *Qué tiranía,* or *What Tyranny.* These words can be related to the constable, a symbol of authority who in Goya's world stands for the perversion of authority. Using the concept of a "personal iconography" to help in understanding the sense of certain subjects, we find a "mini-series" of constable scenes in Album F, nos. 81, 82, and 84. In the first two, the constable is presented as a force for both good and evil, beating a woman with his stick in F. 81, breaking up a fight between two men in F. 82. In F. 86, however, Goya delivers his verdict (fig. 76). This drawing, as the inscription explains, depicts the "death of Constable Lampiños, because he

Fig. 76 *Muerte del Alguacil Lampiños (Death of Constable Lampiños)*, Album F. 86, c. 1812–20, sepia wash on paper, 8¹⁄₈ × 5³⁄₄ (20.5 × 14.5), The Metropolitan Museum of Art, New York, Harris Brisbane Dick Fund, 1935

persecuted students and women of fortune [prostitutes], the latter of whom have given him an enema of quicklime."

If the constable is the symbol of a tyrant, as suggested by the inscription, his action in the drawing of Album G should not be understood as attempting to open the locks that protect the woman but closing them to preserve her chastity. This hypothesis offers an explanation for the twisted but affectionate expression on the constable's unattractive face and the forlorn look of the woman. The constable is locking up his treasure, and she is very unhappy with her fate.

Having thus achieved a measure of clarity for the subject, Goya then proceeded to muddy the waters, nearly effacing the words, *Qué tiranía* and substituting *Ni por esas*. This phrase is difficult to translate and interpret. Gassier's translation renders it as "Nothing doing," which seems excessively free and determined by his interpretation of the image. Roche translates the words as "Not even with those," which is correct as far as it goes but still mystifying. Much depends on the referent of *esas,* here written in its feminine form and thus perhaps relating to the keys, *las llaves,* which is the plural of the feminine noun *la llave.* If this analysis is correct, the inscription might be reformulated as follows: "Not even with these [keys] can the woman's chastity be secured." Is Goya making a sour observation on the fidelity of women or a trenchant comment on man's lust and jealousy (or both)?

Goya's representation of the scene is overtly theatrical. The figures appear to be standing on a low stage, perhaps the entrance to a house, and their expressions and poses create an atmosphere of melodrama. The constable genuflects slightly and gazes at the face of the beautiful young woman whom he has imprisoned in that bizarre prophylactic outfit. She cradles her arms and casts the defeated, mournful glance of a victim at the animated features of her husband.

This drawing is one of many that seem unresolved as far as interpretation is concerned. In this instance, Goya purposefully shifted the meaning from the obvious to the ambiguous, where it remains to this day.

JB

1   Gassier 1973, pp. 560–61.
2   Pérez Sánchez and Sayre 1989, pp. 370–71, no. 166.

Ni por esas

175

35

Mal marido (Bad Husband)

Album G. 13
1824–28
Black crayon on paper, 7¼ × 5¼ (18.5 × 13.5)
Museo Nacional del Prado, Madrid

PROVENANCE: Javier Goya, 1828; Mariano Goya, 1854; Federico de Madrazo and/or Román Garreta y Huerta, c. 1855–60; purchased by the Museo de la Trinidad, 1866; Museo Nacional del Prado, Madrid, 1872.
PRINCIPAL REFERENCES: Gassier 1973, no. 374; Bruxelles 1985, no. 20.

Relationships between men and women are a major theme of Goya's work, and one of his favorite subjects is the unequal marriage. He paid close attention to arranged marriages, which were condemned by social reformers but difficult to suppress. The act of forcing young women into unsuitable marriages of convenience, which were intended to improve the wealth and social status of her family, was targeted for satire by Goya's friend Moratín, among others. However, women were not purely victims of the practice. In the upper classes, marriage even to an ancient ugly suitor was one of the few ways to escape the stifling restrictions imposed on young single women. Once free of her parents' strict control, the female partner of the unequal match could seek solace and pleasure in the arms of a lover.

Goya also observed relations among the working classes, in which marital discord often led to violent conclusions. This "battle of the sexes" is the focal point of four expressive album drawings, which when rearranged from a chronological to a narrative order become a pungent story of spousal abuse and female revenge. In E. 24 (fig. 77), a man already inebriated gulps wine from a wineskin as his partner (wife?) tries vainly to stop him. The menacing caption explains the look of fright on her face—*Después lo beras* (You'll See Later)—and implies that some sort of assault will soon be visited on her. That assault takes place in Album F. 18 (fig. 78), in which a fierce midnight clash occurs in the conjugal bed. The ferocity of this hair-pulling mêlée is conveyed by the slashing movement of the brush. A tear in the paper above the figures has been patched by a crude drawing of an obscene gesture, Goya's explicit but enigmatic commentary on the action.

In both these drawings, the culprit is the man, who uses his physical strength to overpower and impose his will on the woman. He is the *mal marido*, epitomized in Album G. 13, which is an expressive hieroglyph of an abusive

Fig. 77 *Después lo beras (You'll See Later)*, Album E. 24, c. 1815–20, indian ink wash on paper, 10½ × 7⅜ (26.7 × 18.7), The Metropolitan Museum of Art, New York, Harris Brisbane Dick Fund, 1935 (35.103.18)

Mal Marido   177

Fig. 78 (*above left*) *Conjugal Row*, Album F. 18, c. 1812–20, sepia wash on paper, 8¹⁄₈ × 5³⁄₄ (20.8 × 14.6), Museo Nacional del Prado, Madrid

Fig. 79 (*above right*) *Woman Murdering a Sleeping Man*, Album F. 87, c. 1812–20, sepia wash on paper, 8³⁄₈ × 5⁵⁄₈ (20.5 × 14.3), The Metropolitan Museum of Art, New York, Harris Brisbane Dick Fund, 1935

marriage. As shown here, the wife is converted into an oppressed beast of burden who must bear the weight of her malevolent husband and suffer the sting of the whip he brandishes as the instrument of domination.

It is in Album F. 87 (fig. 79) that a woman strikes back with the only means at her disposal—furtive, reciprocal violence. The man, presumably her husband and a

woodcutter by trade, is taking a siesta after his midday meal. The wife has seized his ax and is poised to separate his head from his trunk, making him resemble the logs that lay on the ground beside him. Her haunted expression reveals the depth of her suffering and desperation as she prepares to strike back and end her misery.

JB

36

Enredos de sus vidas (Entanglements of Their Lives)

Album G. 46
1824–28
Black crayon on paper, $7^{1}/_{2} \times 6$ (19.0 × 15.2)
National Gallery of Canada, Ottawa, Purchased 1923

PROVENANCE: Javier Goya, 1828; Mariano Goya, 1854; Valentín Carderera and/or Federico de Madrazo, c. 1855–60; John Savile Lumley, 1st Baron Savile of Rufford, 1858–60; by descent to John Savile, 2nd Baron Savile of Rufford, 1896; Colnaghi, London; purchased by the National Gallery of Canada, 1923.

PRINCIPAL REFERENCES: Gassier 1973, no. 404; Pérez Sánchez and Sayre 1989, no. 171.

Amorous relations between women held a certain fascination for Goya. One of his most imaginative and erotic representations of the subject is a chalk and wash drawing of c. 1797–98 entitled *La Confianza (Trust)* (fig. 80). In B. 113, Goya depicts a caress between two fully dressed women, whose facial expressions subtly combine affection and desire. Another sheet, Album E. h, depicts two women in a loving embrace. The positions of hands and arms and the expression of pleasure on the face of one are unambiguous.

Enredos de sus vidas is more difficult to interpret, although its lesbian content

has been suggested more than once. Certainly the poses reinforce this interpretation, as does the verb *enredar*, which is defined in the *Diccionario de Autoridades* (1726–39) as follows:

> By analogy it means to link, bind and to involve someone, making him [her] incur an obligation and participate in an endeavor from which he can only free himself [herself] with difficulty: as tends to happen to those cohabiting illicitly.[1]

If the poses of the figures and the anticipatory facial expression of the woman on the left are the preface to an impending carnal relationship, the jumble of shapes surrounding the pair, arranged in a circular wreathlike format, is puzzling. When they can be identified, these shapes read as the heads of humans and animals. Some appear to be embryonic, about to assume a recognizable shape, although still incompletely formed. Others can be named, if tentatively. Moving clockwise from the top, one sees what could be the head of a monkey or ape, beneath which is a tangle of lines amid dark shadows. Just at the right shoulder of the woman in the foreground is a pair of disembodied butterfly wings and, below them, what might be a bat and a batwing. More indeterminate shapes follow until we reach a grotesque head immediately at the feet of the

Fig. 80 *La Confianza (Trust)*, c. 1797–98, chalk and wash on paper, $7^{3}/_{4} \times 5^{1}/_{8}$ (19.7 × 13.1), Museo Nacional del Prado, Madrid

foreground figure. Beneath this are three bulbous headlike shapes, which are on the point of materializing. Moving up the left side, there are more emergent heads, ending with another simian head and the head of a dog. Wedged between the two females is another motif, which has been identified as the head of a pig.

The problem of interpreting this strange menagerie cannot be solved definitively. It has been suggested that the monkey and pig, if pig it is, are traditional symbols of lust, and that the dog was regarded in medieval iconography as a symbol of vice and sin. Following this train of thought, the subject has been identified as a criticism of the "sexual excesses" of this lesbian relationship.[2] (The proponent of this theory, by the way, is female.) However, it could just as reasonably be read as the emergence and triumph of same-sex love over the forces of darkness.

Goya has cleverly concealed his hand, as he is wont to do. He has left only a tiny clue. As has been noted, the caption originally read: *Enrredo de su vida*, employing the singular, or *Entanglement of Her Life*. Then he added the letter "s" to the last two words, using a sharper writing instrument.[3] The final version thus reads, "Entanglements of their lives." Mutual consent seems to replace seduction. Nevertheless, "entanglement" implies that the relationship will not be an easy one.

JB

1   Cited in Lorenzo de Marqués 1989, p. 379, note 4.
2   Lorenzo de Marqués 1989, pp. 378–79.
3   The observation is made by Gassier 1973, p. 568.

46

Enrredos de sus vidas

37

Woman with Two Children

Album H. 43
1824–28
Black crayon on paper, $7^{1}/_{2} \times 5^{3}/_{4}$ (19.1 × 14.6)
The Hispanic Society of America, New York

PROVENANCE: Javier Goya, 1828; Mariano Goya, 1854; Federico de Madrazo, c. 1855–60; Raimundo de Madrazo y Garreta; Archer M. Huntington, New York, 1913; The Hispanic Society of America, New York.
PRINCIPAL REFERENCES: Trapier 1963; Gassier 1973, no. 458; Mayor 1974, no. 66; Hofmann 2003, pp. 292–94.

Fig. 81 Jean-Baptiste Greuze (1725–1805), *Maternal Cares (Les Soins maternels)*, c. 1760, brush and gray ink wash over graphite on paper, $16^{3}/_{8} \times 12^{3}/_{8}$ (41.5 × 31.5), Courtesy Galerie Eric Coatalem, Paris

This moving drawing expresses tender emotions of a kind rarely seen in the pell-mell world of Goya's albums. Drawn with impressive economy, the sheet depicts the well-rounded form of a young woman in a robelike dress, wearing a loose-fitting turban on her head. She leans against a soft cushion. In her arms she holds a sleeping or resting small child, clasping him/her against her body. Alongside sits a second small child, who is bundled in a loose-fitting garment with short sleeves. This child bends backward, tilting its head to catch the radiant, benevolent smile of the motherly young woman. (The child's feet once poked out from under the clothing but were partially effaced by the artist.)

Goya's depiction of the soft protective realm of maternal love seems to pose no difficulties of interpretation. Could there be a more natural emotion? However, H. 43 can be inserted into a story of the revolutionary changes in the concept of motherly love advocated by the philosophes in the later years of the eighteenth century.[1] As the nuclear family was coming into being, the roles of men, women, and children were correspondingly altered. One aspect relevant to H. 43 is what has been called maternal "presence and devotion," described by the French historian Elisabeth Badinter in words that seem applicable to the drawing:

The new mother . . . spent much more time with her child than her mother had spent with her. It was indeed the time factor that most clearly marked the distance between these two generations of women. The older generation scarcely noticed their offspring and devoted the bulk of their time to themselves. The new generation lived constantly at their children's side. The child . . . played at his mother's skirt, ate his meals by her side and had a place reserved for him in his parents' parlor. . . . Bonds formed that made the separation of former years difficult if not impossible.[2]

These ideals are represented in a drawing by Jean-Baptiste Greuze of c. 1760 that was subsequently engraved by Jacques-Fermin Beauvarlet or his first wife, Cathérine-Jeanne-Françoise Deschamps. The title of the work is *Maternal Cares (Les Soins maternels)* (fig. 81).[3] Whether or not known to Goya, the image incarnates the same enlightened ideals.

Goya's awareness of the new criteria of motherhood also may be glimpsed in two earlier drawings. In D. b (c. 1819; Musée du Louvre) a fierce, witchlike creature seizes a naked baby as if ready to tear it apart. As the title says, she is a *mala muger*, a bad woman, although it is not entirely clear that the woman is a human being and not a witch. Given

the use of *muger* instead of *bruja* (witch), it is conceivable that the drawing is a condemnation of bad mothering. A drawing from Album C, no. 9 (c. 1808–14) once again shows a nurturing mother, comparable to the woman in H. 43. However, the title is perplexing—*Buena muger parece (She Seems Like a Good Woman)*—and possibly admits a ray of doubt into this scene of motherly love.[4] It is probably wise to take the composition at face value and to interpret the inscription as a reflection of Goya's veiled bemusement at the new criteria of motherhood. If this is the case, the sense of the inscription would be, "It now seems that this is a good woman."

JB

1   For the full story of the profound and complex changes in family life and motherhood proposed by the philosophes, see Badinter 1981, pp. 115–201.
2   Ibid., pp. 177–78.
3   We are grateful to Edgar Munhall for information about this drawing and print.
4   See the interpretation by Wilson-Bareau 2001, p. 179, no. 39.

38

Old Woman with Mirror

Album H. 33
1824–28
Black crayon on paper, $7^1/_2 \times 5^7/_8$ (19.1 × 14.8)
Museo Nacional del Prado, Madrid

Signed, lower left: *Goya*

PROVENANCE: Javier Goya, 1828; Mariano Goya, 1854; Federico de Madrazo and/or Román Garreta y Huerta, c. 1855–60; purchased by the Museo de la Trinidad, 1866; Museo Nacional del Prado, Madrid, 1872.

PRINCIPAL REFERENCES: Gassier 1973, no. 449.

Fig. 82 *Hasta la muerte (Until Death)*, Capricho No. 55, 1799, etching and aquatint, $8^5/_8 \times 6$ (21.8 × 15.2), The Metropolitan Museum of Art, New York, Gift of M. Knoedler & Co., 1918

This satirical drawing is in the spirit of Los Caprichos (1799), which in fact provides a precedent for this subject. In No. 55, entitled *Hasta la muerte (Until Death)*, Goya depicts a decrepit old woman seated at her dressing table, preening before a mirror and trying on a new hat (fig. 82). She refuses to acknowledge the ravages of time (painfully apparent to the three onlookers, who can barely suppress their amusement) and is determined to fight to the end. As Nigel Glendinning has noted, the title of the print mockingly echoes a phrase usually uttered to express valor or loyalty, as on a battlefield.[1]

Goya revived the concept in a painting of c. 1810–12, known as *Time* or the *Old Women* (Palais des Beaux-Arts, Lille). The mortal blow predicted in *Hasta la muerte* is about to be delivered by Father Time, armed with a broom that will sweep the protagonists away. The two old women, with their shrunken grotesque features (one appears to have an advanced case of syphilis), are oblivious to the threat. The woman in white clasps what is thought to be a portrait miniature, showing her as she looked in her prime, while the other holds a tablet inscribed with words often used to initiate a session of gossip—QUÉ TAL?—What's up? The answer is arriving from an unexpected quarter.

The drawing in Album H plays with the same concepts of physical decay and vain self-absorption. Indeed, it may intensify the latter because the old woman requires a magnifying glass to study her countenance in the mirror. She clutches it with both hands and holds it to her left eye; the mirror clearly reflects the frame of the glass. The drawing represents vanity taken to the extreme. The glass is used to compensate for failing eyesight, and without its use the woman cannot reassure herself that her appearance has not changed.

The compact, huddled pose, also used in Album E. 8 (private collection) to represent an old woman, is emphasized by bold reinforced strokes that model the folds of the shawl. Her clasped hands are defined by a few strokes, which suggest the effort required by the thick fingers to lay hold of the small magnifying glass. Equally effective is the way that Goya captures a look of intense concentration on her face. With the same light touch, he sketches in the dressing table, with its jars of ointments and unguents and, in the background, the indefinite form of a pitcher and a piece of furniture.

JB

1 Glendinning 1996, p. 23.

39

Man Killing Monk

Album H. 34
1824–28
Black crayon on paper, $7^{1}/_{2} \times 6$ (19.1 × 15.3)
Museo Nacional del Prado, Madrid

Signed, lower left: *Goya*

PROVENANCE: Javier Goya, 1828; Mariano Goya, 1854; Federico de Madrazo and/or Román Garreta y Huerta, c. 1855–60; purchased by the Museo de la Trinidad, 1866; Museo Nacional del Prado, Madrid, 1872.

PRINCIPAL REFERENCES: Gassier 1973, no. 450; Lafuente Ferrari 1980, no. 95; Bruxelles 1985, no. 7.

The Liberal censure of the monastic establishment in eighteenth-century Spain was fierce and unremitting.[1] And no wonder, because the orders harbored a large number of unproductive monks, friars, and nuns. The census of 1787 recorded 78,113 religious of both sexes (52,300 men and 25,813 women), who lived in 2,067 monasteries and convents belonging to forty different orders.[2] They were omnipresent, and thus it was easy to see that they contributed little to the common good. In fact, 84 percent were mendicants, who begged for a living and could barely sustain themselves without charitable donations from people in the street. The problem was aggravated by the lax rules governing monastic life, particularly the rule that permitted entrance to the orders at an early age. For those without talent, ambition, or wealth, profession in an order looked like an easy way to solve the material problems of life.

Goya agreed with the Liberals and had a dislike of monks and nuns, especially the former, that bordered on loathing, and he never tired of mocking them. His opinion first emerges in several plates of Los Caprichos. (See, for example, plate 13, *Están calientes (They Are Hot)*, and the evolution of the image from the semipornographic picture in Album B to the etching.)[3] Goya treads cautiously in Los Caprichos, which was intended for publication. In the privacy of Album C, however, he saw no need to compromise. There are about a dozen sheets in Album C (c. 1808–14) that take deadly aim at monks in particular, casting them in the role of ignorant, gluttonous, lecherous parasites. Goya's convictions are epitomized in Album C. 120 (fig. 83), which shows an overstuffed friar sitting on the back of a downtrodden laborer who is struggling to break the ground with a hoe.

Although Goya was a sworn enemy of the regular clergy (those belonging to monastic orders), it is not until Album H. 34 that he decided to "kill off" one

Fig. 83   *No sabras lo que llebas aquestas? (Will You Ever Know What You're Carrying on Your Back?)*, Album C. 120, c. 1808–14, india ink and sepia wash on paper, $7^{7}/_{8} \times 5^{5}/_{8}$ (20 × 14.2), Museo Nacional del Prado, Madrid

39

difficult to interpret. There is no doubt that a violent act is taking place. The recumbent figure of a religious, wearing a simple hooded habit and sandals, is probably a man and is probably dead or about to die. But why he is being attacked and with what kind of weapon and, indeed, by whom is hard to say. The killer wields a weapon something like an awl that he seems to be driving, with great difficulty, into the skull of the friar. His face wears a look of fierce determination as he marshals every bit of his strength to drive the weapon home. After decades of mocking the religious, it seems that Goya could take no more.

Yet three pages later, in drawing 37, he seems to be having second thoughts. A friar writes or draws with a compass on a blank piece of paper—his mouth is open as if trying to sound a word before writing it. This act could be interpreted as the first step toward literacy and thence to knowledge, which was perhaps a better way to cure the abuses of monastic life than the drastic means seen in H. 34, unless of course Goya is again being ironic.

JB

1   See Alcalá Flecha 1988(c), pp. 36–100, for a discussion of the Liberal critique of the monastic establishment.
2   Ibid., p. 36.
3   See Wolf 1994 for a revealing discussion of the evolution of this composition.

40

Comer mucho (To Eat a Lot)

Album G. b
1824–28
Black crayon on paper, $7^1/_2 \times 5^1/_8$ (19.0 × 13.0)
Museo Nacional del Prado, Madrid

PROVENANCE: Javier Goya, 1828; Mariano Goya, 1854; Federico de Madrazo and/or Román Garreta y Huerta, c. 1855–60; purchased by the Museo de la Trinidad, 1866; Museo Nacional del Prado, Madrid, 1872.

PRINCIPAL REFERENCES: Gassier 1973, no. 418; Moffitt 1996.

Comer mucho seems to be self-explanatory. A heavy man, perhaps a tonsured friar, is poised above a toilet, either rising or, more likely, about to descend to relieve himself after having consumed a large meal. In the shadowy background, a second man observes the operation with a smile or smirk.

This most mundane of human activities has been interpreted as symbolic. In 1989 one commentator

Fig. 84 *Aldeano en el campo remangandose los calzones (Villager in the Field Pulling Up His Trousers)*, Album F. 62, c. 1812–20, sepia wash on paper, $8^1/_4 \times 5^1/_2$ (21 × 14), Museo Zuloaga, Zumaya

read the image as a symbol of lust and/or the sinful nature of man by reference to medieval and Renaissance images in which the equation between defecation and this deadly sin is explicit.[1] The origins of this concept are found in early Christian asceticism, although the imagery only became common in medieval folk culture. Another level of this interpretation is found in the use of the verb "to eat," which also could mean to copulate. Seven years later, an attempt was made to track the visual source to the 1621 edition of a famous emblem book, Andrea Alciati's *Emblematum liber* (1st edition, 1531), which shows a spacious, well-lit room with classicizing décor and furnishings.[2] On the right, a naked man is seen defecating onto a salver. Apart from the fact that the mise-en-scène of the two images is different, there is little likelihood that Goya needed to consult a seventeenth-century emblem book as a source of inspiration for this commonplace occurrence.

These readings of the image seem unnecessarily erudite. Furthermore, there are instances in which Goya depicted a defecating man in an explicitly symbolic composition, such as plate 68 of the Disasters of War. But such attributes are entirely absent from G. b, which has more in common with the straightforward depiction of this act represented in F. 62 (fig. 84).[3] The

element of mockery inserted into the Album G drawing by the man in the background may imply that the composition has a simple moral message as a condemnation of gluttony, a vice also caricatured in two drawings in Album C (21 and 77), one in Album F (64), and one in Album H (63).

Another approach can be based on the changing cultural conception of the act of defecation, as defined by the cultural historian Norbert Elias. In his influential book *The Civilizing Process*, Elias advanced the theory of what he called the "shifting frontier of embarrassment," according to which bodily acts once performed in public or semipublic spaces gradually became "privatized to a high degree and overlain in social life with strong prohibitions."[4] Goya's two drawings illustrate this shift clearly and concisely. In F. 62, the peasant-like figure has unselfconsciously relieved himself out-of-doors, leaving his deposit in the open air. In G. b, the act has been brought indoors to a room with sanitary equipment and is now the subject of amusement or mockery by the figure lurking in the shadows.

JB

1 Lorenzo de Marqués 1989, p. lxxxvi.
2 Moffitt 1996.
3 Published by Lafuente Ferrari 1979.
4 Elias 1994. For an introduction to Elias's thoughts on this subject, see Persels and Ganim 2004.

40

41

Loco furioso (Raging Lunatic)

Album G. 33
1824–28
Black crayon on paper, $7^5/_8 \times 5^3/_4$ (19.3 × 14.5)
Andrea Woodner Collection, New York

Signed, lower left: *Goya*

PROVENANCE: Javier Goya, 1828; Mariano Goya, 1854; Federico Madrazo, c. 1855–60; Jules Boilly, Paris; his sale, Hôtel Drouot, March 19–20, 1869, lot 48 (album), to Leurceau; Hyadès, Bordeaux; private collection, Paris; Alfred Strölin, Lausanne, by 1933; private collection; Ian Woodner, New York, 1972; Andrea Woodner Collection.

PRINCIPAL REFERENCES: London 1963–64(a), no. 192; Gassier 1973, no. 391; Pérez Sánchez and Sayre 1989, no. 168; Klein 1999; Knudsen 2000, no. 54; Fernández Doctor and Seva Díaz 2000, pp. 64–66; Hofmann 2003, p. 292.

This is the third in a group of thirteen drawings in Album G that bear legends beginning with the word *loco* or *locos*. The subject of insanity is announced in *Loco calabozo (Crazy Dungeon)* (G. 17), which depicts a threatening figure raising a baton over his head, about to strike. The majority of the works, however, fall into a more or less cohesive group between *Locos patines* (see cat. no. 32) and *Loca qe bende los placeres (Madwoman Who Sells Pleasures)*—one of the largest and most powerful suites in either Bordeaux albums.[1] In these drawings, Goya continues to plumb the depths of the irrational in man—a subject of abiding interest for him.

In most of the *locos* drawings, Goya depicts a single large figure with a minimum of context; in a few sheets they appear in twos or threes, and in one instance, in a larger group. The *locos* fit in with other figures on the fringes of society whom Goya depicted with deep sympathy—the poor, cripples, criminals, and fairground freaks. In his gallery of *locos*, however, Goya goes further and probes the emotions of his subjects through intense focus on their facial expression, body language, and attention to dress. As a group, the *locos* exhibit a variety of psychological states, from violent,

manic, and delirious, to melancholic and catatonic, to imbecilic. The protagonists are depicted both within the confines of an institution and on the street; some, however, could be either incarcerated or free. The barrier between these realms is given poignant expression in the present drawing, one of three in the series that suggest the setting of an asylum through the shorthand device of a barred window.

In the upper portion of a sheet of grayish-white paper, Goya sketched a square window with a curved top, crisscrossed with heavy wooden slats bolted together. A desperate naked figure, with sunken eyes turned upward in an expression of despair, and disheveled hair, appears in—and partly out of—the window. In a manic fit, he has apparently trapped his head between the slats, while reaching one arm through in an attempt to free himself from the depths of his dark cell—and inner experience. The void of the world beyond the bars is symbolized in the light of the blank paper that surrounds the window, suggestive of a wall. The vertical and horizontal restraining boards segment the key parts of his body—his deformed head, muscular shoulder, clenched fist, open hand that rests passively on the board, and groin—into disconnected squares, a

Locofurioso

Goya

41

metaphor for his fractured self. The dynamic form of the body contrasts with the static grill in an elegant composition that conveys the collision between the lunatic's instinctual striving for freedom and the ordered, rational world from which he is permanently excluded.

Where did Goya encounter his madman, if, in fact, the drawing was inspired by a specific individual? Did he visit Bordeaux's newly renovated asylum, the Hôpital St. Jean, in search of subjects, or did he draw this and the other incarcerated *locos* from memory, imagination, and artistic tradition? According to Antoniol, Goya could well have gained access to the asylum through his connections with the medical community in Bordeaux (he was treated for a near-fatal disease in the spring of 1825 by a leading anatomist, Dr. Jules Laffargue) or one of his wealthy Bordelais patrons, such as Jacques Galos.[2] There is, however, no concrete evidence of a visit, nor would a real-life model have been required to spark this artistic tour-de-force, which belongs to a long continuum in Goya's art.

Goya first turned to the subject of the madhouse in a painting in oil on tin, *Yard with Lunatics* of 1793–94 (fig. 85), one of several small paintings through which he gave vent to his imagination following his illness of the previous year. The basis for this painting, as Goya noted in a letter of January 1794, was the sight he had once witnessed: two stark-naked lunatics fighting while a warder beat them in a courtyard of an asylum in his hometown of Zaragoza.[3] He returned to

the theme of the asylum in a variation on the first in another group scene, *Madhouse* of 1815–19 (Royal Academy of San Fernando, Madrid), painted in the aftermath of the War of Independence.[4] As scholars have shown, in these group scenes Goya represents a variety of psychopathologies—among them mania, melancholy, and idiocy—for which standard representations of facial expression and pose were readily available through such sources as Cesare Ripa's *Iconographia* of 1645 and the physiognomic analysis of expression of Johann Caspar Lavater's *Physiognomische Fragmente*, published in four volumes between 1774 and 1778, as well as in works by other artists.[5] The dungeon-like setting of Goya's asylum paintings and the combination of violent and nonviolent patients in a single open space derive, as Peter Klein has shown, from the artist's imagination to express the claustrophobic, symbolic darkness of the interior worlds of its inhabitants. Goya lived in a time of reform and innovation in the treatment of the mentally ill, and the asylums he depicted had little to do with the actual institutions of his era.[6]

From the mid-seventeenth century, the mentally ill had been grouped together and confined in hôpitaux généraux (or workhouses) with other undesirables—beggars, the infirm, prostitutes, and those suffering from contagious diseases—who could not contribute to the general welfare of society and were considered to be a visual blight on the city streets. Instead of being driven away, as in the past, the unwanted were now locked away. Those of the deranged deemed dangerous or

Fig. 85 *Yard with Lunatics*, 1793–94, oil on tinplate, 17¼ × 12⅞ (43.8 × 32.7), Algur H. Meadows Collection, Meadows Museum, Southern Methodist University, Dallas

unfit for any form of labor were kept chained in dungeons and brought out from time to time for display as freaks for the entertainment of the public.[7] In the second half of the eighteenth century, however, special institutions were set up in France, Spain, and elsewhere for the care and treatment of the insane, and major reforms were instituted.

It is likely that Goya was aware of ongoing developments in the treatment of insanity, a subject of general interest to his enlightened friends. As Klein notes, the connection of madness and genius and the role of the imagination, discussed in the works of Voltaire and Rousseau, were subjects of abiding interest to him, as eloquently expressed in his celebrated etching *The Sleep of Reason Produces Monsters*, the leitmotif of the Caprichos.[8] The artist's own experiences with near-mortal illnesses in his later life would have made the realm of unreason a natural one for him to explore.

In his late drawings of madmen, as in his earlier paintings, Goya represented a variety of types. Dynamic figures in manic states predominated in the earlier paintings; in his late dark drawings, however, the majority are postures that suggest a melancholic, depressive state: heads down, gaze unfocused, limbs drawn in, and hands hidden.[9] The naked raving lunatic depicted here, however, has many elements in common with the standard representation of a "wild man": his active pose, disheveled hair, open mouth, and rolling eyes.[10] In this and Goya's other madman drawings, the artistic and empathic elements override the clinical. It is through the eloquence of his composition, the powerful contrast of light and dark, and the energy and sure handling of his crayon that he conveys to us the inner torment of a figure permanently barred from the world around him.

SGG

1   See Album G. 32, 34, 35, 36, 37, 39, 40, 41, 43, 44, and 45.

2   Antoniol 1998, pp. 106–7. See also Fauqué and Villanueva Etcheverría 1982, p. 618, and Pérez Sánchez and Sayre 1989, pp. 375–76.

3   Canellas López 1981, p. 315, no. 189, cited in Klein 1999, pp. 200–202. The artist would have been referring to Zaragoza's hospital Nuestra Señora de la Gracia, where two of his relatives, an uncle and an aunt, were interned in the 1760s (Klein 1999, p. 210). This asylum was in fact renowned throughout Europe as one of the pioneers in humane and innovative methods of treatment. On its history, see recent texts by Antoniol 1998, Klein 1999, and Fernández Doctor and Seva Díaz 2000.

4   GW no. 968.

5   On the connection of these paintings to earlier portrayals of insanity by Hogarth and Fuseli and others, see Gilman 1996, pp. 129–30; see pp. 62–66 for his discussion of Lavater. See also Nordström 1962.

6   Klein 1999, pp. 206–7.

7   See the classic study on the history of the insane asylum: Foucault 1965 (first published in 1961 as *Histoire de la folie*).

8   Klein 1999, pp. 218–21.

9   See Album G. 34, 36, 37, 40, 44, and 45.

10 Klein 1999, p. 211, notes that violent patients, who often could not tolerate clothing, were still kept in isolated cells in Goya's time.

42

Loco furioso (Raging Lunatic)

Album G. 40
1824–28
Black crayon on paper, $7^{1}/_{2} \times 5^{5}/_{8}$ (19.0 × 14.4)
Private collection

PROVENANCE: Javier Goya, 1828; Mariano Goya, 1854; Federico de Madrazo, c. 1855–60; Jules Boilly, Paris; his sale, Hôtel Drouot, March 19–20, 1869, lot 48 (album), to Leurceau; Hyadès, Bordeaux; private collection, Paris; Alfred Strölin, Lausanne, by 1933; private collection.

PRINCIPAL REFERENCES: Mayer 1933, p. 377; London 1963–64(a), no. 195; Gassier 1973, no. 398; Ribemont and Garcia 1998, no. 13; Klein 1999; Knudsen 2000, no. 57; Fernández Doctor and Seva Díaz 2000, pp. 64–66, no. 13; Wilson-Bareau 2001, no. 102.

If rage against confinement characterized *Loco furioso* (cat. no. 41), this work depicts an individual in a yet more debased state of mental and physical disintegration. The tormented figure melds into darkness and despair, though still rebelling against his fate. Goya's exquisite handling of chiaroscuro for symbolic effect and directness of execution as well as the sheer emotional power of the work make this drawing his most potent statement on the theme of insanity.

A barred window and a thick stone wall suffice to provide a sense of a prison-like cell in which the figure is confined. The spectator's point of view is from within, as if sharing space with the raving man. He is oblivious to human presence, however, and strains toward the light that falls on his face and torso, detaching him from the surrounding darkness. His rolling eyes, grimacing mouth, and thatched hair standing on end—features consistent with standard iconographic representations of maniacs in an extreme state of agitation—reflect his degraded mental condition, which has reduced him to the state—and appearance—of a chained beast. As has been noted, however, his deformed skull departs from the characteristics of a maniac as described in contemporary medical texts: in his *Traité médico-philosophique sur l'aliénation mentale, ou la manie* of 1801, Philippe Pinel (1745–1826), a founder of French psychiatry, compared the skulls of the maniac and the idiot and showed significant deformation in the idiot and only a little in the maniac.[1] Goya, however, is aiming at expressive, not objective, truth.

Goya's monstrous subject wears nothing but a loose sack, which slips down over his shoulders, leaving most of his torso exposed. His arms are pinned behind him, and his hands are bound (perhaps in a straightjacket) to the low wall behind him. His posture, like his physiognomy, deviates from the norm: his massive torso sinks downward, legs buckling under the weight, though his large feet, beautifully drawn, seem to grip the floor in an effort to push himself back up.

We can follow the movement of the artist's hand as he searches for the appropriate form in which to convey the inner drama of the bestial figure. As previously noted, the sheet shows traces of an earlier idea in which Goya depicted the figure with arms shooting upward over his head with hands clutched.[2] There are also numerous pentimenti along the right arm, which was once more bent and extended further from the body. In both cases, Goya opted to draw the limbs into or behind the body, accentuating his inhuman appearance and helplessness; the violent, agitated state of his mind is expressed through the unnatural containment of his body. The open, flowing form of the image and expressive relationship of light and dark, which Goya achieved through a masterful handling of his crayon in a combination of delicate strokes and forceful slashes, perfectly conveys the dynamic content of the work.

SGG

1 Cited in Gilman 1996, p. 73. See also Fernández Doctor and Seva Díaz 2000, p. 66, who note that the skull in this drawing is closer to idiocy than mania.
2 Gassier 1973, pp. 566–67; see also Wilson-Bareau 2001, p. 199, who offers two different interpretations of the pentimenti of the raised arms and hands. See also Wilson-Bareau 2000, pp. 56–57, for further discussion of the alteration.

Loco Furioso

42

43

Gimiendo y llorando (Weeping and Wailing)

Album G. 50
1824–28
Black crayon on paper, $7^{1}/_{2} \times 6^{1}/_{8}$ (19.2 × 15.5)
Private collection

PROVENANCE: Javier Goya, 1828; Mariano Goya, 1854; Valentín Carderera and/or Federico de Madrazo, c. 1855–60; Juan Jorge Peoli, New York; his sale, American Art Association, May 8, 1894, lot 303b; Sir Robert Mond, London, by 1937; by descent to Mrs. Joy Sen Gupta, Calcutta; sale, Sotheby's, London, June 28, 1979, lot 151; private collection; sale, Sotheby's, New York, January 26, 2000, lot 39; private collection.

PRINCIPAL REFERENCES: Borenius and Wittkower 1937, no. 282; Gassier 1973, no. 408; Ilatovskaya 1996, p. 40; Wilson-Bareau 2001, no. 103.

This is one of the most directly expressive drawings in the Bordeaux albums. The legend Goya attached to it, *Gimiendo y llorando (Weeping and Wailing)*, confirms what we see but provides no clue for interpreting it. A man dressed in a robe kneels on the ground. From the pyramidal base of his lower body draped in the skirt of the robe, his torso rises with his arms extended—one shooting upward in a forceful diagonal, the other wavering—and the fingers of his open hands reaching outward. The wide V of his arms is repeated in the open neck of his garment, and both lead to his expressive head, encircled with unkempt hair. Light falls on his forehead and nose and illuminates the hollow recesses surrounding his eyes, which strain upward in an expression of pathos. The figure fills much of the sheet, with his tremulous fingers extending to the very edges.

The wall behind the man provides a vague sense of the setting and anchors the figure. Made up of large stone blocks that the artist has shaded with his lithographic crayon, using the ribbed paper to create a grainy texture, the wall forms a dark band across the center of the sheet that sets off the volumetric forms of the body up to shoulder level. The head, however, is silhouetted against the light ground of the paper.

Similar walls appear in two other drawings in Album G: *Loco calabozo* (G. 17) and *Loco furioso* (cat. no. 42), where they suggest the lugubrious interiors of an asylum. The wall in this drawing—whether interior or exterior—conveys a similar sense of a soulless place from which there is no escape.

Is the subject a prisoner about to be executed and pleading for his life? As has been noted, the man's posture recalls that of one of Goya's most memorable figures: the patriot on his knees before the firing squad in the *Third of May 1808* (1814), though here the figure exhibits a greater sense of resignation than defiance.[1] Or does he belong to the *locos*, representing a general sense of anguish rather than a particular psychological state? In his Bordeaux albums (and throughout his work), Goya made frequent use of figures on their knees or with legs tucked under—a compact form of the body that concentrates attention on the face and gestures of the arms and hands—in a variety of situations: fleeing from fire, in prayer, brandishing a knife, and in flight.[2] The unspecified context of this drawing allows for multiple readings of this figure, which appears both to rise in supplication and sink back in despair. This openness on the level of meaning, and the beautifully thought-out, abstract nature of the composition, make it one of Goya's most powerful graphic works.

SGG

1 GW no. 984. Noted in Gassier 1973, pp. 569–70, who also connects the figure with that of Christ in Goya's *Christ on the Mount of Olives* (GW no. 1640). Wilson-Bareau 2001, p. 199, notes similarities with the figure in the frontispiece of the Disasters of War (GW no. 993), who conveys a sense of foreboding, and with the ecstatic figure in the Inquisition Album "who will welcome the arrival of 'Divine Liberty (Album C. 115).'"
2 Album G. 22 and 23; Album H. 47 and 52.

Gimiendo y llorando

44

El perro volante (The Flying Dog)

Album G. 5
1824–28
Black crayon on paper, $7\frac{1}{2} \times 5\frac{7}{8}$ (19.0 × 15.0)
Museo Nacional del Prado, Madrid

PROVENANCE: Javier Goya, 1828; Mariano Goya, 1854; Federico de Madrazo and/or Román Garreta y Huerta, c. 1855–60; purchased by the Museo de la Trinidad, 1866; Museo Nacional del Prado, Madrid, 1872.

PRINCIPAL REFERENCES: Gassier 1973, no. 369; Pérez Sánchez and Sayre 1989, no.165.

This is one of several highly enigmatic drawings that form part of the Bordeaux Albums. The image is at once striking and puzzling. A strange hybrid creature, part canine, part avian, part amphibian, is caught midair in a headlong dive, fangs bared. In the distance is a patch of terrain that cannot be identified. It may be occupied by a group of people or a village or a wood.

The animal has several constituent parts. There is no doubt that the head, body, and tail are doglike, as are the front legs and paws. In fact, the dog has been identified as a mastiff, used by shepherds to protect their flocks.[1] The formidable wingspan closely resembles the artificial wings manufactured by Daedalus as depicted in Album H. 52 (fig. 86). The webbed rear paws seem to come from some sort of amphibious bird. Two other elements are worthy of note. Around his neck, the animal wears a collar fitted with short spikes, typically used to protect mastiffs from attacks by wolves.[2] A final item is what appears to be an open book, somehow attached to the back of the "dog."

The significance of the drawing has never been ascertained. Perhaps there is a textual source, but as yet none has been discovered. The most developed hypothesis interprets the drawing as a political satire.[3] According to this theory, the "dog" symbolizes a clergyman who, instead of tending to

his flock, is preparing to ravage it. As evidence, the author notes that dogs sometimes symbolize greed, while the verb "to fly" was slang for "to rob." The message of the drawing is thus a Liberal indictment of mercenary clerics who plunder rather than protect their flocks. Little about this interpretation convinces. Dogs are more commonly understood as symbols of fidelity. Furthermore, there are no obvious ecclesiastical connotations to the drawing, creating the impression that the interpretation has arbitrarily been applied to the composition.

Another hypothesis takes a realistic turn and draws attention to an animal act at the Bordeaux fair which featured a Monsieur Margat, who performed an aerial trick with a stag. Both plunged to earth at the end of the performance. The relevance to the drawing is not evident.[4]

For all these well-intentioned efforts at explication, the meaning of the drawing remains cryptic. Only one point is certain, that it is an extraordinary feat of artistic imagination.

JB

1 Pérez Sánchez and Sayre 1989, p. 369.
2 Ibid.
3 Ibid., pp. 369–70.
4 Fauqué and Villanueva Etcheverria 1982, p. 650.

Fig. 86 *Daedalus Seeing Icarus Fall*, Album H. 52, 1824–28, black crayon on paper, $7\frac{1}{2} \times 5\frac{7}{8}$ (19.1 × 14.8), Museo Nacional del Prado, Madrid

El perro volante

172

44

45

Man on a Swing

Album H. 58
1824–28
Black crayon on paper, $7^1/_2 \times 5^7/_8$ (19.0 × 15.1)
The Hispanic Society of America, New York

PROVENANCE: Javier Goya, 1828; Mariano Goya, 1854; Federico de Madrazo, c. 1855–60; Raimundo de Madrazo y Garreta; Archer M. Huntington, New York, 1913; The Hispanic Society of America, New York.

PRINCIPAL REFERENCES: Trapier 1963; Gassier 1973, no. 470; Stoichita and Coderch 1999, pp. 284–87; New York 2000, no. 129.

This remarkable image converts a commonplace activity into something extraordinary. An older man of indeterminate age rockets through the air on a makeshift swing consisting of a single rope. His legs are mostly extended, and he appears to be approaching the apex of the trajectory. With thick-fingered hands, he grasps the rope, and his face breaks into a broad leering grin, as if he is enjoying his temporary respite from the pull of gravity. Only one element is strange: the rope is attached to nothing. Furthermore, neither the ground beneath the man nor the sky above can be seen; he floats freely in the void.

Two interpretations have been applied to this enigmatic drawing. The first has erotic connotations, based partly on Goya's occasional use of floating figures with leering expressions to convey this meaning (D. 2, *Suben alegres* [*They Rise Up Happily*], Musée du Louvre, and D. 4, *Recozijo* [*Mirth*], The Hispanic Society of America). Another hint of possible erotic significance might be found by the inclusion of the motif of the swing, which appears in French paintings and engravings of the eighteenth century. In these works, a woman on a swing was understood to represent inconstancy or fickleness in matters of love. The repetitive, up-and-down movement of the swing also made it a suitable

metaphor for lovemaking.[1] This concept has been applied to the *Man on a Swing*.[2] However, as has been pointed out, there is a major difference between Goya's drawing and its French counterparts: all the French versions show a woman on the swing.[3] The drawing might then be a literal "send-up" or mockery of its aristocratic French antecedents, which included compositions by Watteau and Fragonard. Another thought is that the drawing is a metaphor for masturbation. This might explain the ambivalent grin on the man's face.

The second interpretation views the drawing as a metaphorical construct based on another traditional meaning of the swing as indicative of the fickleness of life.[4] At one moment you are riding high, and at the next you are brought low. As such, the drawing demonstrates Goya's awareness of life's sudden reversals of fortune, of which he was both a victim and a witness. Despite these hypotheses, this energetic drawing guards its secrets.

Related to the drawing is an etching with aquatint that has been identified as part of a small group of prints intended to initiate a new set of caprichos, sometimes known as the Nuevos Caprichos. The project supposedly never advanced beyond a preliminary stage. This notion depends on the letter written by Goya to Joaquín María de

58

45

58

Ferrer (December 20, 1825), from which it may be inferred that Ferrer had previously rejected the artist's proposition to sell the Bulls of Bordeaux in Paris.[5] Instead Ferrer wanted to know if Los Caprichos (1799) could be reissued, which, as Goya informed him, was no longer possible because the plates had been sold to the crown. The artist goes on to say that, in any event, he would not copy them because "tengo mejores ocurrencias en el día para que se vendieran con más utilidad" ("I have better ideas today that may be sold with greater profit"). This phrase is difficult to translate; Goya's choice of words does not make clear what these ideas might be.

Nevertheless, in 1971 Eleanor Sayre, the distinguished Goya scholar, translated the phrase as if it were more explicit than it really is—"Nor would I copy them because right now I have better ideas [for Caprichos]."[6] The editorial parenthesis imparts a sense of certainty to Goya's ambiguous intentions. Nevertheless, this phrase leaves ample room to doubt that he was planning to embark on a sequel to Los Caprichos. Also problematic is that the authenticity of some of the four plates supposedly made to start the series has been questioned. One of these is based on H. 58, which in 1996 was considered "doubtful" by Juliet Wilson-Bareau.[7] These doubts seem worth entertaining. In the print version (fig. 87), the swing has come to a halt and with it the sense of rollicking movement through space so crucial to the spirited composition; the drawing of the legs and feet is confused; the subtle, expressive grin now looks merely crude. (The demons visible in the background behind the figure may be remnants of a different, earlier composition.) If the print were made by Goya, it is easy to see why he no longer wished or perhaps was able to make etchings.

JB

1   Posner 1982, pp. 75–88.
2   Lorenzo de Márquez 1989, pp. 392–93.
3   Patrick Lenaghan in New York 2000, p. 376.
4   Stoichita and Coderch 1999, pp. 284–87. There is no compelling reason to identify the swinging man with Goya.
5   Canellas López 1981, pp. 389–90, no. 273.
6   Sayre 1971, p. 15.
7   Wilson-Bareau 1996(b), pp. 49–50. There is only one artist's proof known to exist: Staatliche Museen Preussischer Kulturbesitz, Kupferstichkabinett, Berlin.

Fig. 87   *Man on a Swing*, 1825–27, etching and aquatint, $7^{1}/_{4} \times 4^{3}/_{4}$ (18.5 × 12), Courtesy of The Hispanic Society of America, New York

46

Young Witch (Woman?) Flying with a Rope

Album H. 19
1824–28
Black crayon on paper, $7^{1}/_{2} \times 6^{1}/_{8}$ (19.1 × 15.5)
National Gallery of Canada, Ottawa, Purchased 1923

Signed, lower right: *Goya*

PROVENANCE: Javier Goya, 1828; Mariano Goya, 1854; Valentín Carderera and/or Federico de Madrazo, c. 1855–60; John Savile Lumley, 1st Baron Savile of Rufford, 1858–60; by descent to John Savile, 2nd Baron Savile of Rufford, 1896; Colnaghi, London; purchased by the National Gallery of Canada, 1923.

PRINCIPAL REFERENCES: Martin-Méry 1951, no. 9; London 1963–64(a), no. 203; Popham-Fenwick 1965, no. 306; London 1969, no. 69; Sayre 1971, p. 21; Gassier 1973, no. 436; Sayre 1974–75, no. 261; Guillaud and Guillaud 1979, no. 180; Wilson-Bareau 2001, no. 110.

The voluptuous young woman floating through space holding a rope, her dress billowing behind her, is one of the most sensual creatures in Goya's late work. Here he returns to his fascination with figures in the air—both human and supernatural—that fly, float, swing, or fall. As in *Se quieren mucho* (cat. no. 49) and *Man on a Swing* (cat. no. 45) there is no context or ground line; space is created on the blank sheet of paper solely through the position of the body.

Light falls on the girl's face, neck, breasts, and abdomen, which, along with her upraised arms, hold the frontal plane; her shaded lower body and angled legs drift back into space, and the train of her skirt further still. She seems to float toward the spectator on some invisible carrier like a deus ex machina. Goya captures the key details of her fashionable costume in a few summary strokes. Her loose curly hair piled up on her head falls over a wide bandeau that has slipped over her eyes.[1]

Exactly what this agile creature is doing is unclear. As others have noted, she is neither skipping nor swinging; the suggestion that she is performing a rope trick seems more likely.[2] Visually, the rope serves as a frame for the body. It follows the hemline of her dress and encloses the train, forming a kind of imaginary doorway for her to pass through in her swing through space. Is this vivacious young woman based on a figure from real life, perhaps a circus performer, or is she an allegory? She has tentatively been identified as a witch, although she bears no familiar attributes of a supernatural except for her levitating powers and a small set of wings attached to her shoes. The winged shoes, however, are not necessarily connected with witches and could as easily be part of a performer's

Fig. 88 *Volaverunt (Gone for Good)*, Capricho No. 61, 1799, etching and aquatint, $8^{1}/_{2} \times 6$ (21.7 × 15.2), The Metropolitan Museum of Art, New York, Gift of M. Knoedler & Co., 1918

46

costume.[3] It is equally possible that the bewitching young woman was inspired partly from life and embellished in imagination.

This drawing has been compared with Goya's famed Capricho No. 61, *Volaverunt (Gone for Good)* (fig. 88).[4] In this drawing, a figure from real life, the duchess of Alba, is carried aloft on the backs of three fiends, her mantilla held in her outstretched arms as a kind of sail. She too sports a small set of so-called butterfly wings, which are attached to her head. The young woman with a rope repeats the position of the duchess, though in reverse.[5] *Volaverunt* has been interpreted as an allegorical figure that may allude to "the flightiness of the female sex,"[6] and possibly a similar meaning could be attributed to the pneumatic girl with the rope. The protagonist of the late drawing, however, differs markedly from her aristocratic predecessor. She is all softness and curves, an earth mother freed from gravity. Goya's spirited handling of the greasy crayon in bold, slashing, and zigzag strokes and strong contrasts of light and dark emphasize the volumes of the figure and underline her vitality.

SGG

1   The coiffure and bandeau recall the early nineteenth-century revival of the antique style, as for example in David's *Mme Récamier* of 1800.
2   Gassier and Wilson 1971, p. 358; Sayre 1971, p. 21. See also Gassier 1973, p. 637, who notes that neither the wings on her feet nor the bandeau are connected with the depiction of witches.
3   Gassier 1973, p. 637.
4   Wilson-Bareau 2001, p. 202.
5   Ibid.
6   Pérez Sánchez and Gállego 1995, p. 69.

47

Wolf and Man

Album H. 5
1824–28
Black crayon on paper, $7^1/_2 \times 6^1/_4$ (19.1 × 15.8)
Museo Nacional del Prado, Madrid

Signed, lower right: *Goya*

PROVENANCE: Javier Goya, 1828; Mariano Goya, 1854; Federico de Madrazo and/or Román Garreta y Huerta, c. 1855–60; purchased by the Museo de la Trinidad, 1866; Museo Nacional del Prado, Madrid, 1872.

PRINCIPAL REFERENCES: Lafuente Ferrari 1980, no. 88; Gassier 1973, no. 422.

Although Goya used animal symbolism from time to time, he rarely enlisted a wolf for this purpose. Wolves appear most conspicuously in the section of the Disasters of War known as *caprichos enfáticos* (c. 1815), specifically in plates 74 and 78. While there is some disagreement about the precise meaning of the wolf in these compositions, most recent writers agree that it has a negative connotation, citing a contemporary satire as the source.[1] In plate 74, entitled *Esto es lo peor (This Is the Worst),* the wolf is thought to represent the inner circle of Ferdinand VII, which was charged with repressing the constitution of 1812 at the conclusion of the Peninsular War and the restoration of the monarchy. In plate 78, *Se defiende bien (It Defends Itself Well),* a pack of five wolves attacks a white horse as four mastiffs placidly look on. Here again, a political interpretation presently holds sway, in which the horse symbolizes a "noble and rational creature and stands for [the] constitutional monarch," while the wolves represent the forces of the conservative opposition.[2]

The interpretation of the wolf as a symbol of reactionary government in these prints is of course supported by their inclusion in the Disasters of War and is a viable visual source. In Album H. 5 there are no such obvious connections, and what Goya has drawn is very strange. A wolf, standing erect on its hind feet and covered by a voluminous robe, is approached by a half-naked man, wearing only a rough shawl or mantle, possibly made of animal skins, with sandals on his feet. The man extends his hat, turned upside down, toward the wolf, as if begging for alms. The encounter takes place out-of-doors, as indicated by the summary depiction of vegetation that appears between the figures. Evidently the point of the encounter depends on the reversal of roles between man and beast, but how this plays out is known only to Goya.

JB

1 For the most cogent interpretation, see Glendinning 1978.
2 Ibid., p. 188.

5.

Goya

47

48

Struggling Man and Woman with Devil

Album H. 57
1824–28
Black crayon on paper, $7^{1}/_{2} \times 5^{7}/_{8}$ (19.1 × 15.0)
Museo Nacional del Prado, Madrid

PROVENANCE: Javier Goya, 1828; Mariano Goya, 1854; Federico de Madrazo and/or Román Garreta y Huerta, c. 1855–60; purchased by the Museo de la Trinidad, 1866; Museo Nacional del Prado, Madrid, 1872.

PRINCIPAL REFERENCES: Gassier 1973, no. 469.

Albums G and H contain several drawings with utterly undecipherable subjects. In addition to G. 5 and H. 5 in this catalogue, there are others in which Goya's imagination escapes the boundaries of logic and reason. One striking example is G. 9, *Gran disparate (Great Folly),* which depicts a strangely deconstructed man, feeding his own decapitated head with a spoon, while another man pours liquid through a funnel into the empty space between his shoulders (see fig. 63). Number 15 of Album H is a composition featuring a fierce-looking winged creature on whose back sits a warlike figure brandishing sword and shield (see fig. 66). He appears to be mounted on the back of the bird, and together they confront viewers with a strange image of power and danger. It is very tempting to look for sources in the traditional emblematic literature, but this approach tends to be reductive, blotting out the nuances that make these drawings so compelling. Goya's inspiration is not a book or visual prototype but rather a gift for using recognizable forms to construct irrational narratives.

In H. 57 we have no difficulty in identifying the three figures. One is a woman who has a shirtless man in a stranglehold. His arms are pinned behind his back, and his legs are splayed, with one of them folded uncomfortably beneath his body.

Looming over the conflict is a horned devil with outspread wings. Gassier interprets the drawing as follows:

> This union of a half-naked old man and a much-younger woman who pinions his arms behind his back is truly diabolical. He makes a grimace of pain and exasperation; she smiles with an air of victory. This is not a squabble between husband and wife . . . but a demonstration of a young woman's tyranny over an old man, which the horrid devil behind them consecrates in the name of the lust he symbolizes.[1]

This reading depends on a number of debatable assumptions. Is the woman noticeably younger than the man? Does his grimace bespeak pain and exasperation? How exactly does the element of tyranny (as opposed to victory) come into play? On what grounds can the devil be equated with lust? (Devils, by the way, are very rare among Goya's midnight creatures.)

Yet it would be imprudent to dismiss this reading as invalid, especially in the absence of a convincing alternative. There is always the possibility that Goya had nothing specific in mind except to create conditions for multiple responses, in fact much like the varying interpretations of Los Caprichos construed by the artist's contemporaries. Not every Goya problem may have a

solution. In other words, images like this one could have been made to open the way to imaginative interpretation rather than to enclose meaning within the narrow confines of certainty.

JB

1 Gassier 1973, pp. 645–46.

57

146

48

49

Se quieren mucho (They Love Each Other Very Much)

Album G. 59
1824–28
Black crayon on paper, 7$\frac{1}{2}$ × 5$\frac{7}{8}$ (19.2 × 15.0)
Museo Nacional del Prado, Madrid

PROVENANCE: Javier Goya, 1828; Mariano Goya, 1854; Federico de Madrazo and/or Román Garreta y Huerta, c. 1855–60; purchased by the Museo de la Trinidad, 1866; Museo Nacional del Prado, Madrid, 1872.

PRINCIPAL REFERENCES: Gassier 1973, no. 415.

Goya's dark sardonic universe abounds with winged creatures. Witches, demons, and sorcerers entered his work in full force in the second half of the 1790s following the critical illness of 1792–93 that left him deaf and transformed his life and art, opening the way to "caprice and invention."[1] As has been shown, Goya's interest in the supernatural developed in the context of the widespread fascination with the irrational, occult, and macabre that flourished among intellectuals as a delightfully lurid escape in the age of reason.[2] In the early eighteenth century, Padre Benito Jerónimo de Feijóo (1646–1746), a scholarly Dominican and famed university reformer in Spain, launched an attack on the belief in witches, sorcerers, and the like in his essay, "Duendes y espíritus familiares" (in *Cartas Eruditas,* 1742–60), claiming that everything attributed to them could be explained by natural phenomena, while the so-called confessions of those accused of wielding occult power were the result of torture-induced derangement. As Edith Helman has noted, the educated elite of the late eighteenth century shared Feijóo's views, though his vivid evocation of the depraved satanic world stimulated their interest and spurred lighthearted debate.[3] Enlightened intellectuals used the subject of witchcraft and demonology—a holdover from pagan

rites that continued alongside Christianity—as a satirical vehicle to condemn popular belief, mock the rituals of the church (which satanic rites parody), and criticize the Inquisition, as well as to indulge their penchant for fantasy.[4] It was with similar intent that Goya engaged with the topic in drawings, etchings, and paintings in the late 1790s.

There were many sources available to Goya, whose own native province of Aragon was rich in witch lore. The black arts and witchcraft played a strong role in some of the enduring classics of Spanish literature, such as *La Celestina* (1502) by Fernando de Rojas, a book beloved by Goya, as well as works by Cervantes and Quevedo.[5] Plays about witchcraft by seventeenth-century authors, such as Antonio de Zamora, remained popular in the late eighteenth century and provided inspiration for Goya, as did work by earlier artists.[6] The artist undoubtedly shared an interest in sorcery with some of his close literary friends, such as the playwright Leandro Fernández de Moratín (see cat. no. 10). The poet-playwright brought out a new edition in 1811 or 1812 of one of the most famous texts on witchcraft, *Auto de fe celebrado en la cuidad de Logroño en los días de 6 y 7 de noviembre de 1610* (published in 1611), accompanied by his own satirical commentary on the text.[7] The book—a

238

Se quieren mucho

49

report of the most infamous witch trial in Spain, written by two inquisitors who presided over it—offered detailed accounts of witches' depraved deeds from their "confessions": their orgies with the devil in the form of a he-goat, the sucking of the blood of infants, cannibalism, and so on.[8] Whether Moratín was at work on the project in the late 1790s is a matter of debate, though he may have owned the book then and discussed its lurid contents with Goya, who was at work on his Caprichos.[9]

Some of Goya's earliest representations of witches appear in his Madrid Album (Album B, 1796–97): *Brujas a bolar (Witches About to Fly)* and *La tia chorriones enciende la óguera (Auntie Bellows Lights the Fire)*.[10] These images are developed further in drawings known as the Sueños of 1797, studies for his suite of eighty etchings, Los Caprichos, which Goya published in 1799.[11] Ten of the Sueños drawings were devoted to the subject of witchcraft; the most well known of these, Sueño No. 1, was intended to serve as the frontispiece of Los Caprichos.[12] In it, the artist depicts himself asleep at his worktable with ominous winged creatures circling overhead; in the legend below Goya states his aim for the series: "The author dreaming. His only intention is to banish harmful common beliefs, and to perpetuate with this work of *Caprichos* the sound Testimony of the Truth."[13] When the set of eighty prints was offered for sale in February 1799, however, the etching based on Sueño No. 1 became Capricho No. 43, *The Sleep of Reason Produces Monsters*, and was used as a subsidiary title page to

introduce the section on the theme of witchcraft, which makes up a third of the set. In these sheets, ugly witches and goblins anoint one another; humans change into animals; hags corrupt and train nubile youths; and figures with and without wings, and on broomsticks, fly through the air on their way to evildoings.

During the period that Goya was engaged in work on the Caprichos, he also painted a set of six paintings in oil on tin plate on the theme of witchcraft on a commission from the duchess of Osuna, who with her husband was one of the leading *ilustrados* of their time and a major patron of Goya's. Delicately painted in gay colors, these works depict amusing and salacious scenes of a witches' sabbath or orgy and other fantastic and sinister occurrences; two of the series were based on scenes from plays by Antonio de Zamora and others on pictorial sources and popular beliefs.[14] They were installed in the duchess's boudoir of their country house, the Palacio de la Alameda, outside Madrid, where she had a private theater.

Goya returned to the subject of witches and witch lore nearly two decades later in a different medium. In the fantastic and macabre Black Paintings (1820–23), executed in oil directly on the walls of his country house, the Quinta del Sordo, witches and demons appear in several works: *The Great He-Goat* (or *Witches' Sabbath*), *Asmodea* (or *To the Witches' Sabbath*), and *The Fates*. Around the same time, drawings of witches in brush and India ink appear in Album D.[15]

Fig. 89 (*above left*)   *Allá vá eso (There It Goes)*, Capricho No. 66, 1799, etching and aquatint, 8¼ × 6½ (20.9 × 16.6), The Metropolitan Museum of Art, New York, Gift of M. Knoedler & Co., 1918

Fig. 90 (*above right*)   *Y aun no se van! (And Still They Don't Go!)*, Capricho No. 59, 1799, etching and aquatint, 8½ × 6 (21.7 × 15.2), The Metropolitan Museum of Art, New York, Gift of M. Knoedler & Co., 1918

Se quieren mucho depicts a pair of desiccated old wizards floating in the air in broad daylight, a work as enigmatic as it is beautifully rendered and artfully composed. Despite their spindly frames, the couple pulse with life; their facial features and gestures convey their all-too-human emotions. The probably female figure in a loose drapery, with bony legs widely spread, grips the male with large mannish hands that seem to push and pull. Her death's head is fully equipped with mouth, fleshy nose, and expressively rolling eyes. The nearly nude male guides his partner in their ascent, his eyes closed and mouth fixed in a foolish, lascivious grin. Are they off to some extraterrestrial sexual encounter or are the old fiends merely levitating to the final resting place for spent supernaturals?

The delicately shaded angular wings set off the couple's heads and intertwined arms, while their bent legs and the diagonal position of their bodies contribute to the effect of movement. Below the figures Goya added the ironic rubric *Se quieren mucho (They love each other very much)*; his carefully constructed composition, deft strokes of the lithographic crayon, and acute attention to detail seem to reflect his affection for his creatures.

The drawing is a late reflection of the witchcraft works in the Caprichos. It has been compared with *Linda Maestra* (Capricho No. 68), and *Allá vá eso* (Capricho No. 66) (fig. 89), both of which depict couples in flight—the first, an old hag and young girl astride a broomstick, and the second, which is closer to this drawing, two winged figures dangling from a crutch and flying through the air.[16] It also recalls the drawing *Buen Viaje*, Goya's first of a wizard in flight, with a gaggle of figures on his back.[17] The position of the bony rump and legs of the creature to the left in the present drawing is strikingly similar to the lower part of the body of the skeleton emerging from the tomb in one of the most famous and bleak of his Caprichos, No. 59, *Y aun no se van* (*And Still They Don't Go*) (fig. 90).

While belonging to the type of drawings and prints that Goya carried out in the Caprichos, *Se quieren mucho* differs from them in ways that are characteristic and revealing of his late work. In the Caprichos, Goya used a combination of etching and aquatint to create precise modeled forms and strong contrasts of light and dark to construct an illusion of depth. Here the winged pair is abstracted from its setting, and they float in empty space with no ground line. Goya summons them up with a combination of delicate and precise strokes in which details of faces and limbs stand out against softer areas and makes use of the ribbed texture of the paper to achieve a sense of lightness, almost transparency. The drawing evokes the experience of weightlessness and flotation rather than malfeasance, nor does there appear to be a moralizing message. The satire is self-directed: these oldsters are nostalgic evocations of Goya's past creations, superhumans who have become humanized and subjected to the same indignities of the passage of time as he has, and who exhibit the same foolish foibles of old age—a theme recurrent in his late drawings.

SGG

1 Letter from Goya to the vice-protector of the Royal Academy of San Fernando, Bernardo de Iriarte, of January 1794; excerpt in Tomlinson 1994, p. 94.

2 See Helman 1959.

3 Ibid., p. 109.

4 Davidson 1987, p. 91.

5 Heckes 1985, p. 52, cites Miguel de Cervantes's *El casamiento engañoso y el coloquio de los perros* of 1613 and Francisco de Quevedo's *Historia de la vida del Buscón* of 1626; on eighteenth-century literary sources, see Julio Caro Baroja, *Teatro popular y magia* (1974), which is cited in Heckes 1985, p. 112, note 116.

6 Davidson 1987, pp. 91–92 and 94; she notes the witchcraft scenes of the Netherlandish painter David Teniers the younger (1610–1690) and other possible sources of influence in Northern European art and literature.

7 Fernández de Moratín 1871, pp. 617–31.

8 See Fernández-Salvador 1998, pp. 23–25, for more on the text.

9 Helman believes that Moratín was at work on his *Auto de Fe* by 1797, but Andioc and others argue that the much later date of publication refutes this theory. See cat. no. 10 of this book for more on this debate. The writer and politician Gaspar Melchor de Jovellanos, a patron of Goya's, purchased a copy in 1795 of one of the most famous and exhaustive tomes on witchcraft: Sprenger and Kramer's *Malleus Maleficarum* (*Hammer of Witches*) of 1487 (republished in sixteen editions and translated from Latin into many Romance languages). See Helman 1959, p. 121, note 20, who suggests that Goya may have known this book.

10 Album B. 56 and 57.

11 Sueño Nos. 2 and 7; Capricho Nos. 60 and 69.

12 Gassier 1975, p. 76.

13 Ibid.

14 Nordström 1962, p. 153; Sayre 1991, p. 67.

15 Juliet Wilson-Bareau has now dubbed Album D (first recognized as a separate group by Eleanor Sayre) the "Witches and Old Women Album." See Wilson-Bareau 2001, p. 135.

16 See an extended discussion of this work in Sayre 1991, pp. 70–77.

17 Gassier 1975, p. 155, no. 118. Capricho, No. 64, was transformed into a night scene.

50

Traveling Witch

Album H. 27
1824–28
Black crayon on paper, $7^1/_2 \times 5^7/_8$ (19.1 × 15.1)
Museo Nacional del Prado, Madrid

Signed, lower right: *Goya*

PROVENANCE: Javier Goya, 1828; Mariano Goya, 1854; Federico de Madrazo and/or Román Garreta y Huerta, c. 1855–60; purchased by the Museo de la Trinidad, 1866; Museo Nacional del Prado, Madrid, 1872.

PRINCIPAL REFERENCES: Lafuente Ferrari 1980, no. 92; Gassier 1973, no. 443.

Old women play a prominent role in Goya's art and return frequently in his late work as both ordinary and superhuman beings. In his Bordeaux albums, he depicted them moving around the city streets in odd conveyances (see fig. 72); dancing (Album H. 35); and sitting in front of a mirror (see cat. no. 38). Others, exercising their magical powers, take flight astride a bird of prey (see fig. 66); ascend heavenward with a mate (see cat. no. 49); and, as seen here, travel through space on the backs of winged demons.

Women transported on the backs of others seem to have intrigued Goya in scenes drawn both from real life and from imagination. He devoted four drawings in Album G to the strange spectacle encountered in Bordeaux of ladies being carried in shoulder chairs on the backs of laborers. In his Caprichos, a mortal rides on the back of supernatural beings in *Volaverunt* (Capricho No. 61), while a witch who has lost her flying power is carried aloft by others in his comical Capricho No. 65, *Donde vá Mamà? (Where Is Mama Going?)*.

There is nothing particularly witchlike about the huddled old crone in this drawing. She might well have been lifted from a figure glimpsed on a sidewalk in Bordeaux; her companions, however, and the surrounding blank space place her in the supernatural sphere. The trio is compactly organized in a pyramidal composition, which Goya invests with maximum tension. The bodies of the two fiends (more like gargoyles with an Asiatic air) form the base. Their demonic, grimacing faces and bat-wings emerge from under a cloth that covers most of their bodies. The flyers face in opposite directions and cut a diagonal path through space, though it is not clear in which direction they are going. The body of the huddled crone wrapped in a shawl is also concealed, directing attention to her skull-like face, frozen in a grimace of fear or amazement. Is this old witch being put out to pasture? The focus in this air-borne *folie-à-trois* is on their exaggerated facial expressions.

These supernaturals appear to have served Goya here as yet another opportunity to exercise his fascination with expressive heads, perhaps grounded in the physiognomic studies of the period, and to vent his humor. Each is highly specific, though whether the demons' faces express ignorance, greed, lasciviousness, or evil is not clear. Like some of his other late drawings on the subject of witchcraft, this one also seems to be a commentary on human emotions and frailties and the foibles of growing old. Goya's technique is direct and assured with forceful strokes of the crayon, strong contours, and carefully constructed alternations of areas of light and dark.

SGG

51

Young Woman Swooning, Surrounded by Witches

Album H. 25
1824–28
Black crayon on paper, $7\frac{1}{2} \times 6$ (19.1 × 15.3)
Private collection

Signed on verso: *Goya*

PROVENANCE: Javier Goya, 1828; Mariano Goya, 1854; Federico de Madrazo, c. 1855–60; Jules Boilly, Paris; his sale, Hôtel Drouot, March 19–20, 1869, lot 48 (album), to Leurceau; Hyadès, Bordeaux; private collection, Paris; Alfred Strölin, Lausanne, by 1933; private collection.

PRINCIPAL REFERENCES: Mayer 1933, p. 381; London 1963–64(a), no. 205; Sayre 1971, p. 20; Gassier 1973, no. 442; Martigny 1982, no. 21; Ribemont and Garcia 1998, no. 18; Wilson-Bareau 2001, no. 112.

Fig. 91 *El Sueño (The Dream)*, 1819–22, crayon lithograph on paper, $5\frac{1}{8} \times 6\frac{1}{4}$ (13 × 16), Kupferstichkabinett, Staatliche Museen zu Berlin

In this magnificent drawing, Goya pushes further his experimentation with the rich painterly effects that can be achieved with a combination of sharp strokes and the soft rubbing of a greasy lithographic crayon on a sheet of laid paper.[1] His subject—a swooning woman whose mind is temporarily released from conscious control—works in perfect harmony with his experimental technique. To look at this drawing is to enter into an experience of lost and found in which form and meaning remain in the realm of suggestion.

Goya draws his forms out into veiled light from a predominately dark ground. In the center of the composition, a young woman in a loose shift, her hair drawn up in a cone-shaped bonnet, leans back on a chair or bed, with a pillow supporting her head. Her delicately shaded body has a strong sense of volume, and her head—the lightest note in the composition and its focus—is thrown back with her mouth open in an expression of indeterminate meaning. With summary strokes, Goya conjures up a cast of evocative figures that hover around her. Supporting the swooner is an old woman who stands over the bed; the vague indication of wings on the left, which appear to be touching her shoulder, evokes a witch. A younger female figure with dark hair emerges

partially from the shadows at the right. Lower down on the left are one or possibly two beaked creatures with threatening open mouths. These spectral and actual attendants appear to have been developed by Goya into shapes and figures from areas of light and dark through the semiautomatic process he made use of in his paintings on ivory carried out around the same time.

Women fainting, in a trance, under a spell, or dreaming go back a long way in Goya's oeuvre. In his Madrid Album of 1796, for example, Goya depicted in a relatively realistic manner a *maja* overcome (by what is only implied) on a country outing; she leans back in the center of a group of fashionable friends who have gathered around to attend her.[2] Closer to the time of the present drawing is Goya's lithograph of 1819–22, representing a young woman in a trance lying back on the lap of an old Celestina-like crone, who has hypnotized her, while other women look on (fig. 91).[3] In these works, the viewer, like the bystanders, also observes the scene from the outside. Here, however, Goya appears to take the perspective from within the mind of the swooning figure, who conjures up the hallucinatory figures that surround her, much as the artist generates forms from suggestive marks and shapes.

Tangentially related to *Young Woman Swooning*, though different in subject matter, is Goya's famous oil painting *Self-Portrait with Dr. Arrieta* of 1820, in which the half-conscious artist is held up by his doctor and surrounded by shadowy figures (see cat. no. 3). The observation that the arrangement of figures of the painting has echoes of a religious art, alluding to the traditional composition of the Pietà (though an entombment would be more apt in this case), could also be applied to the drawing, though in both cases the central figure is alive. Here, however, the expression on the woman's face could be interpreted not only as physical pain, as in the self-portrait with Dr. Arrieta, or fear, but also as sexual ecstasy, a theme that appears in a different context in one of Goya's most powerful etchings, the *Abducting Horse*

(*Caballo raptor*), plate number 10 of Los Disparates (fig. 92). The multiplicity of interpretations of this drawing attest to Goya's remarkable powers of suggestion as he grew old. Subject, process, and formal qualities come together in this provocative and open-ended drawing that affirms the primary place of imagination in Goya's art.

SGG

1   Gassier 1973, p. 639, notes that the present drawing introduces a group of three contiguous sheets in Album H on the theme of witchcraft, which concludes with *Traveling Witch* (cat. no. 50). He explains that the intermediary drawing (whose whereabouts were unknown at the time) was described by Eleanor Sayre as depicting a "witch sitting on the ground writing in a tablet." That work, *Malefic Prophet* (Album H. 26; private collection), has since been published in Pérez Sánchez and Sayre 1989, no. 176.
2   Album B. 7. Noted by Wilson-Bareau 2001, p. 202.
3   GW no. 1700. This comparison has been noted in Gassier 1973, p. 639, and London 1963–64(a), p. 100.

Fig. 92   *Abducting Horse (Caballo raptor)*, Disparate No. 10, c. 1815–24, etching and aquatint, 9⅝ × 13¾ (24.5 × 35), The Metropolitan Museum of Art, New York, Harris Brisbane Dick Fund, 1924

Chronology   JOANNA SHEERS

GOYA'S LIFE AND CAREER	GOYA'S SUBJECTS AND CIRCLE OF HIS LAST YEARS	SPANISH HISTORY	FRENCH / BORDELAIS HISTORY
			1715–74: Louis XV is king of France
1746: Born on March 30 in Fuendetodos, Spain, to José Goya, master gilder, and Doña Engracia Lucientes, a member of an impoverished noble family		**1746:** Death of Philip V; Ferdinand VI becomes king of Spain (reigns until his death in 1759)	**1743–57:** Louis-Urbain Aubert, marquis de Tourny, is intendant of Guyenne (Aquitaine); his work contributes greatly to Bordeaux's transformation from a medieval city to a modern cosmopolitan metropolis
1749: Goya's family moves to Zaragoza		**1752:** Real Academia de Bellas Artes is established in Madrid	
			1755: Bordeaux's Place Royale, initiated in 1729 by Claude Boucher (intendant of Guyenne 1720–43) is inaugurated under Tourny
1757: Sent to school of the Piarist Order—Escuelas Pias			**1756–63:** Seven Years' War; results in France's loss of several North American colonies; Treaty of Paris signed February 10, 1763; France's trade with West Africa and the West Indies—a mainstay of Bordeaux's economy in the 18th century—continues to prosper
		1759: Charles III inherits the throne (reigns until his death in 1788)	**1758–88:** Louis-Armand Duplessis, Maréchal de Richelieu, is governor of Guyenne

GOYA'S LIFE AND CAREER	GOYA'S SUBJECTS AND CIRCLE OF HIS LAST YEARS	SPANISH HISTORY	FRENCH/BORDELAIS HISTORY
1760: Receives some art training in Zaragoza from the painter José Luzán y Martínez (1710–1785)	**1760:** Leandro Fernández de Moratín born in Madrid (March 10)	**1761–79:** Anton Raphael Mengs (1728–1779) serves as Court Painter	
1763: Has by this time left Luzán's studio for Madrid in order to study with future brother-in-law, Francisco Bayeu; enters scholarship competition of the Real Academia de Bellas Artes de San Fernando, Madrid (Dec. 1763–Jan. 1764), but is rejected (applies unsuccessfully once more in 1766)		**1762:** Giovanni Battista Tiepolo (1696–1770) arrives in Madrid **1765:** Marriage of María Luisa and the future Charles IV	**1768:** Joseph Bonaparte born in Ajaccio, Corsica (Jan. 7); the Bordeaux Académie des Arts is created by a group of local artists and Enlightenment philosophers
1770: Has by this time arrived in Rome to study painting			**1769:** Napoleon Bonaparte born (Aug. 15)
1771: Awarded second prize in a competition arranged by the Academy of Fine Arts, Parma, for his painting *Victorious Hannibal Seeing Italy for the First Time from the Alps* (now in the Selgas-Fagalde Foundation, Cudillero); returns to Zaragoza in June			
1772: Receives commission from the Cathedral of Nuestra Señora del Pilar in Zaragoza for fresco decorations (completed by June); begins murals in the Carthusian monastery church of Aula Dei, outside Zaragoza (completed 1774)			

GOYA'S LIFE AND CAREER	GOYA'S SUBJECTS AND CIRCLE OF HIS LAST YEARS	SPANISH HISTORY	FRENCH / BORDELAIS HISTORY
1773: Marries Josefa Bayeu, sister of Francisco, in Madrid, but continues to work in Zaragoza			
1774: Called to Madrid by Mengs late in the year to paint oil-on-canvas cartoons for the Royal Tapestry Manufactory with brother-in-law Ramón Bayeu (an ongoing project through 1792)	**1775:** José Duaso y Latre born in Aragon		**1774:** Louis XV dies; Louis XVI and Marie-Antoinette become king and queen of France (reign until 1792)
			1776–85: Nicolas Dupré de Saint Maur is intendant of Guyenne
1778: Begins series of prints after paintings by Velázquez, which are announced for sale on July 28 and Dec. 22	**1777:** Joaquín María de Ferrer born (Dec. 7); Cyprien Gaulon born in Santo Domingo (Haiti)		**1778:** France participates in the American Revolution
1779: Applies unsuccessfully for position of Court Painter			
1780: Admitted to the Real Academia de Bellas Artes de San Fernando (May), having qualified with the painting *Christ Crucified* (Museo Nacional del Prado); works in Zaragoza on another fresco commission for the Cathedral of Nuestra Señora del Pilar		**1780:** In light of financial problems, the monarchy closes the Royal Tapestry Manufactory (March 15) for a three-year period	**1780:** The Grand Théâtre is inaugurated in Bordeaux
1781: Returns to Madrid; Goya's father dies (Dec. 17)	**1781:** Manuel Silvela born in Valladolid (Oct. 31)		
1783: Receives important portrait commission from the count of Floridablanca (now in the Banco de España, Madrid)			

GOYA'S LIFE AND CAREER	GOYA'S SUBJECTS AND CIRCLE OF HIS LAST YEARS	SPANISH HISTORY	FRENCH/BORDELAIS HISTORY
1784: Birth of Goya and Josefa's son (and only child to survive to adulthood), Javier Goya y Bayeu (Dec. 2); baptized Xavier (Jan. 1785)	**1784:** Approximate year of birth of Juan de Muguiro	**1784:** The future Ferdinand VII, eldest son of Charles IV, is born	
1785: Appointed Adjunct Director of Painting at the Real Academia de San Fernando; receives commissions from the duke and duchess of Osuna; attains increasing popularity in the 1780s as a portrait painter among royal, aristocratic, and professional patrons			
1786: Appointed Painter to the King (Pintor del Rey) by Charles III	**1786**: Tiburcio Pérez y Cuervo born in Oviedo, Asturias		
	1788: Leocadia Weiss (née Zorrilla y Galarza) born in Madrid (Dec. 9)	**1788:** Death of Charles III (Dec. 14)	
1789: Promoted to Court Painter (Pintor de Cámara) by the new king and queen, Charles IV and María Luisa (April)		**1789:** Charles IV and María Luisa crowned (Jan. 27; reign ends with their abdication in 1808)	**1789:** French Revolution begins; storming of the Bastille in Paris (July 14); revolutionaries issue the Declaration of the Rights of Man (Aug. 26)
1790: Accompanies Josefa to the saltwater baths at Valencia; elected to the Royal Academy of San Carlos	**1790:** First performance of Moratín's play *El viejo y la niña*	**1790:** Fear of revolution thwarts progressive inroads begun during Charles III's reign	**1791:** Slave revolt in Santo Domingo (Haiti) led by Toussaint l'Ouverture, resulting in the island's freedom from French rule; the French constitution is written

GOYA'S LIFE AND CAREER	GOYA'S SUBJECTS AND CIRCLE OF HIS LAST YEARS	SPANISH HISTORY	FRENCH/BORDELAIS HISTORY
1792: Sends by request a written address to the Real Academia de San Fernando on the method of teaching the visual arts; travels to Cádiz and stays for several months with the collector Sebastián Martínez; paints his portrait there (The Metropolitan Museum of Art); Goya is seriously ill during this time and loses his hearing as a result		**1792:** Charles IV dismisses his prime minister, the Conde de Floridablanca, who attempted to censor news of the French Revolution in Spain; the Conde de Aranda is appointed, only to be replaced shortly thereafter by Manuel Godoy, favorite of the king and queen; he is charged with resuming relations with France	**1792:** The French National Convention and First Republic are established; Louis XVI is convicted of treason and the monarchy is abolished; in Bordeaux the convents of the Jacobins and the Recollets are sold and torn down (to be replaced later by the Place des Grands Hommes); the Musée du Louvre opens to the public in Paris
1793: Ramón Bayeu dies in March; Goya, now deaf, returns to Madrid by July 11; chooses to discontinue his work with the tapestry cartoons; paints small cabinet paintings on tinplate of various subjects, which he submits to the Real Academia in Jan. 1794		**1793:** Spain declares war on France	**1793:** Reign of Terror commences in Paris under Robespierre and the Committee of Public Safety; Louis XVI and Marie-Antoinette are executed at the guillotine; execution of the twenty-one Girondins; in Bordeaux the guillotine stands in the Place Dauphine (1792–94); the Palais Galien is torn down
			1794: Robespierre overthrown; end of Reign of Terror; the Convention emancipates all slaves in French colonies
1795: Becomes Director of Painting at the Real Academia de San Fernando; death of Francisco Bayeu		**1795:** Peace of Basel ends hostilities with France; Godoy is named Prince of Peace	**1795:** the Directory, the last stage of the Revolution, is established (1795–99)

GOYA'S LIFE AND CAREER	GOYA'S SUBJECTS AND CIRCLE OF HIS LAST YEARS	SPANISH HISTORY	FRENCH/BORDELAIS HISTORY
1796: Stays with Juan Agustín Ceán Bermúdez in Seville, then travels to Sanlúcar, where he spends some months with the widowed Duchess of Alba; paints her portrait, 1797; approximate beginning of his production of the album drawings (Albums A and B)		**1796:** Spain at war with England	**1796:** Napoleon's Italian campaign
[**1796–99:** Lithography is invented by Aloys Senefelder (1771–1834) in Munich]			
1797: Returns to Madrid; resigns as Director of Painting at the Real Academia because of poor health (April 1); the Duchess of Alba includes Goya's son, Javier, in her will		**1797:** Gaspar Melchor de Jovellanos, Francisco de Saavedra, Juan Meléndez Valdés, and other reformists appointed to government positions by Godoy	
1798: Paints series of witchcraft pictures for the duke and duchess of Osuna (June); completes a fresco cycle in the Hermitage church of San Antonio de la Florida, Madrid (Aug.–Nov.)		**1798:** Godoy resigns; Charles IV appoints Jovellanos and Saavedra as heads of the government	
1799: The Caprichos are published and announced for sale on Feb. 19, but are withdrawn from the market two days later (after twenty-seven sets are sold); Goya paints his first portrait of Leandro Fernández de Moratín in July; appointed First Court Painter (Oct. 31)		**1799:** Godoy reinstated	**1799:** Napoleon Bonaparte enters Paris and crowns himself First Consul; marks beginning of the Consulate in France (1799–1804)

GOYA'S LIFE AND CAREER	GOYA'S SUBJECTS AND CIRCLE OF HIS LAST YEARS	SPANISH HISTORY	FRENCH / BORDELAIS HISTORY
1800: Goya spends the spring in Aranjuez working on preparatory sketches for a group portrait of the royal family, which he completes 1800–1; about this time he also paints portraits of Godoy and his wife, the Countess of Chinchón		**1801:** With support of the French, Godoy declares war on Portugal (War of the Oranges) and is victorious	**1801:** The Musée des Beaux-Arts de Bordeaux is established; Pierre Lacour (1745–1814) is considered the founder and first curator of the museum
1802: Duchess of Alba dies (July 23)			**1802–3:** Peace of Amiens
1803: Goya gives the original copperplates and all unsold sets of the Caprichos to the crown in exchange for an annuity for Javier	**1804:** Antonio de Brugada born in Madrid	**1803:** Spain and France at war with Great Britain	**1803–15:** Napoleonic Wars
			1804: Napoleon names himself Emperor of France; marks beginning of the First French Empire (1804–14); Haiti achieves full independence from France
1805: Javier marries Gumersinda Goicoechea on July 8 in Madrid; Leocadia attends the wedding; Goya gives the couple his house at 7, calle de los Reyes in Madrid and paints a set of portrait miniatures on copper of the newlyweds and his in-laws		**1805:** Battle of Trafalgar (Oct. 21); ends with British victory over Spain and France and control of European waters	
1806: Goya's grandson, Mariano Goya y Goicoechea, is born	**1806:** Moratín's play *El sí de las niñas* is performed for the first time		**1806:** Napoleon declares the Continental Blockade with the intention of injuring England's trade; instead the blockade creates a shortage of colonial products in continental Europe; port activity in Bordeaux is severely affected
	1807: Leocadia marries Isidoro Weiss in Madrid (Oct. 10)	**1807:** French troops pass through Spain en route to Portugal	

GOYA'S LIFE AND CAREER	GOYA'S SUBJECTS AND CIRCLE OF HIS LAST YEARS	SPANISH HISTORY	FRENCH / BORDELAIS HISTORY
1808: The Real Academia commissions Goya to paint an equestrian portrait of Ferdinand VII following Charles IV's abdication; Goya called to Zaragoza to record the city's efforts against the French (Oct.); possibly begins Album C drawings		**1808:** Napoleon's troops, now focused on Spain, seize Barcelona and Pamplona (Feb.); Mutiny of Aranjuez calls for removal of Godoy (March 17); Charles IV is forced to abdicate, ceding the throne to his son, Ferdinand VII; French troops enter Madrid in April, while Ferdinand, Charles IV, María Luisa, and Godoy are held in Bayonne; Napoleon convinces Ferdinand to abdicate in favor of Charles IV, but Napoleon ultimately takes the crown; while some welcome the French rule, local resistance to the occupation is strong; citizens of Madrid revolt in uprisings (May 2) but are defeated by French forces; executions staged at Príncipe Pío (May 3); beginning of the Spanish War of Independence (or Peninsular War) (1808–14); Napoleon crowns his brother, Joseph Bonaparte, King José I of Spain (June 6; he reigns until 1813); French troops defeated at Bailén (July 19); Charles III and María Luisa go to Rome; Napoleon enters Spain (Nov.)	**1808:** Napoleon goes to Bayonne because of events in Spain and makes a stop in Bordeaux in April before sending additional troops to the peninsula
	1809: Silvela attains position of royal judge in Joseph Bonaparte's administration	**1809:** Under Sir Arthur Wellesley (later 1st duke of Wellington), British forces enter Spain to help fight against the French	

GOYA'S LIFE AND CAREER	GOYA'S SUBJECTS AND CIRCLE OF HIS LAST YEARS	SPANISH HISTORY	FRENCH / BORDELAIS HISTORY
1810: Begins Disasters of War series; commissioned to paint portraits of Joseph Bonaparte and French general Nicolas Guye			
1811: Awarded the Royal Order of Spain by Joseph Bonaparte; Goya and Josefa draft a will leaving their estate to Javier and Mariano	**1811:** Moratín made Director-General of Libraries in Madrid; Guillermo Weiss born (Jan. 31); Leocadia is accused of infidelity by her husband		
1812: Josefa dies (June 20); property divided between Goya and Javier; Goya paints portrait of Wellington while he is in Madrid; possibly begins Album F drawings	**1812:** Moratín's Auto de Fe is published	**1812:** The constitution of Cádiz is written (March 18); French defeated at the Battle of Arapiles (or Salamanca; July 22); Wellington in Madrid (Aug.)	**1812:** Napoleon defeated at the Battle of Leipzig in Russia
	1813: Silvela leaves Spain with the army and court of Joseph Bonaparte and settles in Bordeaux; many *josefino*s, supporters of Bonaparte, flee as well	**1813**: Office of the Inquisition temporarily abolished (Feb.); Joseph Bonaparte abdicates and leaves Madrid (March 17); Spanish-British victory at the battle of Vitoria forces the French army to withdraw from Spain (June 21); Treaty of Valençay (Dec. 11); Ferdinand VII is released by Napoleon	
1814: Goya's *Maja* paintings denounced as obscene by the Inquisition; he is investigated as a French sympathizer; Goya paints the famous canvases *Second of May 1808* and *Third of May 1808* as well as another commissioned portrait of Ferdinand VII	**1814:** Rosario Weiss born (Oct. 3); divorce proceedings between Leocadia and Isidoro are ongoing; Moratín is exiled from Madrid	**1814:** Ferdinand VII returns to Spain and is restored to the throne; issues decree against the Liberals; the constitution is abolished (May 4); the Inquisition and absolute monarchy are reinstated; Vicente López Portaña (1772–1850) appointed Court Painter	**1814:** Napoleon abdicates and is exiled to Elba; Louis XVIII takes the throne, marking the beginning of the Restoration in France; wine export and colonial trade resumes in Bordeaux and other French port cities following the Treaty of Paris of May 30

GOYA'S LIFE AND CAREER	GOYA'S SUBJECTS AND CIRCLE OF HIS LAST YEARS	SPANISH HISTORY	FRENCH / BORDELAIS HISTORY
1815: Goya summoned to appear before the Inquisition; pardoned for his affiliation with Joseph Bonaparte largely thanks to his paintings the *Second of May* and *Third of May*; possibly begins Album E drawings; Goya reported to be impoverished			**1815:** Napoleon returns to France for the "100 Days"; defeated at Waterloo in June; Atlantic slave trade abolished at the Congress of Vienna (Oct. 1, 1814–June 9, 1815)
1816: Completes Tauromaquia print series; begins Disparates series (published in 1864 as the Proverbios)	**1816:** Joaquín Ferrer returns to Spain from Peru (where he traveled during the Napoleonic occupation) and marries Manuela de Álvarez Coiñas y Thomas in Madrid		
1817: Goya spends time in Seville			
	1818: Cyprien Gaulon establishes his lithographic workshop in Bordeaux	**1818:** Dismissal of Finance Minister Garay; Spain falls into anarchy	
1819: Goya purchases the Quinta del Sordo (Feb.); Leocadia Weiss and her children move in; Goya's friend José María Cardano establishes the Real Establecimiento Litográfico in Madrid, and Goya experiments with lithography; he is commissioned by the Escolapian Order to paint the *Last Communion of St. Joseph Calasanz* for the church of San Antón in Madrid (May); possibly begins Album D drawings; is taken gravely ill late in the year and is treated by Dr. Arrieta		**1819:** Charles IV and María Luisa die in Rome; the Museo Nacional del Prado, Spain's first public museum, is founded by Ferdinand VII and his wife, María Isabel de Braganza; the peste (or yellow fever) is rampant in parts of Spain	

GOYA'S LIFE AND CAREER	GOYA'S SUBJECTS AND CIRCLE OF HIS LAST YEARS	SPANISH HISTORY	FRENCH/BORDELAIS HISTORY
1820: Goya's attends the session of the Real Academia for the last time to swear allegiance to the constitution and to the king (April 4); begins Black Paintings (1820–23); completes the eighty-four Disasters of War etchings (which would remain unpublished until 1863); paints portraits of Dr. Arrieta and Tiburcio Pérez y Cuervo	**1821:** Moratín arrives in Bordeaux, having fled from Spain, and moves into Silvela's home (Oct. 11)	**1820:** Revolt of Riego in Cádiz (Jan. 1): Rafael del Riego y Nuñez leads officers in a successful Liberal rebellion against Ferdinand VII; the king is forced to accept the constitution of 1812 (March 9); beginning of the Liberal Triennium, a three-year period in which the Spanish monarchy remained impotent, while local governments supported the constitution (1820–23)	**1821:** Napoleon dies in St. Helena at age 52 (May 5)

1822: Bordeaux's Pont de Pierre, which connects the banks of the Garonne River, opens to traffic |
| **1823:** Goya deeds the Quinta del Sordo to his grandson, Mariano (Sept. 17); paints portrait of Ramón Satué, nephew of José Duaso y Latre | **1823:** Ferrer is sentenced to death, but escapes to France via England; Brugada emigrates to Bordeaux; José María Cardano leaves Madrid for Paris | **1823:** Ferdinand VII imprisoned by Spanish Liberals and taken to Cádiz; France sends an expeditionary force called the 100,000 Sons of Saint Louis into Spain on April 7 to aid Ferdinand's restoration to the throne; occupying Madrid by May 24, they defeat the constitutional army at the Fort of Trocadero (August 30–31); Surrender of Cádiz (Sept. 30); Ferdinand VII released and restored to the throne; Absolutist regime reinstated; Riego imprisoned and publicly executed (Nov. 7); Ferdinand VII reenters Madrid (Nov. 13) | |

GOYA'S LIFE AND CAREER	GOYA'S SUBJECTS AND CIRCLE OF HIS LAST YEARS	SPANISH HISTORY	FRENCH/BORDELAIS HISTORY
1824: MADRID: Goya takes refuge in the home of José Duaso y Latre (beginning probably in Jan.); paints Duaso's portrait during this period (probably after March 30); on May 2, immediately following the declaration of amnesty, Goya requests a leave of absence from Ferdinand VII to go to France to take the mineral waters at Plombières for medical reasons (request granted May 30); the ten-year-old Rosario is entrusted by Goya and Leocadia to the care of Tiburcio Pérez; Goya executes small portrait on paper of Javier before departing from Madrid. BORDEAUX: Goya, who never goes to Plombières, arrives in Bordeaux in late June; stays with Moratín and Silvela for three days, then leaves for Paris. PARIS: paints portraits of Joaquín and Manuela de Ferrer, who have themselves just settled in Paris; also paints for them a bullfighting scene. BORDEAUX: Goya returns to Bordeaux on Sept. 1, having traveled with Martín Miguel de Goicoechea and his family; Leocadia and her children arrive in Bordeaux in mid-September; they settle with Goya in a house on 24 cours de Tourny; Goya paints second portrait of Moratín and possibly begins the drawings of Albums G and H.		**1824:** Period of absolutist repression and persecution of Liberals under Ferdinand VII (1824–33); on May 1 Ferdinand VII declares temporary amnesty for constitutional sympathizers	**1824:** Louis XVIII dies; his brother Charles X ascends to the throne (Sept. 16; reign ends with the July Revolution of 1830); Exhibition of Living Artists opens in Paris (Aug. 25) and includes works by Delacroix, Ingres, and Constable, as well as lithographs and miniature paintings; construction and development continues in Bordeaux

GOYA'S LIFE AND CAREER	GOYA'S SUBJECTS AND CIRCLE OF HIS LAST YEARS	SPANISH HISTORY	FRENCH/BORDELAIS HISTORY
1825: First renewal of Goya's leave of absence granted by Ferdinand VII (Jan.); Goya at work on the miniatures on ivory (winter 1824–25); in the spring serious illness sets in; second renewal of his leave of absence granted July 4; Goya and his family move into a house at 10 Chemin de la Croix-Blanche, where they live for two years; Martín Miguel de Goicoechea dies; Goya at work on the Bulls of Bordeaux lithographs (completed by Dec. 6, printed and registered by Cyprien Gaulon); Goya also makes a lithographic portrait of Gaulon in this year			**1825:** A bronze statue of Tourny is erected in the Place Tourny, very near Goya's residence of the time; the construction of the Quinconces baths is completed
1826: Paints portrait of Jacques Galos in Bordeaux at some point between March 30 and the end of the year; makes his first return trip to Madrid in May to present a petition for retirement as Court Painter with full salary; his request is granted by Ferdinand VII in June; while in Madrid, Goya's portrait is painted by Vicente López, who is by this time First Court Painter; Goya returns to Bordeaux and moves with his family to 13 rue Saint-Seurin late in the year			

GOYA'S LIFE AND CAREER	GOYA'S SUBJECTS AND CIRCLE OF HIS LAST YEARS	SPANISH HISTORY	FRENCH / BORDELAIS HISTORY
1827: Paints portrait of Juan de Muguiro in May; second visit to Madrid (summer); paints portrait of Mariano during this trip; upon his return to Bordeaux on Sept. 19, Goya moves to his final home at 39 Fossés de l'Intendance	**1827:** Moratín and Silvela move to Paris; Gaulon is honored at the exhibition of the Société Philomatique de Bordeaux in the Wauxhall on Fossés de l'Intendance— opposite Goya's home		
1828: Javier and his family make plans to come to Bordeaux in Jan.; Gumersinda and Mariano arrive March 28; Goya sends an undated letter to Javier expressing his desire for his son's presence; paralysis sets in April 1; Goya dies April 16; funeral mass is held April 17 at Goya's parish church of Nôtre Dame; he is buried in the cemetery of the Chartreuse in Bordeaux beside Martín Miguel de Goicoechea (Leocadia, Rosario, Antonio de Brugada, Pío de Molina, and Braulio Poc were present); Javier arrives in Bordeaux on April 20 to take possession of his inheritance	**1828:** Moratín dies in Paris (June 21); Javier begins to sell his father's work (May 23–24)		
	1829: Leocadia writes to Juan de Muguiro to offer him the *Milkmaid of Bordeaux* (Dec. 9; letter posted Jan. 13, 1830)		**1830:** Louis Philippe, duke of Orléans, takes the throne (reign ends 1848)
	1832: Silvela dies in Paris (May 9)		
	1833: Leocadia, Guillermo, and Rosario return to Spain	**1833:** Death of Ferdinand VII (Sept. 29); amnesty is declared; many exiles, including the Ferrers, return to Spain; Isabella II reigns as queen (until exiled in 1868; abdicates officially in 1870)	

GOYA'S LIFE AND CAREER	GOYA'S SUBJECTS AND CIRCLE OF HIS LAST YEARS	SPANISH HISTORY	FRENCH/BORDELAIS HISTORY
	1840: Rosario, in pursuing a career as an artist, becomes a member of the Real Academia de Bellas Artes de San Fernando		
	1842: Rosario is appointed drawing teacher to Isabella II (Jan. 18), but dies the following year at the age of twenty-nine (July 3, 1843)		
	1854: Javier dies		
	1856: Leocadia's death (Aug. 7)		
1863: Disasters of War series is published			
1864: Disparates series is published, then called the Proverbios because of the association of its subject matter with Spanish proverbs	**1874:** Death of Mariano (Jan. 8)		
1900: Major retrospective exhibition of Goya's work in Madrid; the Bordeaux portraits of Moratín and Silvela are on view			
1900–1: Goya's remains repatriated from France to Spain (along with Moratín's)			
1929: His remains exhumed once more and reburied under the floor of San Antonio de la Florida			

Selected Bibliography IRAIDA RODRÍGUEZ-NEGRÓN

Books, Articles, and Archival Material

Alcalá Flecha 1988(a). Roberto Alcalá Flecha. "De la sociedad estamental a la sociedad clasista," *Literatura e ideología en el arte de Goya.* Zaragoza: Diputación General de Aragón, 1988.
——**1988(b).** Roberto Alcalá Flecha. "El combate ideológico contra las viejas instituciones," *Literatura e ideología en el arte de Goya.* Zaragoza: Diputación General de Aragón, 1988.
——**1988(c).** Roberto Alcalá Flecha. *Literatura e ideología en el arte de Goya.* Zaragoza: Diputación General de Aragón, 1988.
——**1997.** Roberto Alcalá Flecha. "Goya y el mito de las parcas," *Goya* 258 (May–June 1997): 337–51.
Álvarez Lopera 1997. José Álvarez Lopera. "La carrera de Rosario Weiss en España: a la búsqueda de un perfil," *La mujer en el arte español: VIII Jornadas de Arte / Departamento de Historia del Arte "Diego Velázquez," Centro de Estudios Históricos.* Madrid: Editorial Alpuerto, 1997.
——**2001.** José Álvarez Lopera. "Rosario Weiss no pintó 'La Lechera,'" *Descubrir el Arte* 3: 23 (May 2001): 50–1.
——**2003.** José Álvarez Lopera. "Rosario Weiss. Vida y obras," *Goya y lo goyesco en la Fundación Lázaro Galdiano.* Exh. cat. Mercedes Águeda Villar, ed. Segovia: Fundación Lázaro Galdiano, 2003.
Andioc 1973. René Andioc, ed. *Epistolario de Leandro Fernández de Moratín.* Madrid: Editorial Castalia, 1973.
——**1982.** René Andioc. "Sobre Goya y Moratín hijo," *Hispanic Review* 50: 2 (Spring 1982): 119–32.
——**1998.** René Andioc. "Sobre Moratín y Goya," *Goya y Moratín: (en Burdeos, 1824–1828).* Exh. cat. Bilbao: Museo de Bellas Artes de Bilbao, 1998.
Ansón Navarro 1995. Arturo Ansón Navarro. *Goya y Aragón: Familia, amistades y encargos artísticos.* Zaragoza: Caja de Ahorros de la Inmaculada de Aragón, 1995.
Antoniol 1998. Bernard Antoniol. "Goya, peintre de la folie," *Goya, Hommages: Les années bordelaises, 1824–1828: Présence de Goya aux XIXe et XXe siècles.* Exh. cat. Francis Ribemont and Françoise Garcia, eds. Bordeaux: Musée des Beaux-Arts de Bordeaux, 1998.
Arías Anglés 1989. Enrique Arías Anglés. *Antonio de Brugada: pintor romántico y liberal.* Madrid: Ayuntamiento de Madrid; El Arapiés, 1989.
Autobiografía de Moratín 1962. Autobiografía de Moratín in the Biblioteca Nacional, Madrid, ms. 5617 (1962).

Badinter 1981. Elisabeth Badinter. *Mother Love, Myth and Reality. Motherhood in Modern History.* New York: Macmillan 1981.
Baldwin 1985. Robert W. Baldwin. "Healing and Hope in Goya's *Self-Portrait with Dr. Arrieta,*" *Source* IV: 4 (Summer 1985): 31–36.
Baticle 1989. Jeannine Baticle. "Goya and the Link with France at the End of the Old Regime," *Goya and the Spirit of Enlightenment.* Exh. cat. Alfonso E. Pérez Sánchez and Eleanor A. Sayre, eds. Boston: Museum of Fine Arts, 1989.
——**1992.** Jeannine Baticle. *Goya.* Paris: Fayard, 1992.
——**1998(a).** Jeannine Baticle. "La pintura de Goya en París y Burdeos, 1824–1828," *Goya y Moratín: (en Burdeos, 1824–1828).* Exh. cat. Bilbao: Museo de Bellas Artes de Bilbao, 1998.
——**1998(b).** Jeannine Baticle. "L'oeuvre peint de Goya à Paris et à Bordeaux 1824–1828," *Goya, Hommages: Les années bordelaises, 1824–1828: Présence de Goya aux XIXe et XXe siècles.* Exh. cat. Francis Ribemont and Françoise Garcia, eds. Bordeaux: Musée des Beaux-Arts de Bordeaux, 1998.
Bean 1964. Jacob Bean. *100 European Drawings in the Metropolitan Museum of Art.* New York: The Metropolitan Museum of Art, 1964.
Bériac 1983. Jean Pierre Bériac. "La litografía: técnica y primeras aplicaciones," *La litografía en Burdeos en la época de Goya.* Exh. cat. Zaragoza: Excmo. Ayuntamiento de Zaragoza. Delegación de Extensión Cultural, 1983.
Bernadau 1844. Pierre Bernadau. *Le viographe bordelais, ou Revue historique des monuments de Bordeaux.* Bordeaux: Gazay, 1844.
Beruete y Moret 1916–18. A. de Beruete y Moret. *Goya, pintor de retratos.* Madrid: Blass y Cía., 1916–18.
——**1924.** A. de Beruete y Moret. "Goya pintor de retratos," *Conferencias de Arte.* Madrid: 1924.
——**1928.** A. de Beruete y Moret. *Goya: Goya, pintor de retratos; Goya, composiciones y figuras y Goya grabador.* Madrid: Blass, 1928.
Bilbao 1999. *Museo de Bellas Artes de Bilbao: Maestros antiguos y modernos.* Bilbao: Fundación BBK, 1999.
Blackburn 2002. Julia Blackburn. *Old Man Goya.* 1st American edition. New York: Pantheon Books, 2002.
Blanco Mozo 1998. José L. Blanco Mozo, "El retrato de doña Catalina de Erauso, la monja alférez, obra de Juan van der Hamen (1596–1631)," *Boletín del Museo e Instituto Camón Aznar* 71 (1998): 33.

Boime 2004. Albert Boime. *Art in an Age of Counterrevolution 1815–1848.* Chicago: University of Chicago Press, 2004.

Boix 1922(a). Félix Boix. *Los dibujos de Goya.* Madrid: Gráficas Reunidas, 1922.

Boletín del Clero Español 1849. "Duaso," *Boletín del Clero Español en . . .* 2 (1849): 49–55.

Bordeaux 1856. *Nouveau guide de l'étranger à Bordeaux.* Bordeaux: Chaumas, 1856.

——**1988(a).** *Deux siècles d'art à Bordeaux: au-delà de la Revolution.* Bordeaux: Nouvelle édition Corail, 1988.

——**1988(b).** *Images des Espagnols en Aquitaine.* Bordeaux: Presses Universitaires, 1988.

Borenius and Wittkower 1937. Tancred Borenius and Rudolf Wittkower. *Catalogue of the Collection of Drawings by the Old Masters, Formed by Sir Robert Mond.* London: Eyre and Spottiswoode, [1937].

Boston 1955. "Goya: Drawings and Prints," *Bulletin of the Museum of Fine Arts* LIII (1955): 43–66.

Bouvy 1918. Eugène Bouvy. *L'imprimeur Gaulon et les origines de la lithographie à Bordeaux.* Bordeaux: Imprimeries Gounouilhou, 1918.

Bozal 1996. Valeriano Bozal. "Goya, dibujos de Burdeos," *Reales Sitios* 33: 128 (1996): 2–11.

——**2000.** Valeriano Bozal. *Goya. Entre Neoclasicismo y Romanticismo.* Madrid: Historia 16, 2000.

Calvo Serraller 1996. Francisco Calvo Serraller. *Goya.* Madrid: Electa, 1996.

Camón Aznar 1980–82. José Camón Aznar. *Fran. de Goya.* 4 vols. Zaragoza: Caja de Ahorros de Zaragoza, Aragón y Rioja, 1980–82.

Canellas López 1981. Angel Canellas López, ed. *Diplomatario / Francisco de Goya.* Zaragoza: Institución "Fernando el Católico" de la Exma. Diputación de Zaragoza, 1981.

Carderera y Solano 1835. Valentín Carderera y Solano. "Biografía de D. Francisco de Goya, pintor," *El Artista* II (1835): 253–55. Reprinted in Ricardo Centallas Salomera. *Valentín Carderera y Solano. Estudios sobre Goya (1835–1885).* Zaragoza: Institución "Fernando El Católico," 1996.

——**1838.** Valentín Carderera y Solano. "Goya," *Semanario Pintoresco* 120 (1838): 631–33. Reprinted in Ricardo Centallas Salomera. *Valentín Carderera y Solano. Estudios sobre Goya (1835–1885).* Zaragoza: Institución "Fernando El Católico," 1996.

——**1860.** Valentín Carderera y Solano. "François Goya: sa vie, ses dessins et ses eaux-fortes," *Gazette des Beaux-Arts* (1860): 215–27.

Caro Baroja 1974. Julio Caro Baroja. *Teatro popular y magia.* Madrid: Ediciones de la Revista de Occidente, 1974.

Carr 1982. Raymond Carr. *Spain 1808–1975.* 2nd edition. Oxford: Clarendon Press, 1982.

Caveda y Nava 1867. José Caveda y Nava. *Memorias para la historia de la Real Academia de San Fernando y de las bellas artes en España, desde el advenimiento al trono de Felipe V, hasta nuestros días, por el excmo. sr. d. José Caveda, consiliario de dicha academia. Se publican por acuerdo unánime de la misma.* 2 vols. Madrid, Imprenta de M. Tello, 1867.

Christie's 1997. *Important Old Master Paintings.* Christie's New York, Friday, January 31, 1997.

Ciofalo 2001. John J. Ciofalo. *The Self-Portraits of Francisco Goya.* Cambridge; New York: Cambridge University Press, 2001.

Cleveland 1982. *European Paintings of the 16th, 17th, and 18th Centuries.* Cleveland Museum of Art, 1982.

Comini 1987. Alessandra Comini. *The Changing Image of Beethoven: A Study in Myth Making.* New York: Rizzoli, 1987.

Courteault 1908. Paul Courteault. *À propos du séjour de Goya à Bordeaux.* Bordeaux: Gounouilhou, 1908.

——**1909.** Paul Courteault. *Bordeaux à travers les siècles.* Bordeaux: Feret, 1909.

Coustet and Saboya n.d. Robert Coustet and Marc Saboya. *Bordeaux. Le Temps de l'histoire: Architecture et urbanisme au XIXe siècle (1800–1914).* Bordeaux: Éditions Mollat.

Cruz Valdovinos 1987. José M. Cruz Valdovinos. "La partición de bienes entre Francisco y Javier Goya a la muerte de Josefa Bayeu y otras cuestiones." *Goya. Nuevas visiones: homenaje a Enrique Lafuente Ferrari.* Madrid: Amigos del Museo del Prado, 1987.

Davidson 1987. Jane P. Davidson. "Goya's Devil's Domain," *The Witch in Northern European Art, 1470–1750.* Freren: Luca Verlag, 1987.

De Angelis 1974. Rita De Angelis, ed. *L'opera pittorica completa di Goya.* Milan: Rizzoli, 1974.

De Salas 1964. Xavier de Salas. "A Group of Bullfight Scenes by Goya," *The Burlington Magazine* 106 (January 1964): 37–38.

——**1973.** Xavier de Salas. "Sur deux miniatures de Goya récemment retrouvées," *Gazette des Beaux-Arts* LXXXI (March 1973): 169–72.

——**1979(a).** Xavier de Salas. *Goya.* Translation by G. T. Culverwell. London: Studio Vista, 1979.

——**1979(b).** Xavier de Salas. "Une miniature et deux dessins inédits de Goya," *Gazette des Beaux-Arts* XCIII (April 1979): 168–71.

Deacon 1995. Philip Deacon. "Introduction," *El sí de las niñas (Leandro Fernández de Moratín).* London: Bristol Classical Press, 1995.

Desgraves 1954. Louis Desgraves. *Bordeaux au cours des siècles.* Bordeaux: Clèdes, 1954.

Desparmet Fitz-Gerald 1928–50. X. Desparmet Fitz-Gerald. *L'oeuvre peint de Goya.* 2 vols. Paris: F. de Nobele, 1928–50.

Díez 2004. José Luis Díez. "The Spanish Portrait in the Nineteenth Century: The Triumph of a Genre," *The Spanish Portrait: From El Greco to Picasso.* Exh. cat. Javier Portús, ed.

Madrid: Museo Nacional del Prado; London: Scala Publishers, 2004.

Dormandy 2000. Thomas Dormandy. *Old Masters: Great Artists in Old Age.* London; New York: Hambledon and London, 2000.

Elias 1994. Norbert Elias. *The Civilizing Process. Sociogenetic and Psychogenetic Investigations.* Translated by Edmund Jephcott. Oxford; Cambridge, Mass.: Blackwell, 1994.

Fauqué 1983. Jacques Fauqué. "Goya y la litografía en Francia," *La litografía en Burdeos en la época de Goya.* Exh. cat. Zaragoza: Excmo. Ayuntamiento de Zaragoza. Delegación de Extensión Cultural, 1983.

———**1988(a).** Jacques Fauqué. "La famille de la Torre à Bordeaux (1824–1833)," *Images des Espagnols en Aquitaine.* Bordeaux: Presses Universitaires, 1988.

———**1988(b).** Jacques Fauqué. *Les nouveaux Caprices de Goya.* Agen: Musée des Beaux-Arts, 1988.

———**1998.** Jacques Fauqué. "Les amis de Goya à Bordeaux," *Goya, Hommages: Les années bordelaises, 1824–1828: Présence de Goya aux XIXe et XXe siècles.* Exh. cat. Francis Ribemont and Françoise Garcia, eds. Bordeaux: Musée des Beaux- Arts de Bordeaux, 1998.

Fauqué and Villanueva Etchevarría 1982. Jacques Fauqué and Ramón Villanueva Etchevarría. *Goya y Burdeos 1824–1828.* Zaragoza: Ediciones Oroel, 1982.

Fernández 1996. Pedro Jesús Fernández. *Quién es quién en la pintura de Goya.* Madrid: Celeste, 1996.

Fernández de Moratín 1871. *Obras de D. Nicolás y D. Leandro Fernández de Moratín.* 3 vols. Madrid: Imprenta y Estereotipia de M. Rivadeneyra, 1871.

———**1968.** Leandro Fernández de Moratín. *Diario, mayo 1780–marzo 1808.* René Andioc and Mireille Andioc, eds. Madrid: Editorial Castalia, 1968.

Fernández Doctor and Seva Díaz 2000. Asunción Fernández Doctor and Antonio Seva Díaz. *Goya y la locura.* Zaragoza: INO Reproducciones, 2000.

Fernández-Salvador 1998. Carmen Fernández-Salvador. "The Witches of Goya," *Athanor* XVI (1998): 23–29.

Figeac 2002. Michel Figeac, ed. *Histoire des Bordelais.* Vol. 1. Bordeaux: Mollat / Fédération historique du sud-ouest, 2002.

Florisoone 1966. Michel Florisoone. "La raison du voyage de Goya à Paris," *Gazette des Beaux-Arts* LXVIII (December 1966): 327–32.

Forrest 1975. Alan Forrest. *Society and Politics in Revolutionary Bordeaux.* London; New York: Oxford University Press, 1975.

Foucault 1965. Michel Foucalt. *Madness and Civilization; a History of Insanity in the Age of Reason.* Translated by Richard Howard. New York: Vintage Books Edition, 1965.

Gállego 1978(a). Julián Gállego. *Autorretratos de Goya.* Zaragoza: Caja de Ahorros de Zaragoza, Aragón y Rioja, 1978.

———**1978(b).** Julián Gállego. "Goya y Burdeos," *Seminario de Arte Aragones* XXVII–XVIII (1978): 13–23.

———**1979.** Julián Gállego. "Francia y Goya," *Goya* 148–50 (January–June 1979): 250–59.

———**1997.** Julián Gállego, "La figura de la maja, desde Goya hasta Zuloaga," *La mujer en el arte español: VIII Jornadas de Arte / Departamento de Historia del Arte "Diego Velázquez," Centro de Estudios Históricos.* Madrid: Editorial Alpuerto, 1997.

García de la Rasilla and Calvo Serraller 1987. Isabel García de la Rasilla and Francisco Calvo Serraller, eds. *Goya. Nuevas visiones. Homenaje a Enrique Lafuente Ferrari.* Madrid: Amigos del Museo del Prado, 1987.

García Guatas 1996. Manuel García Guatas. "Nuevos datos sobre dos aragoneses retratados por Goya," *Goya* 252 (May–June 1996): 326–30.

Garrido 2003. Carmen Garrido. "El Retrato de la Condesa de Chinchón. Estudio técnico." *Boletín del Museo del Prado* 21, no. 39 (2003): 44–55.

Gassier 1971. Pierre Gassier. "Goya à Paris," *Goya* 100 (January–February 1971): 246–51.

———**1973.** Pierre Gassier. *The Drawings of Goya: The Complete Albums.* New York: Praeger Publishers, 1973.

———**1975.** Pierre Gassier. *The Drawings of Goya: The Sketches, Studies, and Individual Drawings.* Translated by James Emmons. London: Thames & Hudson, 1975.

———**1983.** Pierre Gassier. *Goya: A Witness of His Times.* Secaucus, N.J.: Chartwell Books, 1983.

———**1990.** Pierre Gassier, ed. *Tout l'oeuvre peint de Goya.* Paris: Flammarion, 1990.

———**1998.** Pierre Gassier. "Les dessins de Bordeaux," *Goya, Hommages: Les années bordelaises, 1824–1828: Présence de Goya aux XIXe et XXe siècles.* Exh. cat. Francis Ribemont and Françoise Garcia, eds. Bordeaux: Musée des Beaux-Arts de Bordeaux, 1998.

Gassier and Wilson 1971. Pierre Gassier and Juliet Wilson. *The Life and Complete Work of Francisco Goya.* New York: Harrison House, 1971.

Gaya Nuño 1955. Juan Antonio Gaya Nuño. *Historia y Guía de los Museos de España.* Madrid: Espasa-Calpe, S. A., 1955.

———**1964.** Juan Antonio Gaya Nuño. *La pintura española en los museos provinciales.* Madrid: Aguilar, 1964.

Gerard Powell 1998–99. Véronique Gerard Powell. "Goya Portraitist," *Goya: un regard libre.* Exh. cat. Paris: Réunion des Musées Nationaux; Lille: Palais des Beaux-Arts, 1998–99.

Gil 1990. Rafael Gil. *Asensi Julià: el deixeble de Goya.* Valencia: Edicions Alfons el Magnànim, Institució Valenciana d'Estudis i Investigació, 1990.

Gil Salinas 1996. Rafael Gil Salinas. "Goya y la difusión del arte español en América," *Congreso Internacional "Goya 250 años después, 1746–1996."* Marbella: Museo del Grabado Español Contemporáneo, 1996.

Gilman 1996. Sander L. Gilman. *Seeing the Insane.* Revised edition. Lincoln: University of Nebraska Press, 1996.

Glendinning 1977. Nigel Glendinning. *Goya and His Critics.* New Haven; London: Yale University Press, 1977.

——**1978.** Nigel Glendinning. "A Solution to the Enigma of Goya's 'Emphatic Caprices.' Nos. 65–80 of *The Disasters of War,*" *Apollo* 107 (1978): 186–91.

——**1980.** Nigel Glendinning. "Convention and Character in Goya's Portraits," *Biography in the 18th Century.* J. D. Browning, ed. New York; London: Garland Publishing, 1980.

——**1989.** Nigel Glendinning. "Art and Enlightenment in Goya's Circle," *Goya and the Spirit of Enlightenment.* Exh. cat. Alfonso E. Pérez Sánchez and Eleanor A. Sayre, eds. Boston: Museum of Fine Arts, 1989.

——**1996(a).** Nigel Glendinning. "El arte satírico de *Los Caprichos,* con una nueva síntesis de la historia de su estampación y divulgación," *Caprichos de Francisco de Goya, una aproximación y tres estudios.* Madrid: Calcografía Nacional, Real Academia de Bellas Artes de San Fernando; Barcelona: Fundació Caixa de Catalunya; Fundación El Monte, 1996.

——**1996(b).** Nigel Glendinning. "Goya at 250," *Apollo* (September 1996): 73–75.

——**2002.** Nigel Glendinning. "El problema de las atribuciones desde la exposición Goya de 1900," *Goya 1900: catálogo ilustrado y estudio de la exposición en el Ministerio de Instrucción Pública y Bellas Artes.* 2 vols. Madrid: Dirección General de Bellas Artes y Bienes Culturales; Instituto del Patrimonio Histórico Español, 2002.

——**2004.** Nigel Glendinning. "Las Pinturas Negras de Goya y la Quinta del Sordo. Precisiones sobre las teorías de Juan José Junquera," *Archivo Español de Arte* LXXVII: 307 (July–September 2004): 233–45.

——**2004–5.** Nigel Glendinning. "The Spanish Portrait in the Eighteenth Century," *The Spanish Portrait: From El Greco to Picasso.* Exh. cat. Javier Portús, ed. London; Madrid: Scala Publishers, 2004.

Gómez-Moreno 1941. María Elena Gómez-Moreno. "Un cuaderno de dibujos de Goya," *Archivo Español de Arte* 14 (1941): 155–63.

Gudiol 1971. José Gudiol. *Goya, 1746–1828: Biography, Analytical Study and Catalogue of His Paintings.* 4 vols. Translated by Kenneth Lyons. Barcelona: Ediciones Polígrafa, 1971.

Guía de arquitectura y urbanismo de Madrid 1982–83. *Guía de arquitectura y urbanismo de Madrid / Colegio Oficial de Arquitectos de Madrid.* 2nd edition. Madrid: El Colegio, 1982–83.

Harris 1975. Enriqueta Harris. *Goya.* London: Phaidon, 1975.

Harris 1964. Tomás Harris. *Goya: Engravings and Lithographs.* 2 vols. Oxford: B. Cassirer, 1964.

Hart 1962. Harold W. Hart. "The Sedan Chair as a Means of Public Conveyance," *The Journal of Transport History* V: 4 (November 1962): 205–18.

Heckes 1985. Frank Irving Heckes. "Supernatural Themes in the Art of Francisco de Goya." (Volumes I and II). Ph.D dissertation. University of Michigan, 1985.

Held 1994. Jutta Held, ed. *Goya, Neue Forschungen: das Internationale Symposium 1991 in Osnabrück.* Berlin: Gebr. Mann Verlag, 1994.

Helman 1959. Edith F. Helman. "The Younger Moratín and Goya: On *Duendes* and *Brujas,*" *Hispanic Review* XXVII: 1 (January 1959): 103–22.

——**1963.** Edith F. Helman. *Trasmundo de Goya.* Madrid: Revista de Occidente, 1963.

——**1987.** Edith F. Helman. "Algunos sueños y brujas de Goya," *Goya. Nuevas visiones. Homenaje a Enrique Lafuente Ferrari.* Isabel García de la Rasilla and Francisco Calvo Serraller, eds. Madrid: Amigos del Museo del Prado, 1987.

Herranz Rodríguez 1996. Concha Herranz Rodríguez. "Glosario de Indumentaria," *Vida cotidiana en tiempos de Goya.* Exh. cat. Madrid: Ministerio de Educación y Cultura, Dirección General de Bellas Artes y Bienes Culturales; Barcelona: Lunwerg Editores, 1996.

Hiéret 1986. J.-P. Hiéret. "Vivre l'âge d'or a Bordeaux (XVIIIᵉs): Négoce et prospérité," *Histoire et ethnographie régionale. L'Aquitaine de 1715 a nos jours.* Bordeaux: Musée d'Aquitaine; Guitel Frères, 1986.

Hofmann 2003. Werner Hofmann. *Goya: "To Every Story There Belongs Another."* New York: Thames & Hudson, 2003.

Hughes 2003. Robert Hughes. *Goya.* New York: Alfred A. Knopf, 2003.

Junquera 2003(a). Juan José Junquera. "Los Goya: de la Quinta a Burdeos y vuelta," *Archivo Español de Arte* 76 (2003): 353–70.

——**2003(b).** Juan José Junquera. *The Black Paintings of Goya.* Translated by Gilla Evans. London: Scala Publishers, 2003.

Klein 1999. Peter K. Klein. "Insanity and the Sublime: Aesthetics and Theories of Mental Illness in Goya's *Yard with Lunatics* and Related Works," *Journal of the Warburg and Courtauld Institutes* LXI (1999): 198–252.

Lafond 1907(a). P. Lafond. "Les dernières années de Goya en France," *Gazette des Beaux-Arts* XXXVII (1907): 114–31.

——**1907(b).** P. Lafond. *Nouveaux caprices de Goya. Suite de trente-huit dessins inédits.* Paris: Société de Propagation des Livres d'Art, 1907.

Lafuente Ferrari 1947. Enrique Lafuente Ferrari. *Antecedentes, coincidencias e influencias del arte de Goya.* Madrid: Sociedad Española de Amigos del Arte, 1947.

——**1979.** Enrique Lafuente Ferrari. "Un dibujo inédito de Goya de la serie sepia (Cuaderno F)," *Goya* 148–50 (1979): 206–9.

——1980. Enrique Lafuente Ferrari. *Goya: Drawings*. Bilbao: Silex, 1980.

Lasterra 1967. Crisanto de Lasterra. *Museo de Bellas Artes de Bilbao*. Madrid: Aguilar, 1967.

Levitine 1983. George Levitine. "Goya and l'Abbé Bordelon," *Studies on Voltaire and the Eighteenth Century* 216 (1983): 135–36.

Lhéritier 1920. Michel Lhéritier. *L'Intendant Tourny (1695–1760)*. 2 vols. Paris: Librairie Felix Alcan, 1920.

Licht 2001. Fred Licht. *Goya*. New York: London: Abbeville Press Publishers, 2001.

Llanos de Torriglia 1946. F. de Llanos de Torriglia. "Moratín retrata a Goya en casa de Silvela," *Boletín de la Real Academia de la Historia* (1946): 63–73.

López 1988. François López. "Les Espagnols à Bordeaux de 1808 à 1823," *Images des Espagnols en Aquitaine*. Bordeaux: Presses Universitaires, 1988.

López-Rey 1947. José López-Rey. *Goya y el mundo a su alrededor*. Buenos Aires: Editorial Sudamericana, 1947.

——1956(a). José López-Rey. *A Cycle of Goya's Drawings: The Expression of Truth and Liberty*. New York: The Macmillan Company, 1956.

——1956(b). José López-Rey. "Goya and His Pupil María del Rosario Weiss," *Gazette des Beaux–Arts* XLVII (May–June 1956): 251–84.

——1964. José López-Rey. "Goya at the London Royal Academy," *Gazette de Beaux-Arts* LXIII (May–June 1964): 359–69.

López Tabar 2001. Juan López Tabar. *Los famosos traidores: los afrancesados durante la crisis del Antiguo Régimen (1808–1833)*. Madrid: Biblioteca Nueva, 2001.

Lorenzo de Márquez 1989. Teresa Lorenzo de Márquez. "Carnival Traditions in Goya's Iconic Language," *Goya and the Spirit of Enlightenment*. Exh. cat. Alfonso E. Pérez Sánchez and Eleanor A. Sayre, eds. Boston: Museum of Fine Arts, 1989.

Luna 1996. Juan J. Luna. "Goya. La singularidad de un proceso vital y estético," *Goya: 250 aniversario*. Juan J. Luna and Margarita Moreno de las Heras, eds. Exh. cat. Madrid: Museo del Prado, 1996.

MacDonald 1976. Lyn Macdonald. *Bordeaux and Aquitaine*. London: B. T. Batsford Ltd., 1976.

Madrid 1900(b). "La exposición de cuadros de Goya," *La época* (May 11, 1900).

——1996. *Catálogo de las estampas de Goya en la Biblioteca Nacional*. Madrid: Ministerio de Educación y Cultura, Biblioteca Nacional; Barcelona: Lunwerg Editores, 1996.

——2002. *Goya 1900: catálogo ilustrado y estudio de la exposición en el Ministerio de Instrucción Pública y Bellas Artes*. 2 vols. Madrid: Dirección General de Bellas Artes y Bienes Culturales; Instituto del Patrimonio Histórico Español, 2002.

Marbella 1996. *Congreso Internacional "Goya 250 años después, 1746–1996."* Marbella: Museo del Grabado Español Contemporáneo, 1996.

Marrast 1988. Robert Marrast. "Les espagnols à Bordeaux de 1823 à 1834," *Images des espagnols en Aquitaine*. Bordeaux: Presses Universitaires, 1988.

Martínez-Novillo 1998. Álvaro Martínez-Novillo. "Les taureaux des Bordeaux," *Goya, Hommages: Les années bordelaises, 1824–1828: Présence de Goya aux XIXe et XXe siècles*. Exh. cat. Francis Ribemont and Françoise Garcia, eds. Bordeaux: Musée des Beaux-Arts de Bordeaux, 1998.

Matheron 1996. Laurent Matheron. *Goya*. Madrid: Ayuntamiento de Madrid; Bordeaux: Mairie de Bordeaux, 1996.

Matilla Tascón 1978. Antonio Matilla Tascón. "La familia de Goya en el Archivo Histórico de Protocolos," *Villa de Madrid* 59 (1978): 29–38.

Mayer 1924. August L. Mayer. *Francisco de Goya*. Translated by Robert West [pseud.]. London; Toronto: J. M. Dent & Sons, 1924.

——1930. August L. Mayer. "A Goya Drawing," *The Burlington Magazine* LVI: CCCXXVI (May 1930): 272–73.

——1933. August L. Mayer. "Dibujos desconocidos, de Goya," *Revista Española de Arte* II: 7 (September 1933): 376–84.

——1934. August L. Mayer. "Some Unknown Drawings by Francisco Goya," *Old Master Drawings*. 9: 34 (September 1934): 20–22.

Mayor 1974. A. Hyatt Mayor. *Goya: 67 Drawings*. New York: The Metropolitan Museum of Art, 1974.

Medrano Basanta 2003. José M. Medrano Basanta, "Sobre Goya y el mundo de los toros," *La Tauromaquia de Goya: fuentes y significado*. Valencia: Diputación Provincial de Valencia, 2003.

Mena Marqués 2004–5. Manuela B. Mena Marqués. "Goya, a Free 'Disciple' of Velázquez," *The Spanish Portrait: From El Greco to Picasso*. Exh. cat. Javier Portús, ed. London; Madrid: Scala Publishers, 2004.

Miller 1940–1941. M. Miller. "Géricault's Paintings of the Insane," *Journal of the Warburg and Courtauld Institutes* 4 (1940–41): 151–63.

Moffitt 1981–82. John F. Moffitt. "Observations on the Origins and Meanings of Goya with the Devils in the 1820 *Self-Portrait with Dr. Arrieta*," *The Minneapolis Institute of Arts Bulletin* LXV (1981–82): 36–49.

——1996. John F. Moffitt. "Francisco Goya, Andrea Alciati, and Emblematic Evacuation," *Source* XV: 3 (Spring 1996): 20–27.

Moniot 1986. François Moniet. "Vivre l'âge d'or à Bordeaux (XVIIIᵉs): Navigation," *Histoire et ethnographie régionale. L'Aquitaine de 1715 a nos jours*. Bordeaux: Musée d'Aquitaine; Guitel Frères, 1986.

Morales y Marín 1987. José Luis Morales y Marín. *Los toros en el arte*. Madrid: Espasa-Calpe S.A., 1987.

——1994. José Luis Morales y Marín. *Goya: Catálogo de la pintura*. Zaragoza: Real Academia de Nobles y Bellas Artes de San Luis, 1994.

Moreno de las Heras 1997. Margarita Moreno de las Heras. *Goya: pinturas del Museo del Prado*. Madrid: Museo del Prado, 1997.

Muller 1984. Priscilla E. Muller. *Goya's "Black" Paintings: Truth and Reason in Light and Liberty*. New York: Hispanic Society of America, 1984.

New York 1968. *The Frick Collection: An Illustrated Catalogue*. Vol. II (Paintings: French, Italian and Spanish). New York: The Frick Collection, 1968.

——1971. *European Paintings from the Minneapolis Institute of Arts*. New York: Praeger Publishers, 1971.

——2000. *The Hispanic Society of America: Tesoros*. New York: The Society, 2000.

——2002. *The Robert Lehman Collection. Nineteenth- and Twentieth-Century European Drawings*. New York: The Metropolitan Museum of Art; Princeton: Princeton University Press, 2002.

Nordström 1962. Folke Nordström. *Goya, Saturn, and Melancholy: Studies in the Art of Goya*. Stockholm: Almquist & Wiksell, 1962.

Núñez de Arenas 1950. M. Núñez de Arenas. "Manojo de Noticias: La suerte de Goya en Francia," *Bulletin Hispanique* LII: 3 (1950): 229–73.

Pardo Canalís 1968. Enrique Pardo Canalís. "Bosquejo histórico de Don José Duaso," *Anales del Instituto de Estudios Madrileños* III (1968): 253–80.

Paris 1838(a). *Comedias de Don Leandro Fernández de Moratín*. Paris: 1838.

——1838(b). "Noticia de la vida y escritos de D. Leandro Fernández de Moratín," *Comedias de Don Leandro Fernández de Moratín*. Paris: 1838.

Pérez Sánchez 1987. Alfonso E. Pérez Sánchez. "Goya en el Prado. Historia de una colección singular," *Goya. Nuevas visiones. Homenaje a Enrique Lafuente Ferrari*. Isabel García de la Rasilla and Francisco Calvo Serraller, eds. Madrid: Amigos del Museo del Prado, 1987.

Pérez Sánchez and Gállego 1995. Alfonso Pérez Sánchez and Julián Gállego. *Goya: The Complete Etchings and Lithographs*. Munich; New York: Prestel, 1995.

Persels and Ganim 2004. Jeff Persels and Russell Ganim, eds. *Fecal Matters in Early Modern Literature and Art: Studies in Scatology*. Aldershot, England; Burlington, Vermont: Ashgate Publishers, 2004.

Piquero López and González de Amezúa y del Pino 2002. María Ángeles Blanca Piquero López and Mercedes González de Amezúa y del Pino. *Los Goyas de la Academia*. 2nd revised edition. Madrid: Real Academia de Bellas Artes de San Fernando; Sociedad Estatal Goya 96; Barcelona: Lunwerg, 2002.

Pita Andrade 1989. José Manuel Pita Andrade. *Goya: obra, vida, sueños . . .* Madrid: Silex, 1989.

Popham and Fenwick 1965. A. E. Popham and K. M. Fenwick. *Catalogue of Paintings and Sculpture. European Drawings [and two Asian drawings] in the Collection of the National Gallery of Canada*. Vol. 4. Ottawa: Published for the Trustees of the National Gallery of Canada by the University of Toronto Press, 1965.

Posner 1982. Donald Posner. "The Swinging Women of Watteau and Fragonard," *The Art Bulletin* 64 (1982): 75–88.

Poussou 1989. Jean-Pierre Poussou. "Introduction," *Le port des Lumières: Architecture et art urbain: Bordeaux, 1780–1815*. Bordeaux: C.E.R.C.A.M., 1989.

Rascón 1843. J. A. Rascón. "Necrología. Doña Rosario Weiss," *Gaceta de Madrid* No. 3286 (September 20, 1843): 3–4.

Rèche 1979. Albert Rèche. *Naissance et vie des quartiers de Bordeaux: mille ans de vie quotidienne*. Paris: Seghers, 1979.

——1996. Albert Rèche. "Bordeaux," *The Dictionary of Art*. Vol. 4. Jane Turner, ed. New York: Macmillan Publishers Limited, 1996.

Ribemont 1998. Francis Ribemont. "Goya et Bordeaux. Grandeur et servitude d'un mythe," *Goya, Hommages: Les années bordelaises, 1824–1828: Présence de Goya aux XIXe et XXe siècles*. Exh. cat. Francis Ribemont and Françoise Garcia, eds. Bordeaux: Musée des Beaux-Arts de Bordeaux, 1998.

Ribeiro 1988. Aileen Ribeiro. *Fashion in the French Revolution*. New York: Holmes & Meier, 1988.

Rodríguez Torres 1993. María Teresa Rodríguez Torres. *Goya, Saturno y el saturnismo: su enfermedad*. Madrid: M. T. Rodríguez, 1993.

——1996. María Teresa Rodríguez Torres. "Economía de guerra en Goya. Cuadros pintados con caña," *Congreso Internacional "Goya 250 años después, 1746–1996."* Marbella: Museo del Grabado Español Contemporáneo, 1996.

Rosenfeld 1991. Daniel Rosenfeld. *European Paintings and Sculpture, ca. 1770–1937 in the Museum of Art, Rhode Island School of Design*. Providence: The Museum, 1991.

Royo Villanova 1927. R. Royo Villanova. *Goya y la Medicina*. Zaragoza: La Académica, 1927.

Ruiz Morcuende 1962. F. Ruiz Morcuende. "Prólogo," *Moratín Teatro*. Madrid: Espasa-Calpe, 1962.

Saltillo 1952. Marqués del Saltillo. *Miscelanea madrileña, histórica y artística. Primera Serie: Goya en Madrid: Su familia y allegados (1746–1856)*. Madrid: Imprenta y Editorial Maestre, 1952.

Sambricio 1956. Valentín de Sambricio. *Tapices de Goya*. Madrid: Patrimonio Nacional, Archivo General de Palacio, 1946.

——1986. Carlos Sambricio. "La tercera generación ilustrada: la arquitectura de la Revolución," *La arquitectura española de la ilustración*. Madrid: Consejo Superior de los Colegios de Arquitectos de España; Instituto de Estudios de Administración Local, 1986.

Sánchez Cantón 1946. F. J. Sánchez Cantón. "Como vivía Goya. I—El inventario de sus bienes. II—Leyenda e historia de la Quinta del Sordo," *Archivo Español de Arte* 19 (1946): 73–109.

——1947. F. J. Sánchez Cantón. "De la estancia bordelesa de Goya," *Archivo Español de Arte* 77 (1947): 60–63.

——1951. F. J. Sánchez Cantón. *Vida y obras de Goya*. Madrid: Editorial Peninsular, 1951.

——1954. F. J. Sánchez Cantón. "Goya, refugiado," *Goya* 3 (1954): 130–35.

——1964. F. J. Sánchez Cantón. *The Life and Works of Goya*. Madrid: Editorial Peninsular, 1964.

Saugera 1995. Eric Saugera. *Bordeaux Port Négrier XVII–XIX siècles*. Paris: Karthala; Biarritz: J & D Editions, 1995.

Sayre 1958. Eleanor A. Sayre. "An Old Man Writing: A Study of Goya's Albums," *Boston Museum Bulletin* LVI: 305 (Autumn 1958): 116–36.

——1966. Eleanor A. Sayre. "Goya's Bordeaux Miniatures," *Boston Museum Bulletin* LXIV: 337 (1966): 84–123.

——1971. Eleanor A. Sayre. *Late Caprichos of Goya. Fragments from a Series*. New York: Philip Hofer Books; Walker and Company; Department of Printing and Graphic Arts, Harvard College Library, 1971.

——1979. Eleanor A. Sayre. "Le témoignage d'une lettre de Goya," *Goya, 1746–1828: Peintures, Dessins, Gravures*. Exh. cat. Jacqueline Guillaud and Maurice Guillaud, eds. Paris: II Le Centre, 1979.

——1989. Eleanor A. Sayre. "Introduction to the Prints and Drawing Series," *Goya and the Spirit of Enlightenment*. Exh. cat. Alfonso E. Pérez Sánchez and Eleanor A. Sayre, eds. Boston: Museum of Fine Arts, 1989.

——1991. Eleanor A. Sayre. "Goya's Caprichos: A Sampling of Witches," *Goya, Neue Forschungen: das Internationale Symposium 1991 in Osnabrück*. Jutta Held, ed. Berlin: Gebr. Mann Verlag, 1994.

Schwarz 1957. Heinrich Schwarz. "Goya's Portrait of Gaulon," *The Wesleyan University Alumnus* XLI: 3 (May 1957): 19–20.

Seville 1991. *Museo de Bellas Artes de Sevilla*. 2 vols. Sevilla: Ediciones Gever, 1991.

Silvela(a) 1845. Francisco Agustín Silvela. "Noticia de la vida y escritos de Don Manuel Silvela," *Obras póstumas de d. Manuel Silvela*. Francisco Agustín Silvela, ed. Madrid: Establecimiento Tipográfico de don Francisco de Paula Mellado, 1845.

Silvela(b) 1845. Manuel Silvela. "Vida de Moratín," *Obras póstumas de d. Manuel Silvela*. Francisco Agustín Silvela, ed.

Madrid: Establecimiento Tipográfico de don Francisco de Paula Mellado, 1845.

——1867–68. Manuel Silvela, ed. *Obras póstumas de D. Leandro Fernandez de Moratín*. Madrid: Imprenta. y Estereotipia de M. Rivadeneyra, 1867–68.

Soria 1949. Martín Sebastián Soria. "Las miniaturas y retratos miniaturas de Goya," *Cobalto* 49 (1949): 1–4.

Stein 1995. Susan Alyson Stein. "Goya in the Metropolitan: A History of the Collection," *Goya in the Metropolitan Museum of Art*. Exh. cat. New York: The Metropolitan Museum of Art, 1995.

Stoichita and Coderch 1999. Victor I. Sotichita and Anna Maria Coderch. *Goya: The Last Carnival*. London: Reaktion Books, 1999.

Stoll 1954. Robert Th. Stoll. *Goya Dessins*. Paris: Les éditions Braun, 1954.

Straus 1912. Ralph Straus. *Carriages & Coaches: Their History & Their Evolution*. London: Martin Secker, 1912.

Symmons 1991. Sarah Symmons. "The Virtuoso Self: A Study of Goya's Self-Portraits," *Goya, Neue Forschungen: das Internationale Symposium 1991 in Osnabrück*. Jutta Held, ed. Berlin: Gebr. Mann Verlag, 1994.

——1998. Sarah Symmons. *Goya*. London: Phaidon, 1998.

Taillard 1997. Christian Taillard. *Bordeaux à l'âge classique*. Bordeaux: Éditions Mollat, 1997.

Tild 1921. Jean Tild. *Goya*. Paris: Librairie F. Alcan, 1921.

Tomlinson 1989. Janis Tomlinson. *Francisco Goya: The Tapestry Cartoons and Early Career at the Court of Madrid*. Cambridge; New York: Cambridge University Press, 1989.

——1992. Janis Tomlinson. *Goya in the Twilight of Enlightenment*. New Haven; London: Yale University Press, 1992.

——1994. Janis Tomlinson. *Francisco Goya y Lucientes 1746–1828*. London: Phaidon, 1994.

Tormo y Monzó 1902. Elías Tormo y Monzó. "Las pinturas de Goya y su clasificación y distribución cronológica," *Varios estudios de artes y letras*. Vol. 1. Madrid: Est. tip. de la Viuda é hijos de M. Tello, 1902.

Tortora and Eubank 1998. Phyllis G. Tortora and Keith Eubank. *Survey of Historic Costume. A History of Western Dress*. 3rd edition. New York: Fairchild Publications, 1998.

Trapier 1963. Elizabeth du Gué Trapier. *Unpublished Drawings by Goya in the Hispanic Society of America*. New York: The Society, 1963.

——1964. Elizabeth du Gué Trapier. *Goya and His Sitters: A Study of His Style as a Portraitist*. New York: The Hispanic Society of America, 1964.

Tréverret 1882. A. de Tréverret. "Moratín à Bordeaux," *Annales de la faculté de lettres de Bt.* IV (1882): 192–205, 413–45.

Vallentín 1951. Antonina Vallentín. *Goya*. Paris: Éditions Albin Michel, 1951.

Vega 2002. Jesusa Vega. "Goya 1900. La Exposición," *Goya 1900: catálogo ilustrado y estudio de la exposición en el Ministerio de Instrucción Pública y Bellas Artes.* 2 vols. Madrid: Dirección General de Bellas Artes y Bienes Culturales; Instituto del Patrimonio Histórico Español, 2002.

Viñaza 1887. El Conde de la Viñaza. *Goya: su tiempo, su vida, sus obras.* Madrid: Tipografía de Manuel G. Hernández, 1887.

Vischer 1997. Bodo Vischer, "Goya's Still Lifes in the Yumuri Inventory," *The Burlington Magazine* 139 (1997): 121–23.

Von Loga 1921. Valerian von Loga. *Francisco de Goya.* Berlin: G. Grotesche Verlagsbuchhandlung, 1921.

Wehle 1941. Harry B. Wehle. *Fifty Drawings by Francisco Goya.* 2nd edition. New York: The Metropolitan Museum of Art, 1941.

West 2004. Shearer West. *Portraiture.* Oxford; New York: Oxford University Press, 2004.

Wilson-Bareau 1994. Juliet Wilson-Bareau. "Truth and Fantasy: The Small Paintings. Exile in France 1824–1828," *Goya, Truth and Fantasy: The Small Paintings.* Juliet Wilson-Bareau and Manuela B. Mena Marqués, eds. New Haven; London: Yale University Press, 1994.

——**1996(a).** Juliet Wilson-Bareau. "Goya in The Metropolitan Museum," *The Burlington Magazine* CXXXVIII: 1115 (February 1996): 95–103.

——**1996(b).** Juliet Wilson-Bareau. "Goya pintor y grabador," *Ydioma universal, Goya en la Biblioteca Nacional.* Exh. cat. Elena Santiago Páez, ed. Madrid: Ministerio de Educación y Cultura, Biblioteca Nacional; Barcelona: Lunwerg Editores, 1996.

——**2000.** Juliet Wilson-Bareau. "The Roots of Goya's Realism," *Goya's Realism.* Exh. cat. Vibeke Vibolt Knudsen, ed. Copenhagen: Statens Museum for Kunst, 2000.

——**2002.** Juliet Wilson-Bareau. "La Lechera de Burdeos," *Goya.* Barcelona: Galaxia Gútenberg, 2002.

——**2003.** Juliet Wilson-Bareau. "Goya and France," *Manet/Velázquez: The French Taste for Spanish Painting.* Exh. cat. Gary Tinterow and Geneviève Lacambre, eds. New York: The Metropolitan Museum of Art; New Haven; London: Yale University Press, 2003.

Wind 1978. Barry Wind. "Close Encounters of the Baroque Kind: Amatory Paintings by Terbruggen, Baburen and La Tour," *Studies in Iconography* 4 (1978): 119–22.

Wolf 1994. Reva Wolf. "Sexual Identity, Mask, and Disguise in Goya's 'Los Caprichos,'" *Goya, Neue Forschungen: Das Internationale Symposium 1991 in Osnabrück.* Jutta Held, ed. Berlin: Gebr. Mann Verlag, 1994.

Worldfacts n.d. "Bordeaux," *Worldfacts,* n.d. <http://world-facts.us/France-Bordeaux.htm>

Young 1900. Arthur Young. *Arthur Young's Travels in France during the Years 1787, 1788, 1789.* Miss Betham-Edwards, ed. London: G. Bell, 1900.

Young 1972. Eric Young. "Unpublished Letter from Goya's Old Age," *The Burlington Magazine* 114 (August 1972): 558.

Yriarte 1867. Charles Yriarte. *Goya: sa vie, son oeuvre.* Paris: Typographie de Henri Plon, 1867.

Exhibition Catalogues

Águeda Villar 2003. Mercedes Águeda Villar, ed. *Goya y lo goyesco en la Fundación Lázaro Galdiano.* Segovia: Fundación Lázaro Galdiano, 2003.

Barcelona 1977. *Goya.* Barcelona: Palacio de Pedralbes, 1977.

Berlin 2005. *Goya.* Berlin: Alte Nationalgalerie, Staatliche Museen, 2005. Traveled.

Bilbao 1998. *Goya y Moratín: (en Burdeos, 1824–1828).* Bilbao: Museo de Bellas Artes de Bilbao, 1998.

Boix 1922(b). Felix Boix. *Exposición de dibujos 1750–1860: catálogo general ilustrado.* Madrid: Blass, 1922.

Bordeaux 1971. *Bordeaux: 2000 ans d'histoire.* Bordeaux: Musée d'Aquitaine, 1971.

——**1986.** *Histoire et ethnographie régionale. L'Aquitaine de 1715 à nous jours.* Bordeaux: Musée d'Aquitaine; Guitel Frères, 1986.

——**1989.** *Le port des Lumières: Architecture et art urbain: Bordeaux, 1780–1815.* Bordeaux: C.E.R.C.A.M., 1989.

Bruxelles 1985. *Goya.* Bruxelles: Musées Royaux des Beaux-Arts de Belgique, 1985.

Budapest 1996–97. *Spanyol Mestermüvek a Bilbaói Szépmüvészeti Múzeumból.* Budapest: Szépmuvészeti Múzeum, 1996–97.

Catton Rich 1941. Daniel Catton Rich, ed. *The Art of Goya: Paintings, Drawings, Prints.* Chicago: The Art Institute of Chicago, 1941.

Dupuis-Sabron 1993–94. Geneviève Dupuis-Sabron. *Scènes du Bordeaux d'autrefois.* Bordeaux: Musée d'Aquitaine, 1993–94.

Gassier 1990. Pierre Gassier, ed. *Goya, toros y toreros.* Arles: Actes Sud, 1990. Traveled.

Grasselli 1995–96. Margaret Morgan Grasselli, ed. *The Touch of the Artist: Master Drawings from the Woodner Collections.* Washington, D.C.: National Gallery of Art; New York: Harry N. Abrams, 1995–96.

Guillaud and Guillaud 1979. Jacqueline Guillaud and Maurice Guillaud, eds. *Goya, 1746–1828: Peintures, Dessins, Gravures.* Paris: 11 Le Centre de Marais, 1979.

Harris 1938. Tomás Harris. *From Greco to Goya: Illustrated Souvenir of an Exhibition.* London: The Spanish Art Gallery, 1938.

Hofmann 1980. Werner Hofmann, ed. *Goya: Das Zeitalter der Revolutionen, 1789–1830.* Munich: Prestel, 1980.

Ilatovskaya 1996. Tatiana Ilatovskaya. *Master Drawings*

Rediscovered: Treasures from Prewar German Collections. New York: Harry N. Abrams; Moscow: The Ministry of Culture of the Russian Federation; St. Petersburg: The State Hermitage Museum, 1996.

Ives and Stein 1995. Colta Feller Ives and Susan Alyson Stein. *Goya in the Metropolitan Museum of Art.* New York: The Metropolitan Museum of Art, 1995.

Knudsen 2000. Vibeke Vibolt Knudsen, ed. *Goya's Realism.* Copenhagen: Statens Museum for Kunst, 2000.

Lille 1998–99. *Goya: un regard libre.* Paris: Réunion des Musées Nationaux; Lille: Palais des Beaux-Arts, 1998–99. Traveled.

London 1928. *Catalogue of an Exhibition of Spanish Art Including Pictures, Drawings and Engravings by Goya.* London: Privately printed for the Burlington Fine Arts Club, 1928.

——**1963–64(a).** *Goya and His Times.* London: The Academy, 1963–64.

——**1963–64(b).** *The Graphic Work of Goya.* London: The British Museum, 1963–64.

——**1969.** *European Drawings from the National Gallery of Canada, Ottawa.* London: Colnaghi, 1969.

Luna 1989–90. Juan J. Luna, ed. *Tesoros del Museo de Bellas Artes de Bilbao. Pintura: 1400–1939.* Bilbao: Fundación Rich, 1989–90.

Luna and Cavalli-Björkman 1994–95. Juan J. Luna and Görel Cavalli-Björkman. *Goya.* Stockholm: Nationalmuseum; Bra Böcker, 1994–95.

Luna and Moreno de las Heras 1996. Juan J. Luna and Margarita Moreno de las Heras, eds. *Goya: 250 aniversario.* Madrid: Museo del Prado, 1996.

Madrid 1900(a). *Catálogo de las obras de Goya expuestas en el Ministerio de Instrucción Pública y Bellas Artes.* Madrid: Establecimiento Tipográfico de Fortanet, 1900.

——**1928.** *Catálogo ilustrado de la exposición de pinturas de Goya, celebrada para conmemorar el primer centenario de la muerte del artista.* Madrid: Tipografía Artística, 1928.

——**1932.** *Antecedentes, coincidencias e influencias del arte de Goya.* Madrid: Sociedad Española de Amigos del Arte, 1932. (Published in 1947)

——**1996(a).** *Vida cotidiana en tiempos de Goya.* Madrid: Ministerio de Educación y Cultura, Dirección General de Bellas Artes y Bienes Culturales; Barcelona: Lunwerg Editores, 1996.

——**1996(b).** *Realidad e imagen: Goya, 1746–1828.* Madrid; Zaragoza: Electa, 1996.

Martin-Méry 1951. Gilberte Martin-Méry, ed. *Goya, 1746–1828.* Bordeaux: Delmas, 1951.

New York 1915. *Loan Exhibition of Paintings by El Greco and Goya for the Benefit of the American Women War Relief Fund and the Belgian Relief Fund.* New York: M. Knoedler & Co., 1915.

——**1955.** *Goya: Drawings & Prints.* New York: The Metropolitan Museum of Art, 1955.

Oslo 1996. *Francisco Goya: maleri, tegning, grafikk.* Oslo: Nasjonalgalleriet, 1996.

Páez 1996. Elena Santiago Páez, ed. *Ydioma universal, Goya en la Biblioteca Nacional.* Madrid: Ministerio de Educación y Cultura, Biblioteca Nacional; Barcelona: Lunwerg Editores, 1996.

Paris 1935. *Goya: exposition de l'oeuvre gravé, de peintures, de tapisseries et de cent dix dessins du musée du Prado.* Paris: éditions des Bibliothèques nationales de France, 1935.

——**1938(c).** *Peintures de Goya des collections de France.* Paris: Musée de l'Orangerie, 1938.

Pérez Sánchez and Gállego 1994. Alfonso E. Pérez Sánchez and Julián Gállego. *Goya grabador.* Madrid: Fundación Juan March, 1994.

Pérez Sánchez and Sayre 1989. Alfonso E. Pérez Sánchez and Eleanor A. Sayre, eds. *Goya and the Spirit of Enlightenment.* Boston: Museum of Fine Arts, 1989. Traveled.

Philadelphia 1999. *Goya, Another Look.* Philadelphia Museum of Art, 1999. Traveled.

Portús 2004. Javier Portús, ed. *The Spanish Portrait: From El Greco to Picasso.* Madrid: Museo Nacional del Prado, 2004.

Ribemont and Garcia 1998. Francis Ribemont and Françoise Garcia, eds. *Goya, Hommages: Les années bordelaises, 1824–1828: Présence de Goya aux XIXe et XXe siècles.* Bordeaux: Musée des Beaux-Arts de Bordeaux, 1998.

Sambricio 1961. Valentín de Sambricio. *Exposición Francisco de Goya: IV centenario de la capitalidad.* Madrid: Artes Gráficas, 1961.

Sayre 1974–75. Eleanor A Sayre, ed. *The Changing Image: Prints by Francisco Goya.* Boston: Museum of Fine Arts, 1974–75. Traveled.

Seville 1970. *Exposición de las últimas adquisiciones: Reales Alcázares.* Madrid: Fábrica Nacional de Moneda y Timbre, 1970.

Stuffmann 1981. Margret Stuffmann, ed. *Goya Zeichnungen und Druckgraphik.* Frankfurt am Main: Städtische Galerie im Städelschen Kunstinstitut, 1981.

Sullivan 1982. Edward J. Sullivan. *Goya and the Art of His Time.* Dallas: The Meadows Museum, 1982.

The Hague 1970. *Goya.* The Hague: Mauritshuis, 1970. Traveled.

Tinterow and Lacambre 2003. Gary Tinterow and Geneviève Lacambre, eds. *Manet/Velázquez: The French Taste for Spanish Painting.* New York: The Metropolitan Museum of Art; New Haven; London: Yale University Press, 2003.

Tokyo 1987. *Spanish Paintings of 18th & 19th Century: Goya and His Time.* Tokyo: Seibu Museum of Art, 1987.

Tomlinson 2002. Janis Tomlinson, ed. *Goya: Images of Women.* Washington, D.C.: National Gallery of Art; New Haven; London: Yale University Press, 2002. Traveled.

Vega 1990. Jesusa Vega. *Origen de la litografía en España: El Real*

Establecimiento Litográfico. Madrid: Fábrica Nacional de Moneda y Timbre, 1990.

Washington, D.C. 1955. *Goya, Drawings and Prints from the Museo del Prado and the Museo Lázaro Galdiano, Madrid, and the Rosenwald Collection, National Gallery of Art, Washington, D.C.* Washington, D.C.: Smithsonian Institution, 1955.

Wilson-Bareau 2001. Juliet Wilson-Bareau, ed. *Goya: Drawings from His Private Albums*. London: Hayward Gallery in association with Lund Humphries, 2001.

Wilson-Bareau and Mena Marqués 1994. Juliet Wilson-Bareau and Manuela B. Mena Marqués, eds. *Goya, Truth and Fantasy: The Small Paintings*. New Haven; London: Yale University Press, 1994. Traveled.

Zaragoza 1983. *La litografía en Burdeos en la época de Goya.* Zaragoza: Excmo. Ayuntamiento de Zaragoza. Delegación de Extensión Cultural, 1983. Traveled.

—— **1992.** *Goya.* Madrid: Electa, 1992.

Photograph Credits

Front cover and cat. no. 7: Photography by Richard di Liberto

Back cover, cat. nos. 37 and 45, and fig. 87: Photography by Roberto Sandoval; Courtesy of The Hispanic Society of America, New York

Cat. no. 1: Photograph ©1995 The Metropolitan Museum of Art

Cat. no. 2: Photograph ©1988 The Metropolitan Museum of Art

Cat. no. 4: Photograph ©2005 The Metropolitan Museum of Art

Cat. no. 5: Photograph ©1988 The Metropolitan Museum of Art

Cat. no. 10: Photography © de la fotografía Museo de Bellas Artes de Bilbao; Courtesy of the Archivo fotográfico of the Museo de Bellas Artes de Bilbao

Cat. nos. 11, 12, 34, 35, 38, 39, 40, 44, 47, 48, 49, and 50, figs. 1, 2, 5, 13, 29, 34, 37, 45, 46, 48, 50, 61, 63, 64, 66, 67, 69, 78, 80, 83, and 86: All rights reserved © Museo Nacional del Prado, Madrid

Cat. nos. 13, 17, 20, 30, and 32, figs. 44 and 60: Photography © 2006 Museum of Fine Arts, Boston

Cat. no. 14: Photography by Bruce M. White

Cat. no. 15: Photography by Cathy Carver

Cat. nos. 16, 18, 19, 43, and 51: Photography by Robert Lorenzson

Cat. no. 21: © Christie's Images Limited 2006

Cat. no. 22: © The J. Paul Getty Museum

Cat. nos. 23, 24, and 26: Photograph ©2002 The Metropolitan Museum of Art

Cat. no. 25: Photograph ©1994 The Metropolitan Museum of Art

Cat. nos. 28, 36, and 46: photo © National Gallery of Canada

Cat. no. 31 and figs. 4 and 31: Images © 2005 Board of Trustees, National Gallery of Art, Washington D.C.

Cat. no. 33: © The Pierpont Morgan Library, New York, 2004

Cat. no. 41: Photography by Jim Strong

Figs. 6 and 7: Photography by José Garrido

Figs. 22, 23, 25, and 74: Photography courtesy of the Musée d'Aquitaine, Bordeaux © DEC, Bordeaux

Fig. 32: Photograph ©1998 The Metropolitan Museum of Art

Fig. 33: Photograph Reproduced with the Permission of the Barnes Foundation™ All rights reserved

Fig. 35: Photograph ©1994 The Metropolitan Museum of Art

Figs. 47, 51, and 91: Photography by Joerg P. Anders; Courtesy of the Bildarchiv Preussicher Kulturbesitz / Art Resource, New York

Figs. 49, 71, 75, 82, 88, 89, 90, and 92: All rights reserved, The Metropolitan Museum of Art

Fig. 54: Photography by Lysiane Gauthier © Cliché du M.B.A. de Bordeaux

Figs. 76 and 79: Photograph ©2005 The Metropolitan Museum of Art

Fig. 77: Photograph ©1999 The Metropolitan Museum of Art

Index

Afrancesados, 2, 51, 55, 109
Alba, duchess of, 238, fig. 88
Alban de Lesgallery, Jean-Jacques
   *Les Allées de Tourny et la maison
      Meyer* 44–45, fig. 23
   *Les Allées de Tourny et le Grand
      Théâtre* 44–45, fig. 22
Alciati, Andrea: *Emblematum liber*, 214
Álvarez, José de, 104
Aquitaine, 35, 36; *see also* Bordeaux
Arnao, Vicente González, 6, 100, 102
Arrieta, Dr. Eugenio García, 65, 70–73,
   78, cat. no. 3
Ars moriendi, 72
Ausonius, 35

Basire, Joseph: *Le Grand Théâtre*, 47–48,
   fig. 25
Baudelaire, Charles, 152
Bayeu, Josefa (Goya's wife), 9, 12, 28, 74
Beethoven, Ludwig van, 65, 68
beggars, 186
Beruete y Moret, Aureliano, 97, 105, 116,
   120
Bituriges Vivisci, 35
Bonaparte, Joseph, 2, 4, 5, 51, 112
Bonaparte, Napoleon, 2, 50–51, 53
Bordeaux, 35–59
   architecture and buildings, 39–42;
      Château Trompette, 40, 47;
      churches and cathedrals, 36, 54;
      Dupré du Saint Maur's influence,
      47, 48; fortifications, 36, 38, 51;
      Grand Théâtre, 45, 47–48, figs. 22,
      25; Hôpital St. Jean asylum, 218;
      Nouvelle Place Royale, 40, 41, 42,
      fig. 19; Palais Galien (Roman
      coliseum), 36–37, 49, 53; Pont de
      Pierre, 53–54, fig. 28; Roman
      buildings, 36–37, 47; Tourny's
      influence, 42–46
   city layout, 36–37, 40, 43–44, figs. 18,
      21, 27; Allées de Tourny, 43–46,
      figs. 22–24; Cours de Tourny,
      45–46; Place des Grands Hommes,

50; Place des Quinconces, 51–52,
   fig. 26; quayside, 41–42, 51–52,
   53–54, figs. 20, 28; Restoration and
   urbanization, 51–54; Vincennes,
   188, 190
commercial prosperity, 38–40, 41–42,
   54, 55; decline under Napoleon,
   50–51
education and culture, 47; Collège de
   Guyenne, 37
émigré community, 6–8, 14, 46,
   52–53, 55, 56, 112
Goya's exile in. *See* Goya: exile in
   Bordeaux
Goya's homes in, 15, 46, 52
historical background, 35–36, 38–39;
   and French Revolution, 48–50
population fluctuations, 35, 39, 50–51
slave trade, 38–39, 51
wine trade, 35, 39, 51
Boucher, Claude, 40
Brugada, Antonio de, 13, 14, 20, 24, 26,
   52, 121
   on Goya's lithograph technique,
      150–51
   on Goya's miniature technique,
      125–26
bullfighting: attitudes toward, 150

Caburrús, Conde de, 106
Cardano, José María, 6, 16, 147–48
Carderera, Valentín, 70
Carnicero, Antonio, 16
Ceán Bermúdez, Juan Agustín, 66, 151
Ceballos, Mariano, 156, cat. no. 23,
   fig. 57
Chalifour (architect), 50
Charles IV, king of Spain, 2
Charles X, king of France, 35, 56
Chinchón, countess of, 6
Colbert, Jean-Baptiste, 38
Constant: *2me Vue des Allées de Tourny*,
   45–46, fig. 24
Counter-Reformation, 38
Coustet, Robert, 54

Cuervo, Juan Antonio, 90, 92, fig. 36
Cuervo, Don Tiburcio Pérez y, *see* Pérez
   y Cuervo, Don Tiburio

Delacroix, Eugène, 8, 152
Deschamps, Claude, 53
Duaso y Latre, José, 4, 82, 94–96,
   cat. no. 6
Duplessis, Louis-Armand, Maréchal de
   Richelieu, 47
Dupré de Saint Maur, Nicolas, 47, 48

Eleanor of Aquitaine, 35–36
emblem books, 214, 236
Engelmann, Godefroy, 147

fairs, 191–92, 224
Feijóo, Padre Benito Jerónimo, 238
Ferdinand VII, king of Spain, fig. 2
   and Goya, 4, 12, 14, 18–19, 84
   reign, 2–3, 55, 56, 94, 109, 150
Fernández de Moratín, Leandro.
   See Moratín, Leandro Fernández de
Ferrer, Joaquín María de, 6, 10–11, 15–16,
   80, 82, 100–102, cat. no. 8
   and Bulls of Bordeaux, 148–50, 153
   and miniatures, 125
   and "Nuevos Caprichos" proposal,
      169–70, 178, 180, 226, 229
Ferrer, Manuela de Álvarez Coiñas y
   Thomas de, 6, 80, 82, 97, 104–105,
   cat. no. 9
flagellant processions, 174, 176
France
   Colonies, 38–39, 50, 51
   Goya in. *See* Goya: exile in Bordeaux
   Revolution, 2, 48–50
   and Spain, 2–3
Fronde, the, 38
Fuente, Vicente de la, 94

Gabriel, Anges-Jacques, 42, 43
Gabriel, Infante Sebastián, 31
Gabriel, Jacques Jules, 40
Galard, Gustave de, 120

La Foire, 192, fig. 74
Gaulon's Workshop, fig. 9
Portrait of Gaulon, 148, fig. 58
Galarza, Juana, 11–12, 74
Galos, Jacques, 12, 15, 17, 20, 52, 84, fig. 33
Garneray, Louis: *Vue du port de Bordeaux*, 53–54, fig. 28
Gaulon, Cyprien Charles Marie Nicolas, 53, 148, figs. 9, 58
    Goya's portrait of, 16, 164, cat. no. 27
Gautier, Théophile, 152
Godoy, Manuel, 2, 108, 109
Goicoechea, Cesárea, 98
Goicoechea, Gerónima, 98
Goicoechea, Gumersinda (Goya's daughter-in-law), 8, 11–12, 25, 26, 74, 98, fig. 7
Goicoechea, Jerónimo, 8
Goicoechea, Manuela, 98, fig. 37
Goicoechea, Martín Miguel de, 8, 11–12, 51–52, 74
Goya, Javier (Francisco Javier Pedro Goya y Bayeu) (Goya's son), 3–4, 19, 20, 74, cat. no. 4, fig. 6
    biography of father, 77
    Goya's relationship with, 11–12, 23–24, 65, 74
    inheritance, 23–29, 31, 74; father's works, 12, 31, 68, 121, 167
    marriage to Gumersinda, 11–12, 74
Goya, Mariano (Goya's grandson)
    Goya's portrait of, 22, 84, 88, fig. 14
    Goya's provision for, 3–4, 9, 25
    sells Goya collection, 31, 68, 167
GOYA Y LUCIENTES, FRANCISCO JOSÉ DE
    album drawings, 1, 11, 68, 167–248; everyday scenes, 182–94; fantasy subjects, 17–18, 168, 170–71, 224–48; madness as theme, 168, 170, 216–21; Madrid Album, 240, 246; religious themes, 168, 171, 174, 176, 210–12, 224, 248; sexuality as theme, 168, 178, 195–96, 201–2, 226; social commentary and satire, 168, 170, 195–223; Spanish themes, 174–81
    animal symbolism in work, 234
    deafness, 14, 24, 63, 68, 167
    death, 26, 56, fig. 15
    drawings, *see* album drawings *above*
    exile in Bordeaux, 5–9, 94, 96; daily

routine 13–14, 24; drawings, *see* album drawings *above*; émigré community, 6–8, 14, 46, 52–53, 55, 56, 112; historical background to, 2–5; police surveillance, 5–6; residences, 15, 46, 52; return visits to Madrid, 18–20, 22; visits Paris 5–6, 8, 101, 104, 147–48; working habits 20, 27–28, 52, 121–22, 147–48
    financial affairs, 12, 15; family and legacy, 12, 23–24, 24–25, 26–29, 31, 74
    health: compromises career in Spain, 63; deterioration in exile, 14–15; illness in Spain, 3, 63, 65; last months of life, 24, 25–26; lead poisoning theory, 65n; self-portraits and illness, 63–73
    lithography, 1, 6, 15–17, 102, 120, 147–65; Delacroix's admiration for, 8, 152; and failing eyesight, 151, 152; technique, 150–51, 164
    Madrid retrospective (1900), 116
    miniature paintings, 1, 12–13, 74, 101, 120, 122, 125–45
    political allegiances 3–4, 94, 96
    portraits by, 1, 5, 20, 22, 63–75; self-portraits, 63–73
    portrait of, fig. 13
    relationship with Leocadia Weiss, 9–11, 22–23, 27–28
    relationship with son (Javier), 11–12, 23–24, 65
    will and legacy, 12, 23–24, 24–25, 26–29, 31, 74
    WORKS
Abducting Horse (Caballo raptor), 248, fig. 92
Aguarda que venga (She Is Waiting for Him to Arrive), 128, fig. 45
Aldeano en el campo remangandose los calzones (Villager in the Field Pulling Up His Trousers), fig. 84
Allá vá eso (There It Goes), 242, fig. 89
Allegorical Figure, 171, 236, fig. 66
Andrés del Peral fig. 42
Aun aprendo (I Am Still Learning), 1, fig. 1
Bartolomé Sureda y Miserol, 79–80, fig. 31

Black Paintings, 3, 13, 118, 130, 174, 240
Boy Staring at an Apparition, 126, fig. 44
Bravo toro, 158, cat. no. 24
Buen Viaje, 242–43
Buena muger parece (She Seems Like a Good Woman) 206
Bullfight, 151, fig. 54
Bullfighting Scene, known as Suerte de Varas, 6, 102, 149–50, 153–54, cat. no. 22
Bulls of Bordeaux, 1, 15–17, 122, 148–52, 153, 156–63, cat. nos. 23–26
Los Caprichos, 3, 12, 13, 125–26, 150, 210, 230; "Nuevos Caprichos" proposal, 169–70, 178, 180, 226, 229; witchcraft themes 240, 242–43, 244
caprichos enfáticos, 234
Castigo francés (French Punishment), fig. 59
The Celebrated Picador, Fernando del Toro, 153, fig. 55
Claudio Ambrosio Surat/Llamado el Esquelete vibientel (Claude Ambroise Seurat, Known as the Living Skeleton, 17, 191–92, fig. 10
Comer mucho (To Eat a Lot), 170, 214, cat. no. 40
Cómico descubrimiento (Comical Discovery), 171
La Confianza (Trust), 201, fig. 80
Conjugal Row, 198, 200, fig. 78
Corrida de toros en un pueblo (Bullfight in a Village), 153, fig. 56
Cyprien Charles Marie Nicolas Gaulon, 16, 164, cat. no. 27
Daedalus Seeing Icarus Fall, fig. 86
De secreto (The Secret), 184
De todo sirven (They Can Be Used for Anything), 184
Del avaro no se espera ningun bien . . . (One Can Expect No Good from a Miser . . .), 170, fig. 62
Después lo beras (You'll See Later), 198, fig. 77
Diversión de España (Spanish Entertainment), 160, cat. no. 25
Diligencias nuebas [written over] sillas de moda (New Stagecoaches

[written over] Fashionable Chairs),
182–84, cat. no. 30

Disasters of War, 167, 234

*Don Tiburcio Pérez y Cuervo, the
Architect,* 78–79, 80, 90–93,
cat. no. 5

*Donda vá Mamá? (Where Is Mama
Going?),* 244

Duel, 148, fig. 53

*Enredos de sus vidas (Entanglements
of Their Lives),* 201–2, cat. no. 36

Esto es lo peor (This Is the Worst), 234

*El famoso Americano, Mariano
Ceballos,* 16–17, 156, cat. no. 23

Ferdinand VII, fig. 2

*Feria en Bordeaux (Fair in Bordeaux)
(The Female Giant),* 191–92,
cat. no. 33

Forge, 92

Francisco Bayeu, 122

*Gimiendo y llorando (Weeping and
Wailing),* 222, cat. no. 43

*Gran coloso durmido (Great Sleeping
Colossus),* 17–18, fig. 11

Gran disparate (Great Folly), 171, 236,
fig. 63

Gumersinda Goicoechea, fig. 7

Hasta la muerte (Until Death), 208,
fig. 82

Head of a Man, 140, cat. no. 19

Heads of a Child and an Old Woman,
13, 127, 138, cat. no. 18

Isidoro Máiquez, 122

Jacques (Santiago) Galos, 20, 84,
fig. 33

Javier Goya, fig. 6

*Javier Goya (Francisco Javier Pedro
Goya y Bayeu,* 12, 65, 74,
cat. no. 4

Joaquín María de Ferrer, 80, 82,
100–101, cat. no. 8

José Duaso y Latre, 82, 94–96, 101,
cat. no. 6

Juan Antonio Cuervo, 90, 92, fig. 36

Juan de Muguiro, 20, 22, 88–89, 140,
fig. 34

Judith and Holofernes (1820–23),
144, fig. 50

Judith and Holofernes (1824–25),
144, cat. no. 21

Leandro Fernández de Moratín (1799),
82, 108–9, fig. 39

Leandro Fernández de Moratín (1824),
82–83, 101, 106–11, cat. no. 10

La Lectura (Woman Reading), 132,
fig. 47

La Leocadia, 10, fig. 5

Linda Maestra, 242

Loco calabozo (Crazy Dungeon), 216

Loco furioso (Raging Lunatic)
(Album G. 33) 216–19, 220, 226,
cat. no. 41

Loco furioso (Raging Lunatic)
(Album G. 40) 220, 222,
cat. no. 42

Loco p.r errar (Mad by Error), 170,
fig. 60

*Loco qe bende los placeres (Madwoman
Who Sells Pleasures),* 216

Locos patines (Crazy Skates), 188–90,
cat. no. 32

Madhouse, 218

Maja, 171, 178–80, cat. no. 29

Maja and Celestina, 127, 134,
cat. no. 16

Maja desnuda, 128

Mal marido (Bad Husband), 198–200,
cat. no. 35

Mal sueño, 18

Mala muger, 204, 206

Mala noche (Bad Night), fig. 49

Man Awakened by Bear Cub, 171,
fig. 67

Man Hunting for Lice near a Shack,
127, 136, fig. 48

Man Killing Monk, 171, 210–12,
cat. no. 39

Man Looking for Fleas in His Shirt,
127, 136, cat. no. 17

Man on a Swing (album drawing),
226–29, 230, cat. no. 45

Man on a Swing (etching), 229,
fig. 87

Man Reading, 132

Manuel Silvela, 83, 112–17, cat. no. 11

*Manuela de Álvarez Coiñas y Thomas
de Ferrer,* 80, 82, 97, 104–5,
cat. no. 9

Mariano Ceballos, Alias the Indian,
156, fig. 57

Mariano Goya, 22, 84, 88, fig. 14

The Marquesa de Pontejos, fig. 4

*Mendigos q.e se lleban solos en
Bordeaux (Beggars Who Get About*

on Their Own in Bordeaux), 186,
cat. no. 31

Milkmaid of Bordeaux, 27, 118–23, 138,
cat. no. 12

*Mirar lo qe no ven (They Are Looking
at What They Cannot See),* 192

Monk and Old Woman, 13, 127, 130,
cat. no. 14

Monk Guzzling from a Large Bowl,
171, fig. 64

*Muerte del Alguacil Lampiños (Death
of Constable Lampiños),* 195–96,
fig. 76

*Ni por esas; Que tirania [faintly
written] (Not Even with Those;
What Tyranny),* 195–96, cat. no. 34

*No sabras lo que llebas aquestas? (Will
You Ever Know What You're
Carrying on Your Back),* fig. 83

Old Woman with Mirror, 208,
cat. no. 38

Paseo (Promenade), fig. 70

El perro volante (The Flying Dog), 171,
224, cat. no. 44

Phantom Dancing with Castanets,
fig. 61

*Picador Drawing a Bull in Open
Country,* fig. 51

The Picnic, 178, fig. 69

Pilgrimage of San Isidro, 174

Plaza Partida (Divided Ring), 162,
cat. no. 26

*Portrait of a Lady (María Martínez de
Puga?),* 4, 80, 82, 97–98, 103, 136,
cat. no. 7

Procession of Flagellants, fig. 68

Procession of Monks, 171

Qué sacrificio! (What a Sacrifice!), 192,
fig. 75

Quien vencerá? (Who Will Win?), 18,
fig. 12

Ramón Satué, 79–80, fig. 30

Reclining Nude, 127, 128, cat. no. 13

Se defiende bien (It Defends Itself Well),
234

*Se quieren mucho (They Love Each
Other Very Much),* 230, 240–43,
cat. no. 49

A Seated Majo and Maja, 13, 127,
fig. 8

Sebastián Martínez, 88–89, fig. 35

Self-Portrait, 68, fig. 29

Self-Portrait after Illness of 1792–93, 68, cat. no. 2

Self-Portrait with Dr. Arrieta, 3, 65, 70–73, 78, 248, cat. no. 3

Self-Portrait with Three-Cornered Hat, 63, 66, cat. no. 1

Semana Santa en tiempo pasado en España (Holy Week in a Time Past in Spain), 174–76, cat. no. 28

Serpiente de 4 baras a Bordeaux (Snake 4 meters long at Bordeaux), 171, fig. 65

The Skaters, fig. 73

The Sleep of Reason Produces Monsters, 219, 240

Struggling Man and Woman with Devil, 236, cat. no. 48

El Sueño (The Dream), 128, fig. 91

Sueño drawings, 142, 240

La Tauromaquia, 16–17, 66, 150, 153, 158

Traveling Witch, 171, 244, cat. no. 50

Tu que no puedes (You Who Cannot), 184, fig. 71

Two Children Looking at a Book, 127, 132, cat. no. 15

Two Old Men, 130, fig. 46

El Vito (Andalusian Dance), 148, fig. 52

Volaverunt (Gone for Good), 232, 244, fig. 88

Wolf and Man, 234, cat. no. 47

Woman Murdering a Sleeping Man, 200, fig. 79

Woman with Clothes Blowing in the Wind, 126, 142, cat. no. 20

Woman with Two Children, 204–212, cat. no. 37

Y aun no se van! (And Still They Don't Go!), 243, fig. 90

Yard with Lunatics, 218, fig. 85

Yo lo he visto en Paris (I Saw It in Paris), fig. 72

Young Witch (Woman?) Flying with a Rope, 230–32, cat. no. 46

Young Woman Swooning, Surrounded by Witches, 246–48, cat. no. 51

Greuze, Jean-Baptiste: *Les Soins maternels*, 204, fig. 81

Holy Alliance, 3

Hoogen, Mr. (Leocadia's friend), 27

100,000 Sons of St. Louis, 3

Huguenots in Bordeaux. 37–38

humanism in Bordeaux, 37

Impressionism, 118

Ingres, Jean-Auguste-Dominique, 8
Madame Jacques-Louis Leblanc, 82, 103, fig. 32

Isabella II, queen of Spain, 29

josefinos, 2, 4, 51

Jovellanos, Gaspar Melchor de, 106, 243n

Julian, Camille, 38

Laclotte, Michel, 52

Lacour, Pierre, 42

Laffargue, Dr. Jules, 218

Lasteyrie, Charles Philibert de, 147

Lavater, Johann Caspar, 68n, 218

Légé (after Jules Philippe): *Bains des Quinconces*, 51–52, fig. 26

Lemoyne, Jean-Baptiste, 40, 49

Liberal Triennium 3, 55

López, J. A.: *Portrait of D. Manuel Silvela*, 116, fig. 43

López y Portaña, Vicente: *The Painter Francisco de Goya*, 20, 84, fig. 13

Louis XIV, king of France, 38, 47

Louis XV, king of France, 40, 43
statue in Bordeaux, 40, 49

Louis XVIII, king of France, 54

Louis, Victor 47, 48

Luisa Fernanda, Infanta of Spain, 29

Madrazo, Federico de, 31, 68

Madrazo, Mariano Fortuny y, 68

Madrid
Goya retrospective (1900), 116
Goya visits from exile, 18–20, 22

maja figure, 134, 178

Manet, Édouard, 89, 98

Mariátegui, Francisco Javier de, 92

Marin, Joseph-Charles, 46

marriage
abusive relationships, 198–200
arranged marriages, 192, 198

Martínez, Sebastián, 63, 88–89, fig. 35

Matheron, Laurent, 13, 20, 24, 77, 121, 153–54, 158, 164

Mazarin, Cardinal Jules, 38

Melón, Abate Juan Antonio: Moratín's correspondence, 5, 8–9, 13, 14, 18–19, 47–48

Mengs, Anton Raphael, 125

Montaigne, Michel de, 37

Moratín, Leandro Fernández de, 6, 27, 28, 49, 121–22, fig. 40
correspondence with Mélon, 5, 8–9, 13, 14, 18–19, 47–48
death, 110–11
friendship with Silvela, 106, 109, 110, 111, 112, 114, 117
Goya's portraits of, 82–83, 101, 106–11, cat. no. 10, fig. 39
in praise of Bordeaux, 55–56
witchcraft text, 238, 240

Muguiro, José Francisco, 8

Muguiro (y Iribarren), Juan de, 20, 22, 27, 52–53, 88–89, 138, 140, fig. 34
and *Milkmaid of Bordeaux*, 118, 120, 121, 138,

Muguiro, Manuela, 8

Napoleon Bonaparte. *See* Bonaparte, Napoleon

Nemnich, Philippe-André, 50–51

Osuna, duke and duchess of, 240

Otín, Francisco, 96n

Ozanne, Nicolas: *Le Port de Bordeaux vu du quai des Farines*, 41–42, fig. 20

Paris: Goya in, 5–6, 8, 101, 104, 147–48

Peninsular War (1808–13), 2

Pérez y Cuervo, Don Tiburcio, 5, 78–79, 80, 90–93, cat. no. 5

Pinel, Philippe, 220

Pío de Molina, José, 24, 25, 26, 52

Poc, Braulio, 14, 46

Pontejos, marquise of, 6, 100, fig. 4

Portier, André, 42, 44

Protestant Reformation, 37

Puga, Antonio, 98n

Puga, Dionisio Antonio de, 4, 97

Puga, María Martínez de, 4, 80, 82, 97–98, cat. no. 7

Quinta del Sordo, 3–4, 10

Ramiro, Gabriel, 97

Regency Council, 2

Rembrandt van Rijn, 63, 68
Richelieu, Louis-Armand Duplessis, Maréchal de, 47
Riego, Rafael del, 3
Ripa, Cesare: *Iconographia*, 218
Robespierre, Maximilien Marie Isidore de, 49
Roche, Michael Armstrong, 195, 196
Romans in Bordeaux, 35, 47

Saboya, Marc, 54
Salas, Xavier de, 80
Salon exhibition (1824), 8
San Carlos, duke of, 100
San Fernando, duchess of, 6, 11
Satué, Ramón, 79–80, fig. 30
Senefelder, Aloys, 147
Seurat, Claude Ambroise, 17, 191–92, fig. 10
shoulder chairs, 182, 244
Silvela, Francisco (Manuel Silvela's grandson), 116, 117
Silvela, Francisco Agustín (Manuel Silvela's son), 112, 117
Silvela (y García de Aragón), Manuel, 5, 47, 55, 83, 112–17, cat. no. 11, fig. 43
    death, 114

friendship with Moratín, 106, 109, 110, 111, 112, 114, 117
skating, 188–90
Spain
    attitudes toward bullfighting, 150
    Goya's drawings on Spanish themes, 16–17, 174–81
    historical background to Goya's exile, 2–5
Sureda y Miserol, Bartolomé, 79–80, fig. 31

Torre, F. de la: *Goya on His Deathbed*, fig. 15
Tourny, Louis Urbain Aubert, Marquis de, 42–46, 53

Vauban, Sébastien Le Prestre de, 38
Velázquez, 125
Vernet, Horace, 147–48

Wars of Religion (1563–98), 37–38
Weiss, Guillermo, 4, 9
Weiss, Isidoro, 9–10
Weiss, Leocadia Zorrilla y, 4–5, 8–9, 15, 56, figs. 3, 5
    death, 31

and Goya's legacy, 23–24, 24–25, 26–29, 31, 74
    Milkmaid of Bordeaux sale, 118, 120, 138, 121
    relationship with Goya, 9–11, 22–23, 27–28
Weiss, Rosario, 4–5, 15, 92, 164
    artistic talent and career, 10–11, 29, 31, 65n, 102, 121
    death, 31
    paternity speculation, 9, 10–11
    and provenance of *Milkmaid of Bordeaux*, 120, 121, 122
    Self-Portrait at Drawing Board, fig. 16
    Virgin of Contemplation, 29, fig. 17
Wilson-Bareau, Juliet, 120–22, 158, 229

Young, Arthur, 40, 48
Yriate, Charles, 66
Yumuri, count of, 98n

Zamora, Antonio de, 238, 240
Zapater, Martín, 63, 66

Index compiled by Jane Horton